VAUGHAN WILLIAMS
• AND THE VISION OF ALBION •

Samuel Palmer, 'The Skylark', 1850
(Victoria and Albert Museum)

VAUGHAN WILLIAMS
• AND THE VISION OF ALBION •

WILFRID MELLERS

BARRIE &JENKINS
LONDON

First published in Great Britain by
Barrie & Jenkins Ltd
289 Westbourne Grove
London W11 2QA

British Library Cataloguing in Publication Data
Mellers, Wilfrid
    Vaughan Williams and the vision of Albion.
    1. English music. Vaughan Williams, Ralph, 1872–1958
    – Biographies
    I. Title
    780′.92′4

    ISBN 0–7126–2117–2

Phototypeset by DP Photosetting, Aylesbury, Bucks
Printed and bound by Butler & Tanner Ltd, Frome and London

To Robin and the Old Plaister Pitt
With love and thanks

He represents, in an age the intellectual powers of which tend strongly to agnosticism, that class of minds to which the supernatural view of things is still credible. The mechanical theory of nature has had grave adherents since: to the non-mechanical theory of man – that he is in contact with a moral order on a different plane from the mechanical order – thousands, of the most various types and degrees of intellectual power, always adhere: a fact worth the consideration of all ingenuous thinkers, if (as is certainly the case with colour, music, number, for instance) there may be whole regions of fact the recognition of which belongs to one and not to another, which people may possess in various degrees; for the knowledge of which, therefore, one person is dependent upon another; and in relation to which the appropriate means of cognition must lie among the elements of what we call individual temperament, so that what looks like a prejudgment may be really a legitimate apprehension. 'Men are what they are', and are not wholly at the mercy of formal conclusions from their formally limited premises.

WALTER PATER, OF SIR THOMAS BROWNE,
APPRECIATIONS, 1889

Since we may not stay here, being people but of a dayes abode, and our age is like that of a flie, and contemporary with a gourd, we must look somewhere else for an abiding city.

JEREMY TAYLOR, *HOLY DYING*, 1651

CONTENTS

PREFACE

This book is not a comprehensive study of the life and works of Vaughan Williams. The standard biography is, understandably, the beautiful book by his widow Ursula Vaughan Williams, while the definitive survey of his works is *The Music of Vaughan Williams*, by Michael Kennedy, now justly regarded as the expert on this composer. My book is at once less and more ambitious: less, because it makes no attempt to 'cover the ground' in discussing all Vaughan Williams's music in chronological sequence; more, because it aims to explore, if not define, Vaughan Williams's 'message' as a composer who was actively creative through more than half of our turbulent century. In attempting this I call on extramusical props, mostly literary: for Vaughan Williams was a highly literate composer who consciously and unconsciously found inspiration in English poetry and prose, notably in the works of Whitman, Bunyan and Blake, but also in many other writers, major and minor. Although what Vaughan Williams 'says' through his music is of course intrinsic to the music itself, it none the less helps that there are guidelines, attested to by the composer, as to what it is about.

A number of works which I call 'key' works, are analysed in some detail, and these sections cannot be fully intelligible without reference to the scores. Seventy-four music quotations are given, though such examples can never be adequate and in this case do not pretend to be. Other works are discussed in relation to the key works, but are not exhaustively analysed. I did not read or re-read any of the books about Vaughan Williams before writing my own, though I was certainly influenced by Deryck Cooke's analysis of the Sixth Symphony which, first published in his great book *The Language of Music* in 1959, is brilliant enough to have been remembered over the years. I am deeply indebted to Ursula Vaughan Williams for reading the manuscript, correcting several errors of fact, and modifying some opinions.

The book may have a strong autobiographical element, since it is a rediscovery of my own roots and a tribute to 'the Mind of England'. Its justification is, I hope, in the title of the Postlude: 'A Valediction: forbidding Mourning'.

W.M.
OLIVER SHELDON HOUSE, 17 ALDWARK, YORK
1 November 1988

xi

ACKNOWLEDGEMENTS

The author and publisher are grateful for permission to reproduce extracts from 'The Dry Salvages' and 'East Coker' from *Four Quartets* by T.S. Eliot, published by Faber & Faber Limited; and 'The Skylark' from *Collected Poems* by Ralph Hodgson, published by Macmillan Publishers Limited.

Excerpts from *Fantasia on a Theme of Thomas Tallis*, *On Wenlock Edge* and the Pastoral Symphony are reprinted by permission of Boosey & Hawkes Music Publishers Ltd; from Mass in G Minor and *Sancta Civitas*, by permission of J. & W. Curwen; from *Dona Nobis Pacem*, *Fantasia on the Old 104th*, *Five Tudor Portraits*, *Flos Campi*, *Hodie*, *Job*, *The Lark Ascending*, the *Magnificat*, the Piano Concerto, *Riders to the Sea*, the Fourth Symphony, the Fifth Symphony, the Sixth Symphony, the Seventh Symphony, the Eighth Symphony, the Ninth Symphony, and *Ten Blake Songs*, by permission of Oxford University Press; from the London Symphony, *A Sea Symphony* and *Toward the Unknown Region*, by permission of Stainer & Bell Ltd.

Samuel Palmer, 'The Piper', 1824
(Victoria and Albert Museum)

FIELD AND FACTORY, VICTORIA AND EDWARD VII

THE ENGLISH CHORAL TRADITION

The old man's story had been more fully historical than that of Queen Victoria, because it had been one of simple life. He had run parallel to Europe, making the picture human. Life, which was leaving the body beside him, had been the dependent of great events, but the great events had not been principally important to it. It was life because it had depended, along with that of Queen Victoria, upon the white colour of hayfields which had just been cut; upon the dew-stuck dust of kingcups, powdering the boots in morning grass; upon the almost extra-audible chirrup of a bat in moonlight, plucking like a cricket at the base of the skull.

T.H. WHITE, *Farewell Victoria*

Vaughan Williams has been referred to – originally, it would seem, by Sir Steuart Wilson – as a 'Christian agnostic', even as a 'disillusioned theist': tags which help to define his crucial position in English history. When he was born in 1872 Queen Victoria was still on the throne, and the Empire on which the sun never set seemed invulnerable. The panoply of Britain's material might seem still unassailable, though there was evidence that materialism, and its technical manifestation in mass industrialization, might damagingly take over from 'spirit'. For industrialism on so comprehensive a scale was at once the apotheosis and the nemesis of European man's post-Renaissance pride and presumption. He had learned to dragoon the energy of Nature to his own ends: only to find that these ends were potentially self-destructive.

As one would expect, the material crisis was complemented by a crisis of faith caused by the impact of science on traditional Christianity. *The Origin of Species* is one of those rare books that change history. Interestingly enough, Ralph Vaughan Williams was related on his mother's (English) side to the humanely scientific Darwins and also to the Wedgwoods, who were among the first to fuse traditional craftsmanship with light industry. On his father's (Welsh) side the Law and the Church had long prevailed: so in his ancestry the Establishment sought compromise with scientific and commercial enterprise. Perhaps it was the Celtic strain which steered him through the winds of change, promoting an enquiring mind along with an awareness of the numinous, if not the acceptance of an accredited faith. In the course of a long creative life – he was to compose vigorously from the end of the nineteenth century to his death more than half-way through the twentieth – Vaughan Williams demonstrated that the human spirit, however abused by industrial materialism and bureaucratic institutionalism, lay dormant, awaiting resuscitation. His life's work was to be, in Blake's sense, a rebirth of the Human Imagination, in a new vision of Albion.

If Vaughan Williams was double in being a Christian agnostic, he was double too in being by birth a countryman from rural Gloucestershire, but by nurture a Londoner, a man of the city. Nor is that an end to his doubleness: for as art and science were fused in his background, so he was by temperament an uncommon common man, while being to a degree socially privileged. His awareness of his cultural heritage was naturally abetted by the social advantages he enjoyed. Family life at home did not segregate intellectual enquiry and sensory awareness from the everyday business of life. Poetry, novels, history, biography and philosophy were read aloud in the family circle, introducing the young Ralph to most of the authors who were to mould his future. Interest in history and architecture was further fostered at his public school (Charterhouse), and then at Cambridge. His university friends and colleagues included the great legal historian Maitland, along with George Trevelyan and H.A.L. Fisher to both of whom he was related. The 'mind of England' was thus in his blood and bones, his nerves and intellect. He had had some formal education in music from Sir Hubert Parry, at the Royal College in 1890, before entering Trinity College, Cambridge, in 1892. He graduated with a Mus. B. in 1894, having been tutored by Charles Wood and Sir Charles Villiers Stanford, and with a BA in history in 1895. Though 'musical', Ralph was not in youth musically fanatical; indeed he was not conspicuously encouraged by his teachers, and Charles Wood, who had exceptional gifts as a pedagogue, advised him against a musical career. Even so, music flowered within Vaughan Williams's wide and deep awareness of his English heritage. Its hold was strong enough, by the time he left Cambridge, to encourage him to return to the Royal College in London for further study. Ultimately, music dominated his many other interests because it was the heart of his creativity. With hindsight we may suspect that this was because music is the art most closely related to spiritual values.

At the time when Vaughan Williams began to compose it cannot, however, have been easy to recognize music's spiritual nature, for Edwardian society used it, not surprisingly, to ballast its own unspiritual ethics and purposes. Music's central manifestation in English life was what came to be called the English Choral Tradition, in which 'masses' of poeple banded 'democratically' together to hymn the might of Edwardian affluence and of the imperial dream which was the world-wide consequence of commercial aggrandizement at home. We are apt to refer to Vaughan Williams's main teachers, Parry and Stanford, with their knighthoods appended, because that is the measure of their status (years later, Vaughan Williams was to refuse a knighthood). We should not, however, do so facetiously, for the composers of the English choral tradition were not hypocritical; they genuinely believed that material might could encourage moral aspiration, fostering traditional Christianity in an ethical if not ultimately in a religious sense. Parry, like Vaughan Williams, came of the small gentry. An Etonian and an Oxford man, he eventually occupied the two prime positions in the musical Establishment, being Professor of Music at Oxford and head of the Royal College of Music in London, and knighted on both counts. Again unsurprisingly, he began his composing career with a sequence of oratorios on biblical subjects: works which have been forgotten for reasons exposed, at the time of their original production, by the most devastating of all music critics, George Bernard Shaw. Vaughan Williams, one may suspect, revered Parry more for his general cultivation and for his love of Bach than for his oratorios *per se*. None the less, these works were respectable examples of an (in several senses) established tradition – into the nature and origins of which we must briefly enquire.

When Handel came to England in the early eighteenth century his intention was to sell Italian opera – the central European convention of the classical baroque era – to the English, who, with the rapid growth of the coal industry, were becoming a basically middle-class 'nation of shopkeepers' who ought to be able to afford it. Although he produced over here a number of magnificent heroic operas, sung in Italian with illustrious, largely imported casts, his venture failed. The commonsensical English anticipated the verdict of Dr Johnson in his *Dictionary* that opera – at least of this kind – was 'an Exotick and Irrational Entertainment', and the internationally celebrated composer was bankrupt. With the canniness of genius Handel had the bright idea of adapting his favoured artistic convention to topical and local needs: he continued to write heroic operas, but took his myths and stories not from classical mythology or ancient history but from the Bible, especially the Old Testament, the one book the English middle class knew and relished. Handel's oratorios are identical with his operas in their fundamental theme – that of man as hero and leader who, god-like in pretension, has to admit to human fallibility and mortality and to the consequences of the Fall. From his profound apprehension of human contradiction sprang the dramatic potency of his music, which can none the less be construed as a paean to man's would-be superhuman courage. Technically, too, the oratorios – which were usually performed in theatres, not churches – mirror the operas, being based on interplay between the private life of individual men and women (manifest in recitative and arioso) and the public weal of the dance and chorus, with the solo aria – wherein private passions are disciplined by dance-rhythm, implying concern for the whole – holding the balance. The only difference between opera and oratorio was that the latter gave greater importance to the chorus as representatives of us the people – present-day mercantile Britons momentarily masquerading as ancient Israelites. Significantly, the choruses are prevailingly homophonic, with the parts marshalled from the 'top' downwards; even the fugal choruses are designed so that the counterpoint fits into the pre-ordained harmonic-tonal scheme rather than involving, as do Bach's fugues, a tense interplay between the 'horizontal' and the 'vertical' dimensions.

Most of Handel's heroes were Old Testament leaders such as Saul and Jephtha, variously maimed by human pride and presumption. Only in *Messiah* is the New Testament favoured along with the Old, which explains why *Messiah* came to be esteemed above all the other oratorios by the rising middle class. Increasingly, the celebration of leader and people was fused with ethical morality in the spirit of the Enlightenment. *Messiah* became an English institution, a role it has maintained until the present day, despite the buffets our material complacency has suffered in the two hundred and fifty years since its triumph.

Handel himself, being a composer of dramatic conflict unrivalled except by Mozart, was superb in pride but seldom complacent. The commercialized British, however, gradually transformed his potent reality into wish-fulfilment. Self-righteously asserting pride in their power, they presented Handel's oratorios with giganticized forces in theatres and civic buildings – especially the town halls of the rapidly expanding northern industrial cities. As the Victorian years unfolded, Handel's oratorios were increasingly construed as hymns to the might of industry and empire, a theme to which *Israel in Egypt* readily lent itself; while *Messiah* paid complementary tribute to pseudo-Christian morality and the Victorian ethic of work. If the heart of Handel was sacrificed in the process, what was left was still, given the force of his genius, potentially efficacious. Crystal Palace Handel still thrills, inducing euphoria as well as amnesia. But since the experience was even then wish-fulfilment, and now sounds like hypocrisy, it was unlikely to nurture composers who were worthy successors to Handel. There is point in the fact that Handel was not indigenous to the mind of England but was an alien importation. When other foreigners, such as Mendelssohn and Spohr, took over from him as oratorio manufacturers – the industrial metaphor is appropriate – we are aware of a hollowness at the core.

This evolution in English oratorio was finally put down by Bernard Shaw when he reviewed a performance of Mendelssohn's *St Paul* in September 1889:

> I grant you that Mendelssohn is better than the organist, the professor, the Mus. Bach. and the Mus. Doc.; just as Tennyson is better than Cumberland or Coleman. But compared with Handel, he is what Tennyson is to Shakespeare.... Set all that dreary fugue-manufacture, with its Sunday-school sentimentalities and its Music-school ornamentalities, against your recollection of the expressive and vigorous choruses of Handel; and ask yourself on your honour whether there is the slightest difference in kind between 'Stone him to death' and 'Under the pump with a kick and a thump' in *Dorothy*. ... But of what use is it to complain? If my cry were heeded, the [Crystal] Palace directors would simply say: 'O he likes Handel, does he? How nice! We rather think we can meet his views in that direction.' And they would straightway kidnap five or six thousand choristers; put *Israel in Egypt* in rehearsal; and treat me to a dose of thunder machines on the Handel orchestra. It would be utterly in vain; I should complain louder than ever: the machine thunder is as unimpressive as the noise of a thousand footsteps in Oxford Street.

Mendelssohn, of course, was or had been a composer of precocious gifts; so we shall not be surprised to discover that Shaw was even more severe on Parry, who tempered the oratorio prototype of Handel, Mendelssohn and Spohr with a dose of the stoic sobriety and contrapuntal science of Brahms, by the 1880s established as linchpin of British academicism both in the universities and colleges. Parry's oratorios on biblical subjects, written between 1887 and 1894, preserve less vitality than Mendelssohn's, despite elements of latent drama that may have accrued from his being a confessed, if reluctant, agnostic. Fortunately – though Delius testily remarked that he would have set the whole Bible to music had he lived long enough – Parry did not restrict himself to oratorio. He was, like Vaughan Williams, a man of wide culture and fine literary taste, inspired not so much by contemporary poets as by masters of England's past, especially Milton, who, though mirroring the religious and political divisiveness of the seventeenth century, could also be regarded as a prop to Victorian ethical probity.

Parry's best-known piece – his setting of Milton's *At a Solemn Musick*, retitled from its first line as *Blest Pair of Sirens* – is probably also his best. It certainly encapsulates the qualities that earned the respect of Vaughan Williams, for its subject is the power of music to preserve and restore spiritual values in a fallen world. The sweep of the paragraphs, the soaring diatonic lines and flowing harmonies, beginning as an assertion of pride and will, attain true nobility as aspiration triumphs over complacency, and righteousness ousts self-righteousness. Sir Hubert – who advised the young Vaughan Williams to compose choral music, 'like an Englishman and a gentleman' – was not always confined by the academic cloister and vicarage lawn, not even during the height of his oratorio-fever, with which the date (1887) of *Blest Pair of Sirens* is contemporary. A late choral and orchestral work (an *Ode on the Nativity* which is a setting not of Milton, but of the old Scots poet Dunbar) does not evoke, as Vaughan Williams did later, the message of the boy who was born, but is surprisingly tough and sinewy, combining something of the open, even gauche, quality of Bruckner with the streamlined orchestral expertise of Richard Strauss – who Busoni said was 'an industrialist even in his music'. Perhaps in this equivocation the unease latent in Parry's Christianity finally becomes patent – in 1912, shortly before the world war that was an explosion of Edwardian materialism. At the end of that war, in 1918, Parry composed what is probably his most distinguished work, the *Songs of Farewell*, which although indubitably English and choral, are explicitly valedictory.

Here Parry's sensitivity to the rhythms of English poetry helped to release him from the metrical squareness of Teutonic tradition, though his resolutely diatonic, slightly chromaticized idiom betrays no whiff of the modal variety of English sixteenth- and seventeenth-century music. This is a little surprising because Parry was a pioneer in the rediscovery of Purcell and, to a lesser degree, of Tudor music. There are occasional hints of 'English' false relation in the late *Songs of Farewell* and the *Ode on the Nativity*; on the whole, however, one suspects that Parry was subconsciously reluctant to admit to such vestiges of technical and spiritual dubiety precisely because he was himself vulnerable. A good but by no means goody-goody Victorian gentleman, he must keep a stiff upper lip, nurturing the Imperial Dream. The most obvious instance is his setting of those lines from Blake's 'Jerusalem' which, in defiance and near-reversal of Blake's intention, he transformed into a patriotic hymn, trotted out to defend national sovereignty at war memorials and on celebratory occasions, along with Thomas Arne's 'Rule Britannia'. The contrast between the two tunes, now equally part of Everyman's consciousness, is pointed. In 1740 Arne's perky tune asserted the blithe optimism of the rising Common Man in his martially and materially prosperous nation;

Parry's spacious melody eschews Arne's insouciance in order to inculcate moral uplift. Arne in 1740 was not yet aware – only a Blake could have been – of the debit side to material power and progress; Parry, in the late nineteenth century, needed moral self-justification, as well as wish-fulfilment. This does not mean that 'Jerusalem' is an inferior piece of work. It is a fine tune which elevates hearts as well as lungs; only if we think of Blake does it cause us momentarily to squirm, even to cringe.

Parry lacked what T.S. Eliot called Blake's 'terrifying honesty'; he hadn't electrical charge sufficient to make his well-intentioned energy spiritually recreative. For that, genius as distinct from talent is essential; and when the time was ripe genius was resurgent in English music, after its long desuetude. Taken at his face value, one could hardly conceive of a grander representative of Establishment than Sir Edward Elgar – to whom we accord the accolade of his title, as we do to Parry and Stanford. He accepted, indeed revelled in, the power and glory of the world he celebrated in his *Pomp and Circumstance* marches: one of which, with words attached later, has become, as 'Land of Hope and Glory', a national institution no less potent than 'Rule Britannia' and 'Jerusalem', and with greater justification since it is a magnificent, potently harmonized tune that can still send shivers down reluctant, even resentful, spines. In this jingoistic vein Elgar has a peer in the young Kipling; and the electrical energy of both writer and composer is disturbing enough to indicate that their face value is not the whole truth about them. It is not fortuitous that Kipling's supreme achievement, *Kim*, written at the beginning of the new century in 1901, should be simultaneously about the Imperial Dream and the adolescent innocence necessary to sustain it; nor that Kipling's remarkable late tales became deeply perturbed and perturbing, at times morbidly sado-masochistic. *Kim* would have been inconceivable after the 1919 Amritsar massacre.

The parallel with Elgar is exact, even down to the brilliant technical skill he acquired by hard experience, with little formal training in music. Profoundly English though he was, Elgar's technique was basically German, as was that of all English composers of his day – a fact not without its socio-political aspects. By means of it Elgar was able, in an England whose musical traditions were moribund, to rival the composer-industrialist Richard Strauss in technical virtuosity, and to assume the existence of a symphonic tradition which in Britain had never happened.

Even so, Elgar's dazzling virtuosity is not what makes him a great composer: for his mature work turns out to be a threnody on Edwardian opulence and material might. The top-hatted, morning-coated Sir Edward, chatting with the rich and titled at the races, is a mask for the man of deep spiritual intuition, who conceived his sweeping themes while striding over the Malvern Hills; who found in his Falstaff not a bloated old reprobate, but a portrait of the decline and death of the ideal Englishman he would have liked to be, and in a sense was. The heroic Second Symphony is prefaced by Shelley's words 'Rarely, rarely, comest thou, Spirit of Delight'; and ends with a dying fall. It was composed on the eve of the Great War that destroyed Elgar's England – and stifled his own creative fires, since although he survived until 1934 he produced no music of consequence after 1918. In old age he recognized with pain, though he still had a justifiable pride in the tune, that his land of hope and glory had been savagely belied in the event. His was a vision of Albion that 'never was' on land or sea, except in his heart's truth; and to that the post-war world seemed indifferent.

Shelley was atheistical, but the spirit of delight to which he refers is a premonition of the numinous, which alone validates human pride and presumption. And in Elgar's case the spiritual quality behind the façade had a specifically religious aspect: he was a Roman Catholic and a man of passionate religious sensibility, if not conviction. That his faith was a matter of aspiration makes it, for us, the more impressive. Because he was a genius fervently uncertain in belief, he could revitalize English oratorio, which had tended to equate spiritual with material power, imperial might with social complacency. In his early days Elgar produced oratorio-style works that are respect-worthy but undistinguished except in the light of what was to come. Understandably he was a slow starter whose first quintessential work, the *Enigma Variations*, appeared when he was forty, in the last year of the nineteenth century. In the first year of the twentieth, he composed *The Dream of Gerontius* which, conceiving oratorio as inner strife, refashions the prototype in highly personal music approaching Verdi in lyrical ardour, Wagner in harmonic expressiveness.

The Dream of Gerontius was the first religious work of Elgar's maturity and remained the greatest. Adrian Boult, who knew more about Elgar than most people, matintained that the high point of his church music was the late *The Kingdom*, though this work never caught the popular imagination, as did *Gerontius*. The reason is not far to seek: *The Kingdom* does not centre on a suffering seeker after faith. In this context Cardinal Newman's text for *Gerontius* was exactly what Elgar needed, for it was not an Establishment rehash of biblical precedents, but the personal testament of a man in some ways similar to Elgar. Newman differed from Elgar in that he was a trained theologian and in that he was, as poet, a non-starter. He could therefore provide the theological substructure that Elgar needed but was indifferent to, while leaving the imaginative flesh and blood to be provided by the music. Elgar's choral writing is in the strict sense superb, with an unflagging momentum to its sequential paragraphs that is related to Parry while far outstripping him in exaltation. Parry's genuine nobility is attained to only by evading or trampling over the painful contradictions latent in human pride; Elgar supersedes Parry's plain diatonicism by lines no less grand, yet in perpetual mobility, modulating incessantly, without loss of direction. In the assurance of his genius Elgar could learn more from late Wagner's headiness than could blandly conservative Parry; and there are hints too of 'early' English polymodality which Elgar, without conscious emulation, could accept as part of his heritage. Indeed, if there is an explanation of the powerfully English effect of Elgar's music, notwithstanding the Teutonic origins of his style, it can only be in the unconscious intrusion of inflexions derived not only from the English language, but also from English folk song, and from the modal reflections of those melodies in Tudor polyphony.

On Elgar's own evidence, we know that the second subject of his *Introduction and Allegro for Strings* was inspired by a group of Welsh folk singers overheard by chance in Cardiganshire, in 1901. The principal subject is, however, even more deeply if less patently permeated by the contours of folk song, absorbed into Elgar's European, chromaticized diatonicism. The meandering opening melody of the elegiac Cello Concerto is another instance; while the vocal writing in *Gerontius*, for all its harmonic opulence and textural sophistication, differs from its Germanic sources in its 'winged' quality, borne on Shelley's Spirit of Delight. The transition from Part I into Part II of the oratorio is especially revealing. At the conclusion of the first part a Priest, Parsifal-like in solemnity, calls on Gerontius, whose name makes him an old, dying man, to 'go forth' in the name of the Lord. The chorus launches into a heroic peroration fugally developing the 'faith' theme of the Prelude (*Gerontius* calls on an advanced Wagnerian leitmotif technique); and steers chromatic ambiguity into resonant contrapuntal unity. The typically Elgarian tune is in D major, healing the prelude's anxious D minor into peace; its spaciously arching seventh elevates Parryan nobility into ecstacy, achieving resolution. After this, Part II may begin with the simplest, and perhaps the most beautiful, music Elgar ever wrote. Flowing from god-like fourths, it is at first not only diatonic, but modal, limpidly scored for woodwind. Within this modality, chromatic oscillations and enharmonic mysteries acquire a new significance; for what had been, in relation to the hero's inner life, anxiety, is now release. Materiality becomes spirit; and spirit is materialized, since Gerontius's soul, having 'passed over', converses with an angel whose music is poised between

Gerontius's dreamy enharmony and the modal purity of stepwise-floating alleluyas. This is the first, and perhaps the only direct, prophecy of Vaughan Williams in Elgar's music. As Vaughan Williams did later, it equates the vision of Albion with a New Jerusalem potentially attainable by a reanimation of matter with spirit. For a moment, Edwardian Sir Edward becomes a Blakean bard, 'calling among the ancient trees'.

Elgar, though the greatest, was not the only composer of genius (as distinct from talent) to revitalize our music at the turn of the century. He had a complement, and also a polar opposite, in Delius, whose reaction against his Victorian heritage was violent. Whereas Elgar ostensibly relished the material world he celebrated while being at heart a spiritual seeker assailed by doubts, Delius abominated alike industrial Bradford, where he was born, and all churches, since he considered God a shibboleth born of man's shaming frailty. The experience that fired Delius's imagination was narrow but intense. It is also the heart of his Englishness, despite his partly Teutonic ancestry and his Wagnerian approach to his art. Thanks to the grudging generosity of his businessman father, he had the wherewithal to retreat from Bradford and to seek havens in the bohemian life of Montmartre, the solitudinous mountains of Norway, and the orange and grapefruit groves of Florida. As a composer he carried the Wagnerian deification of self a stage further in that in his most typical music there is no human population, only himself and solitude. Thus the essence of Delius's music is the flow of sensation – to him 'the only thing that matters'. Even in an abstract instrumental work such as the Violin Concerto the initial Wagnerian appoggiaturas – sighs of the overburdened heart – generate a fluctuating woof of chromatic harmonies; yet the lines that make up these harmonies are, individually considered, vocal, modal, often pentatonic in contour, as though each singing melody were seeking a oneness incarnate in the solo violin's winging song, beyond the temporal flux. Delius's music, like Richard Jefferies' prose, is 'The story of my Heart' or, like Whitman's 'free' verse, 'A Song of Myself'; yet this story and song can find consummation only in surrender to the impersonal forces of wind and sky and sea.

The supreme justification of this pantheistic nature-mysticism occurs in a latish work, *A Song of the High Hills*, composed (again shortly before the Great War) in 1912. In this one may trace occasional references to classical precedents such as sonata and sonata-rondo, though the real force of its large-scale structure is its occurrence – the gradual release of those passion-laden sobs in an ecstatic metamorphosis of (chromatic) harmonic Experience into (pentatonic) melodic Innocence, as the wordless chorus wings us to the peopleless peaks. This is a – perhaps *the* – religious experience.

Despite his contempt for English oratorio Delius composed two works that could not have existed but for that tradition. The earlier of them, *A Mass of Life*, was begun at the turn of the century, finished in 1904–5. It is his biggest work, and possibly his greatest, though not his most consummately realized. Certainly it is his most comprehensive testament, wherein he identifies himself with his hero Nietzsche, celebrating man's 'high courage and self-reliance' in the face of the irremediable 'death of God'. For man to be totally self-responsible is an ultimate exaltation, and also an ultimate terror. Delius carried fanatical belief in the self to a point at which he could tolerate no music but his own – except possibly that of Wagner and of younger composers who dedicated pieces to him. This, if magnificent, is foolhardy; to carry it off, an artist needs to be consistently inspired, which – over the nearly two-hour stretch of *A Mass of Life* – is asking a lot. Although Delius is not quite equal to the challenge, he produces in this key work in our (even in Europe's) history enough inspired music to win the day. Despite the post-Wagnerian idiom, the evocations of midnight and of the stillness of summer noon are as original as they are heart-rending; while the opening and closing choruses remind us, in surging impetus and control of the vast paragraph, of the younger Delius's superabundant energy, which gave poignancy to his nostalgia. Both the life-celebrating virility and the life-transcending nature-worship are musical equivalents of Nietzsche's *Also sprach Zarathustra*, which furnished Delius with his text. Since the magic of such music can be explained only as an act of faith, it is not after all surprising that there should be a parallel between the monumental choruses in the *Gerontius* of State-supporting but God-aspiring Elgar and these monumental choruses of a composer who believed only in 'human courage and self-reliance'. Through both rings Shelley's spirit of delight which, if it cometh but rarely, is worth waiting for.

Although it has no connection with the Christian eucharistical Mass, Delius's *Mass of Life* is aptly named. His later *Requiem*, written during the First World War, is a Mass of death, and the two works prove indistinguishable in intention, since for an ultimate humanist death and life can only be interdependent. Though less massive than the *Mass*, the *Requiem* is scored for similar forces; and its text, cobbled together by Delius from fragments of his beloved Nietzsche with a few tags from Ecclesiastes, bears a similar burden. The composer himself said that the piece 'is not a religious work. ... The proud spirit casts off the yoke of superstition, for it knows that death puts an end to all life, and therefore fulfilment can only be found in life itself.' This was not what the British oratorio public expected from a memorial tribute to young men martyred in the war, and in 1916 moral disapproval of the text – especially the second movement's 'Hymn to Free Love' – spilt over into critical dismissal of the music. What used to be liabilities now count as assets; and although the big choruses of the *Requiem* cannot rival those of *A Mass of Life* in exhilaration or intoxication, there are 'progressive' moments in the *Requiem* that suggest how Delius's music might have evolved, but for the syphilitic paralysis that slowly destroyed him.

Again, these moments turn out to be in essence numinous, if not overtly religious: especially in the last movement's transition into glowing sunrise, the E major tonality being here, as so often in European music, Edenic. Real British (or Norwegian) folk songs occasionally crop up in Delius's winging polyphonies; throughout, his music had sought pentatonic innocence as a goal of its harmonic experience. In the final pages of the *Requiem*, pentatonicism takes over unsullied, except for the intermittent intrusion of the sharp fourth of the lydian mode, traditionally associated with healing. Blithe birds and babbling brooks tinkle through sustained drones, in a pentatonic paradise of harp, celesta and glockenspiel. The common view of Delius as an exclusively regressive composer must always be inadequate since his evocation of the life-force may attain such glory. This epilogue, however, is unique in his work: a prelude to life's renewal in the spring of the year, wherein the non-Western, quasi-Balinese sonorities are a harbinger of things to come – including the quasi-oriental elements in Holst and the 'magic music' of Vaughan Williams's last phase.

When Vaughan Williams attained his mature identity, his music was in many ways a reaction against the complementary polar opposites of Elgar and Delius. True, as a disciple of Parry, he began in the same tradition as Elgar. Born a little later, however, he could not share Elgar's apparent but ultimately disillusioned confidence in Edwardian values, nor could he find Delius's hot-blooded post-Wagnerian chromaticism – the atheistical twilight of Europe's ego-mania – temperamentally congenial. What he could share with them was the religious ecstasy that in Elgar's music was linked both to his search for a faith and to his longing for the old, lost, Malvern Hills England; and still more the Nature-mysticism that in Delius's music stemmed from his admission of man's ultimately solitary state. So it cannot be fortuitous that Vaughan Williams's first major work, composed over the same years as Elgar's *Gerontius* and Delius's *A Mass of Life*, was a symphony that is also an Elgarian oratorio; and that it shared both poet and subject with what is perhaps Delius's most perfectly realized work – the choral and orchestral *Sea-Drift*.

This setting of Walt Whitman's verse is pervaded by regret for life once vivid and vital from which one is now separated – as Delius was later to be, in his garden at Grez-sur-Loing. The all-encompassing sea is the eternal unconscious from which emerges and into which dissolves the self, symbolized by the sea bird who sings of his separation from his probably slain beloved. The solo baritone is Delius himself, who translates Whitman into music, and also you and I, 'insensible of mortality', yet, like everyone else, desperately mortal. The soloist is also Delius as a small boy, or any small boy, at the moment when he first recognizes the immutability of death; 'my mate no more, no more, with me; we two together no more'. The loss of innocence and the loss of love are interdependent: which is why Delius's final recollection of happiness past ('O past, O happy life, O songs of love'), again in a traditionally Edenic E major, is even more heart-rending than the immediate cognition of death. The music's dissolution into sighing appoggiaturas on the reiterated 'no more' sounds at once like eternally breaking waves and like the wail of a new born babe: not for nothing are the words *mere* and *mère* etymologically related. Fundamentally, Vaughan Williams is an affirmative artist who eschews nostalgia. It says something, however, about the probity of his optimism – which in the dark light of the Sixth and Ninth Symphonies is hardly the right word – that he should have started from the sea's eternal synthesis of life and death; and that this most English of composers should have been triggered by a poet of the New World.

I

THE PARLOUR
AND THE OPEN SEA

CONFORMITY AND NONCONFORMITY IN
TOWARD THE UNKNOWN REGION AND
A SEA SYMPHONY

> O voyagers, O seamen,
> You who come to port, and you whose bodies
> Will suffer the trial and judgement of the sea,
> Or whatever event, this is your real destination ...
>
> Not fare well,
> But fare forward, voyagers.
>
> T.S. ELIOT, 'THE DRY SALVAGES'

Although Vaughan Williams's creative fires needed a New World fully to stimulate them, his composing career began where one might have expected, in the Edwardian parlour. His first published works are settings of the supreme Victorian lyricist and elegist, Tennyson: a great poet whom Vaughan Williams seems not to have found congenial, for his 1902 settings are respectable without being memorable. The Pre-Raphaelite Rossetti awoke more echoes in the young composer, perhaps because the poet's pseudo-medievalism and his cultivation of the inner dream were potentially visionary. One of the Rossetti songs, 'Silent Noon', is a mini-masterpiece haunting enough to be still frequently performed. However redolent of the Edwardian parlour, it is musically transcendent, as is the love celebrated in the poem. The incipient modality of the tune, the mediant shifts to the harmony, the tranquilly insidious syncopated rhythm, are already essential Vaughan Williams.

There is a precedent for Vaughan Williams's early songs in those of Stanford, who was with Parry the twin representative of English academic conservatism, being a professor at Cambridge and the Royal College, as Parry was a professor at the Royal College and Oxford. Despite Stanford's notorious ill manners, he seems to have been respected, even revered, by Vaughan Williams as by most of his pupils, though they knew they must escape the Teutonic bondage that had enslaved English music and was encapsulated in Stanford's near-idolatry of Brahms. At least Stanford, unlike Parry, was not primarily an oratorio composer; he wrote operas, a dangerous genre, and even in his instrumental music his

Teutonic academicism was often refreshed by draughts of his Irish ancestry; his Clarinet Concerto, for instance, has for slow movement an Irish keening that has an analogy with the gypsy folk-arabesques in the Clarinet Quintet of Brahms. Similarly, many of Stanford's songs are patently by an Irishman who loves Brahms, and the Irishness is detectable not merely when Stanford is 'arranging' a real folk tune, as in the delightful 'Trottin' to the fair', but whenever he is setting Irish verse, or even verse that evokes the other-worldly. The well known 'The fairy lough' and 'A soft day' are beautiful examples, distilling an authentic folk fragrance; the large-scale setting of Keats's 'La Belle Dame sans Merci' is still finer, opening magic casements on perilous seas and faery lands forlorn. Moreover, the setting of 'O mistress mine' has, in its linear and rhythmic flexibility, a genuinely Elizabethan savour, even though its coda is pure Brahams. Clearly there was much in Stanford's songs that the young Vaughan Williams could admire; no doubt he did so the more readily because as pedagogue Stanford discouraged him from dallying with those old modes, which might undermine harmonic stability. Certainly the Irishness of Stanford's songs pointed towards escape-routes from a cosily enclosed world. To such paths of escape Vaughan Williams gave, in the most popular of his early songs, explicit formulation, since they were 'songs of the open road'.

His cycle of *Songs of Travel*, to verses by Robert Louis Stevenson, is still part of the recitalist's repertory, and deserves to be. If written for the parlour, the songs are about a need to break out; and do so more honestly and therefore movingly than the self-conscious bucolics of Chesterton and Belloc. Some of Stevenson's verses were written to pre-existent tunes. Vaughan Williams fashions new tunes that fit them like a glove: not so much in the tramping-rhythmed 'Vagabond' as in a folk-styled love-song like 'I will make you brooches' and in an elegy like 'Bright is the ring of words'. The modal tunes, the false-related harmonies, the shifting mediants sound touching because spontaneous, however artful both words and music, given the milieu they come from.

Breaking out from that milieu was, however, a creative necessity at a deeper level than is indicated by these songs; and it is to the point that the best of Vaughan Williams's early songs hardly conformed to Edwardian *moeurs* at all. 'Linden Lea' became a household word, familiar in several kinds of parlour; many people still recognize the tune, even if they do not know its name. Significantly it appeared, in 1901, in a magazine, a part of parochial life; and was first performed at a concert in the Yorkshire village of Hooton Roberts, where the father of Ivor and Nicholas Gatty, Cambridge contemporaries of Vaughan Williams, was vicar. After its

15

London presentation in the following year the song became a best-seller, for the admirable reason that, masquerading in the guise of an Edwardian parlour song with piano accompaniment, it was a small creation of genius, with the pristine flavour of a genuine folk song. Having heard it, one seems to have known the tune all one's life: so that what Vaughan Williams does in his music directly echoes what William Barnes does in his verse. For Barnes, a most un-Tennysonian poet, was, like Vaughan Williams, a cultivated English gentleman of an enquiring mind. Attempting to conserve the 'true' English language by writing in Dorsetshire dialect, he discovered that his linguistic pursuits had much to teach him about the quality of English rural life. Born in 1800, dying in 1886, he lived among educated Victorians who were intelligent enough to respect his work as more than antiquarianism – even if they did not fully appreciate the superiority of his dialect verse over his genteel poetry. Vaughan Williams, born in the decade before Barnes's death, was an heir to his heritage, both in his research into the origins of an English musical language, and in his recognition that a language was also a way of life. The collusion of composer and poet seems to have been a happy accident, for Vaughan Williams did not comprehensively explore their relationship. 'Linden Lea' is not unique in Vaughan Williams's early songs: as early as 1896 he had composed a gravely beautiful setting of Thomas Vaux's 'How can the tree but wither?' which sounds like authentic Vaughan Williams, not because it is folk-like but because it is consistently modal Tudor re-creation. Still, while this is a fine song atypical of the Edwardian parlour, 'Linden Lea' is a minor miracle: a poignantly unselfconscious fusion of worlds peasant and polite, rural and urban.

As already indicated, Vaughan Williams's breakaway called, however, for the catalyst of a New World more urgently than that of an old. He found one in the American poet Walt Whitman, to whose work he had been introduced, at Cambridge, by Bertrand Russell. Whitman's liberating 'free verse' was widely influential at the time; not only Delius but even pedagogic musicians such as Hamilton Harty, Stanford and Charles Wood found in it some intimation of alternative worlds – as in the next generation did Holst as well as Vaughan Williams. Whitman's *Leaves of Grass* complemented the prose poems of the European Nietzsche, whose celebration of untrammelled self sprang from the death of Europe as well as of God. 'A Song of Myself' was a product of a world that might supersede Europe, and in psychological terms was already so doing – as English Blake had indicated in his accurately titled Prophetic Book, *America*. The free verse of Blake's Prophetic Books has much in common with the even freer verse Whitman hammered out on the 'anvil of his soul', only in Whitman biblical cadences are absorbed into the American vernacular. Imaginations boggled at Whitman, both at home in the Calvinist regions of his native heritage, and in moribund old Europe; his elder colleague Emerson was on the mark in noting, in a famous letter of 1855, that *Leaves of Grass* was 'the most extraordinary piece of wit and wisdom that America has yet contributed'. It defined an American self owing a minimum to anything other than self; and it miraculously adumbrated a universal religion absorbing Christianity along with the great oriental religions, of which Whitman's knowledge was for the most part intuitive. Mystically and philosophically, as well as technically, Whitman has much in common with Blake, for whom 'Jesus Christ IS the Human Imagination'. Similarly, Whitman's God was his and everyone's selfhood: to live one's own life to the full measure of one's capacity is to be one with one's fellow creatures, including the animals; to be one with Nature; and so to *be* God. Here is the ultimate recipe for a New World of the spirit, as well as of place. This spirit still reverberates in the 'free' cadences of Whitman's verse, in which, paradoxically, he worked hard in the pursuit of spontaneity. It may function at white heat, or it may catalogue the tawdry ephemera of everyday experience; inwardly or outwardly, however, it is the ultimate poetic of democracy.

It was probably easy for Englishmen of Vaughan Williams's generation to respond to Whitman because there was an English precedent for him less esoteric and more direct than Blake. In his *Biographia Literaria* Coleridge suggests that Wordsworth's purpose, in the *Lyrical Ballads* of 1798, was 'to give the charm of novelty to a thing of every day, and to excite a feeling analogous to the supernatural, by awakening the mind's attention to the lethargy of custom, and directing it to the wonders of the powers within us; an inexhaustible treasure, but for which, in consequence of the film of familiarity and selfish solicitude, we have eyes that see not, ears that hear not, and minds that neither feel nor understand'. On a more gargantuan scale Whitman, in his New World, certainly assaulted 'the lethargy of custom', directing us to 'unknown powers within', and to the 'novelty' of familiar objects. Such too had been the effect of the notorious address delivered by Emerson to the Divinity School at Harvard in the 'refulgent summer' of 1838, in which it had been 'a luxury to draw the breath of life'. A plea for life that was also an act of self-discovery ruffled the Harvard dovecotes in a way that the self-styled proletarian bard was savagely to intensify. Ripples of the turbulence were still flowing over Vaughan Williams more than half a century later; or, it would be fair to say, a century later, since the impact of Whitman on Vaughan Williams did not entirely cease throughout his creative life.

Much later, Vaughan Williams was to be affected by Whitman's non-Western anti-creeds, and by the 'doubleness' inherent in his having been, as Bunyan had been in England, involved in civil war. At the outset, however, Vaughan Williams latched on to Whitman's basic preoccupation, for in 1906 he set his poem 'Toward the Unknown Region' for chorus and orchestra, and had it successfully launched at the Leeds Choral Festival in 1907. The poem is a fairly generalized statement of Whitman's theme, which Vaughan Williams sought yet was hardly ready for. Perhaps this is why he chose a poem which is, for Whitman, less free than usual, since it is, though without rhyme, in five three-lined stanzas. The poet promises us the ultimate fruition of joy if we loosen all but the eternal ties of time and space; since each of the three lines in a stanza is longer than the previous one, this may count as a 'loosening', albeit controlled in comparison with Whitman's more characteristic afflatus. It suits Vaughan Williams well enough however, as he launches into his initial voyage, beginning with a short orchestral prelude on a phrase that will be a 'fingerprint' throughout his composing life. A pentatonic descent from D to F is rounded off by a stepwise rise from F to A; the bass begins as an inversion of the melody:

Another fingerprint – pizzicato basses in a moderate march rhythm, with 'heroic' horn calls in dotted rhythm – leads into the choral music, introduced by the crucial words 'Darest thou'. The 'dare' is answered with Parryan confidence, slightly compromised by oscillating mediants that tell us we have 'no path to follow', and by whole-tone augmented chords and chromatic undulations to demonstrate what Whitman calls our chartless and mapless condition. The aeolian D minor shifts briefly to D major when the texture becomes fugal. Upwardly arpeggiated entries carry us forward with more than Parryan momentum, the surge growing stronger the more we relinquish human contact. The evocation of the 'unknown region' is on a whole-tone chord of the augmented fifth, inducing floating chromatics that stem from late Wagner by way of Elgar's *Gerontius*, first performed a few years previously.

But the structure of the piece, being a free rondo, prohibits anything like Wagner's 'endless Melos'. After each forward aspiration the pentatonic motto theme both calls us to order and – since each 'take-off' tends to be more exalted than the last – recharges our spiritual batteries. Although not extended, the work thus attempts a journey into the unknown parallel to that of *Gerontius*, and the most thrilling music occurs when, with the 'bounds bounding us' broken, we 'float' through chromatic sequences that are supposed to demolish time and space. Unsurprisingly, given that Vaughan Williams was a relatively unfledged composer, they do not really do so, at least in comparison with the exultation of *Gerontius* or *A Song of the High Hills*. Indeed, when in the final section we have reached the Unknown Region it turns out to be Edwardian England after all, hopefully purged of dross. The music is a pompous and circumstantial march in straight F major – the most Parry-like music in a score that is still fairly frequently performed: more because it is satisfying to sing and supportive of the status quo, socially as well as musically, than because it succeeds in its quest. That initial 'dare, has been answered in the negative, though the negation is temporary.

Vaughan Williams's other early Whitman piece, *A Sea Symphony*, was begun at about the same time as *Toward the Unknown Region*, in 1903, though it was not completed until 1910. The long gestation was due partly to the fact that *A Sea Symphony* was Vaughan Williams's first attempt at a large-scale work; was also attributable to a psychological maturation. By the time he reached the end of *A Sea Symphony* he had a clearer notion of what Whitman's 'dare' was about, though it would be another ten or more years before he ventured into regions genuinely unknown. One may say, however, that the Symphony looked into a New World future, while the clouds gathered and the sun set on the imperial epoch. The contrast with Delius's Whitman setting, *Sea-Drift*, is pointed. Delius, at the date Vaughan Williams started his sea-piece, offered freedom in nirvana, while the Nietzschean self submits to the twilight of Europe. Vaughan Williams, accepting Whitman's optimism, embarks on a journey that has definable human goals. Even so, the work ends on a question mark rather than with the consummation of the quest: which will prove to be the motive force behind Vaughan Williams's life-work. We will discover eventually that that life-work will itself end on a question mark, for the 'unknown regions' of Whitman's time and space are illimitable.

The first movement, 'A Song for all seasons, all ships', is about the relationship between the unknowable sea and the men who ride on it in ships. The key signature is a glorious D major, indicative of human heroism; yet the first sounds we hear are a brass fanfare on B flat minor, which abruptly shifts to its tonic, the upper mediant. Mediant relationships had been one of the means whereby Beethoven, and after him

19

Schubert, had undermined classical diatonic tonality: a process which, especially in works like the Hammerklavier Sonata and the *Missa Solemnis*, involved an exploration of 'unconscious' depths. We will find that mediant relationships increasingly dominate Vaughan Williams's music in ever more subtle ways. Here they point simply to the dichotomy between man and nature, which may offer a trigger for release. We soon realize that the swing of the unconscious sea here offers a freedom beyond that aspired to in the earlier Whitman piece. Fugato, as the choric voices enter, springs from an upward pentatonic phrase but modulates, chromatically and enharmonically, with irresistible impetus, as the 'white sails belly' and the steam ships 'come and go' on the 'dusky and undulating sea'. Whitman's anthropomorphic imagery gives physicality to the musical gestures, reinforced by triplet rhythms before a trenchant recapitulation of the B flat minor–D major fanfares.

Pentatonic arabesques subside into a new section in a brisk duple metre which, since it begins on an aeolian dominant to the basic D major, may serve the function of a symphonic second subject. The perky, martial as well as nautical, music evokes the flags with which men proudly or hopefully festoon their ships. The busy marine music turns into a 'chant' in honour of 'sailors of all nations', sung by solo baritone with choral interjections. The metre is now triple, and spacious; tonality, having shifted down a tone from B flat to A flat, once more oscillates between mediants. Again the music becomes slightly Parryan in its aspiring nobility, but regains its sea-surge in a fugato invocation of 'the soul of man' who must chart the boundless ocean. Man's essence is that he relishes the task, knowing he cannot succeed; interestingly, the free polyphony here merits comparison with *Gerontius*, though Vaughan Williams's seascape is naturally void of ecclesiastical trappings. The upward bouncing pentatonic motif heard at the outset of the movement grows more powerful in many mutations, until a magnificent climax hymns a sea captain, 'emblem of man elate above death' (which again, of course, he cannot be). D major sounds (almost) unambiguously, and the movement concludes with an expansion of the ceremonial flag-music on the words 'a pennant universal'. The ultimate D major climax – 'One flag above the rest', meaning man's unconquerable soul, not one nation against another! – is grandly Elgarian, and justifies its magniloquence. But the solo soprano droops from her high B through a pentatonic melisma to an off-key (modal C minor) reminiscence of the initial invocation; we are invited to 'Behold the sea itself', as distinct from men on it. The coda, in slowly unfolding fugato emerging from the original pentatonic rise, is mysterious as well as noble. Basses, descending *pianissimo* to a low D, become God's all-encompassing ocean while man's 'one flag above all' is hymned simultaneously. The interdependence of man and nature is thus the burden of this big symphonic movement which, if not in sonata form, has an exposition, a middle section or sections if not development, and a transformed recapitulation.

'On the Beach at Night alone' forms the symphonic slow movement and, as the title indicates, concerns man's solitariness in the context of the night of the unconscious and the sea's universality. Yet the poem – one of Whitman's most magical inspirations – envisages human solitude as potential salvation; freed of human contradictions, we may find, on the beach alone in the unknowing night, that the sea is an 'old mother who sways to and fro singing her husky song'. Nursed by her, the 'I' of the poem realizes that 'a vast similitude interlocks all'; time and space, life and death are annihilated. Vaughan Williams's image for this is worthy of Whitman's words, being one of his earliest manifestations of indubitable genius. A mysterious undulation of false-related triads of C minor and E major is richly but tenebrously scored:

We will see later that the doubleness of false relation is perhaps the most crucial feature of Vaughan Williams's language; in this instance it is almost as though darkly tragic C minor 'stands for' our strifeful human lot, while the E major triad is as blissfully oblivious of 'the pain of consciousness' as is the sea itself. Dichotomy is emphasized because the movement is scored for baritone solo with semi-chorus. The soloist begins with a one-note intonation which intermittently wafts to the pentatonic third, as though borne on the swell. Both the vocal and orchestral rhythms emulate the sea's 'swaying', while the softly growling scoring makes its 'huskiness' incarnate. For the 'vast similitude' of Nature tonality veers from the rocking C minor–E major axis to diatonic E flat major, the triple metre pervaded by a padding, passacaglia-like bass to suggest the eternity of time and space. The rhythm is that of a grave, triple-pulsed march; the choral parts are in fugato, with a theme opening with a noble rising fifth. Fugato builds up both in tempo and in harmonic richness as more aspects of 'past, present and future' are invoked. For a climactic statement of the 'vast similitude' full chorus enters in resonant homophony, again rocking between mediants (E flat and C majors). A postlude returns to the original monotone for solo baritone, and the orchestra swings sibilantly to silence. This is one of the first instances of Vaughan Williams's *melodic* undulations between major and minor third.

The third movement, 'Waves', is explicitly described as a scherzo, and is a paean to the 'sea itself'. After the man-made ships a myriad waves hasten, anthropomorphically 'lifting up their necks, a motley procession, flashing and frolicsome under the sun'. Momentarily, on this sunlit morning, men are invigorated by, not scared of, the waves: as is evident in the opening choral and orchestral fanfares, bounding in triple rhythm but with cross accents and false-related triads. The tonality is basically a phrygian G minor, but the more exuberant the waves grow, the more freely the music modulates, with chromatic passing notes and sequences. Orchestrally, the sizzling chromatics are sometimes onomatopoeic; the sea's 'laughing' even promotes an image one might call Handelian. If this is an unconscious reference back to English oratorio, it may have suggested transition into a *largamente* section that for a while imbues the unconscious sea with Parryan nobility, in a straightforward diatonic B flat major. But for the 'motley procession' the sea's animal exhuberance is joyously reinstated. Fanfares bound upwards, leading into a modified recapitulation of the opening section, back in phrygian-tinged G minor. But since the Parry-Elgar triple-rhythmed march recurs – leading to a coda wherein the waves 'follow' humankind's brave ocean-going vessels – it would seem that this scherzo too is really about the relationship between man and nature, rather than about 'the sea itself'. If Whitman's ultimate 'dare' is again evaded, that may afford cause for congratulation; the key is a blessed G major.

The finale, scored for both soprano and baritone soloists, with chorus and orchestra, is by far the longest movement, the title of which – 'The Explorers' – links it with the earlier *Toward the Unknown Region*. Whitman opens his poem with an elemental apostrophe to the universe – 'this unspeakable high procession of sun and moon and countless stars in the firmament', and the teemingly multifarious mini-life in the waters and grasses. From this he proceeds to a vision of Man – 'Adam and Eve descending, their myriad progeny after them'. Man asks his questions: 'Wherefore, unsatisfied soul? Whither, O mocking life?', to which the unknowing sea and impassive earth proffer no reply. In face of this, man's voyage of discovery through 'trackless seas and regions infinite' becomes a voyage of self-discovery. 'We will risk the ship, ourselves and all ... are they not all the seas of God?' Vaughan Williams is not yet equal to this, but who would be? So at first he identifies Whitman's elemental aspiration with that of William Morris's search for a regenerated England, as he had at the end of *Toward the Unknown Region*. The grave opening is in a stable, E flat major, with a fugato theme based on a rising fifth. The noble span of the lines and the diatonically dissonant texture resemble the Elgar of *Gerontius* rather than the blander sobrieties of Parry; this is appropriate to the social aspiration, though not to Whitman's windy metaphysics. Not until many years later, in his Sixth and Seventh Symphonies, will Vaughan Williams confront Whitman's challenge direct. The seas in this early work are not really perilous; despite momentary modulations to G flat and to G majors, calm assurance in E flat major pervades the assertion that 'Now first it seems my thought begins to span thee' – 'thee' being the sea's limitlessness, and therefore unspanability!

Undulating false relations, however, introduce the vision of Adam and Eve, whose ageless legacy to their 'progeny' (including us) is manifest in one of Vaughan Williams's slow marches over a pizzicato bass. The tonality begins as dorian G minor, but modulates fluidly for man's 'feverish' questionings. The questions themselves are sung unaccompanied, in organum-like parallel chords. Each question disrupts the padding gait of the march, but fugato entries impart harmonic drive and rhythmic momentum, ending with the apotheosis of man the (Blakean) poet as God. The fugued climax is earthy, rather than nautical, hinting at the grandeur of Elgar and the majesty of Handel, and ending with Purcellian shifts to chords of the flat seventh, triple *forte*: from which it declines in undulating concords recalling Tudor church music – or at least anticipating the use Vaughan Williams will make, in his next major orchestral work, of this idiom. This apparently regressive section ceases with pentatonic arabesques in descending mediants, G to E to C. Back in E flat, the two soloists sing, sometimes canonically, sometimes in octave unisons, of man's necessary quest over the dark seas, with appropriate enharmony and fluid modulations. Orchestral shimmerings help God to 'lave me all over' until full chorus enters with the words 'O thou transcendent', to a rising pentatonic motif derived from the first theme of the first movement.

The call to the soul to 'speed away' returns to fanfares on rising fourths and fifths, garlanded with trills. The shimmering orchestra sounds like the angelic music in *Gerontius*, though the sounds also have much in common with Delius's nature-noises. The climax is a homophonic choral version of the earlier duet between soprano and baritone, the theme of which – rising minor third, stepwise descent, rising fourth, falling third – is another pentatonic fingerprint which will recur throughout Vaughan Williams's long creative evolution. Here the harmonization is in falsely related concords, of which the final triple *forte* D major triads in first inversion serve as a pivot back to E flat major and a serene coda. Human identity and the unknowing sea are in precarious equilibrium. Fugato entries undulate up and down through a tone, like the wave-music in the nocturnal slow movement; the rising fourths and fifths of the chorus, now distantly soft, are bereft of personality, though the solo voices, soaring aloft, remind us of the pathos of the human condition in this elemental environment. Fleetingly the soprano solo, inspired by the 'daring joy' of the words, induces a perilous enharmonic modulation as she floats to a high B flat. The final pages, however, subside in wave-like undulations in unsullied E flat major, gradually coming to rest in a widely spaced E flat triad in the chorus, anchored to the basses' sepulchral bottom E flat. High up, flutes sustain a chord of the added sixth over almost inaudible, subaqueous thirds in the lowest reaches of the orchestra.

These two choral-orchestral works, *Toward the Unknown Region* and *A Sea Symphony*, initiate the long rite of passage that is the evolution of Vaughan Williams's work. But we have seen that Vaughan Williams cannot, at this stage, fully confront Whitman's 'dare'. To do that he needed a developmental symphony or sonata technique which is no more than embryonic in his symphonic oratorio, but which he was to evolve during the symphonic sequence of his middle years. The sea will return in many of his later works. Immediately, however, Vaughan Williams leaves the uncharted seas, not to return to the deceptively safe heart of Edwardian England but to become an 'interior' pioneer, seeking his English identity beyond or beneath the industrialized world around him. The journey towards an unknown region, over the open sea to a New World, was preludial to Vaughan Williams's rediscovery of Old England, for a new birth could occur only when he had found out what our socially pre-industrial and musically pre-Teutonic identity was. Far from being a merely musical matter, this was happening, to use an appropriate metaphor, in every field.

II

'THE MIND OF ENGLAND'

CONSERVATISM AND CONSERVATION IN
ON WENLOCK EDGE

This empty place was, in its aspect, despite the difference in configuration between down and undulating plain, more like the home of my early years than any other place known to me in the country. I can note many differences, but they do not deprive me of this sense of home feeling; it is the likenesses that hold me, the spirit of the place, one which is not a desert with the desert's melancholy or sense of desolation, but inhabited, although thinly and by humble-minded men whose work and dwellings are unobtrusive. The final effect of this wide, green space with signs of human life and labour on it, and sight of animals – sheep and cattle – at various distances, is that we are not aliens here, intruders and invaders of the earth, living in it but apart, perhaps hating and spoiling it, but with the other animals and children of Nature, like them living and seeking our subsistence under her sky, familiar with her sun and wind and rain.

W.H. HUDSON, *A Shepherd's Life*

We spoke in the last chapter of the Dorset dialect poet William Barnes as a link between pre- and post-industrial Britain, commenting on his affinities with Vaughan Williams. A figure comparable with but much greater than Barnes was Thomas Hardy, whose agrarian revocations in poetry and prose sprang from anguished recognition of loss. What had been lost was that consanguinity between man and Nature described by Hudson in the passage quoted above. Barnes was content to record that intuitive, almost vegetative, state of being; Hardy, burdened with a social and even political conscience, saw its decline in the context of history. This is suggested in the poem he wrote on 31 December 1900 in celebration, at the dark end of the century, of an 'aged thrush' who, 'frail, gaunt and small,'

> In blast-beruffled plume,
> Had chosen thus to fling his soul
> Upon the growing gloom.
>
> So little cause for carollings
> Of such ecstatic sound
> Was written on terrestrial things
> Afar or right around

That I could think there trembled through
His happy good-night air
Some blessed Hope, whereof he knew
But I was unaware.

The poem is not only a statement of personal agnosticism but also an expression of disenchantment with material progress. Hopkins's magnificent sonnet 'God's Grandeur' sees the same situation in a religious context, asking why, though 'The world is charged with the grandeur of God', men no longer 'reck His rod', living as they must in a world 'seared with trade, bleared, smeared with toil': a world wherein 'the soil is bare now, nor can foot feel, being shod'. Hopkins's sestet gives a positive answer to his question, but only in relation to his personal religious experience as a Jesuit priest, which was far from that of representative urban man.

Hardy, without even a pretence of religious faith but with the ultimate integrity of the artist, found no alternative to 'pessimism'; his poems tend to be 'satires of circumstance' and his greatest novels are inescapably tragic. What makes *Tess of the D'Urbervilles* a key book is its vivid contrast between the spontaneous rhythms of life on the summer farm and the wintry bleakness of man's malice and destiny's obliviousness, as they impinge on the unwittingly heroic heroine. Though Vaughan Williams read Hardy's novels avidly, he made little creative use of him, probably because the severity of Hardy's vision was at odds with his sanguine, even optimistic, temperament. Even so, Vaughan Williams was indeed sensitive to the disastrous effects of change from an agrarian to an industrial society, and, significantly, turned to Hardy late in his life. In his carol-sequence *Hodie* he included Hardy's touching poem 'The Oxen', while the implicit scenario of the bleakly powerful Ninth Symphony was shaped by a re-reading of *Tess*. Though Vaughan Williams as usual denied any programmatic intentions, an analogy remains; and Ursula Vaughan Williams tells us that late in life her husband cherished an unfulfilled project to compose music for a cinematic version of *The Dynasts* – a theme 'pessimistic' enough, if congenial to his vision of the mind of England, in the context of history.

The poetry of Hopkins Vaughan Williams read, but without instinctive empathy. One might have expected that Hopkin's spiritually exalted sprung rhythms would have appealed to him; if they did, their positive impact may have been countered by mistrust of the poet's Jesuitical intensity. In his early years Vaughan Williams's sympathies lay not with metaphysical agony and ecstasy, though both exist even in his early music, but rather with the sober physicality of the Arts and Crafts movement and the 'conservation' writers. A favourite among his boyhood books was Borrow's *Lavengro* – a celebration at once of the English countryside and the continuity of rural life, and of the outsider exemplified in the gypsy. More directly in tune with Vaughan Williams's social and family background were Ruskin and especially William Morris, who transformed a vision of Old (quasi-medieval) England into a semi-feudal socialism potentially realizable in the modern world. This legacy was passed down to George Sturt, who wrote under the name of Bourne, the village he lived in: a man who, like Vaughan Williams, was in his own words 'not Christian but naturally religious'. The social and political dimensions in Sturt's writing on rural England look back to Morris, forward to the Nature-pantheism of D.H. Lawrence. The same polarities control the work of Richard Jefferies, who writes in documentary vein about modes of life that are becoming obsolete, but aspires to the prose poem in hymning Nature. We will see that the same earthy-ecstatic double value informs much of the finest music of Vaughan Williams.

For the moment, however, we are concerned with social reality: with the agrarian order as described in books such as Jefferies' *Hodge and his Masters* (published in 1880), Hudson's *A Shepherd's Life* (published in 1910), and Sturt's *The Wheelwright's Shop* (published, retrospectively, in 1923). These books concern life and labour; and contemporaneously Vaughan Williams was interested in English folk song and dance as a human activity. From the early years of the century he was engaged in field-work, collecting songs from still – if sometimes dodderingly – active men and women. He esteemed the human as well as musical qualities of his singers – as did Cecil Sharp, when he movingly related the music made by his singers in the Appalachian Mountains to the lives they led and the traditions they inherited. Given their relation to the seasonal cycle and to the natural poetry of speech uttered by folk living in communion with the earth and with beasts and birds, they had no need of formal schooling. Vaughan Williams attempted to pay homage to what tenuously survived or could be recalled of such a community here at home. In his early 'ballad opera' *Hugh the Drover* he incorporated a few real folk tunes and invented others to match them. His Falstaff operas are later, more ambitious projects with similar intentions. Although entertainingly lively, these are not major works in the Vaughan Williams canon, for the obvious reason that, however much he valued folk music as a way of life, he knew that it was too remote from the life emerging in industrial Britain for him to share it.

Yet if these theatrical pieces are games of let's pretend – as are some of the supreme masterpieces of twentieth-century music, notably Stravinsky's *Le Sacré du Printemps* – Vaughan Williams's interest in folk music was not a bootless attempt to put the clock back and re-enter a vanished world; it was rather discovery that this ostensibly remote music was still pertinent to him and us. As early as 1893 he had lighted on the song 'Dives and Lazarus' in a printed anthology of tunes. Ten years later he encountered it 'in the field'; and knew, through the quavery sounds as he had not through the written script, that 'here's something I have known all my life, though I didn't know that I knew it'. This is, strictly speaking, an act of re-cognition: not just a melody, but a way of feeling, thinking and behaving buried deep in nerves and senses. This is why, when later in life Vaughan Williams composed original works based on folk tunes, he was not indulging in archaism but was making the past present. One supects that the well-known *Fantasia on English Christmas Carols*, written for chorus and small orchestra in 1912, is so oddly affecting precisely because it is not an exercise in anthropological lore or retrospective musical research but a modest re-vision of a life that had once seemed permanent. As T.S. Eliot puts it in 'East Coker':

> Rustically solemn or in rustic laughter
> Lifting heavy loam feet in clumsy shoes,
> Earth feet, loam feet, lifted in country mirth
> Mirth of those long silent under earth
> Nourishing the corn. Keeping time,
> Keeping the rhythm in their dancing
> As in their living in the living seasons
> The time of the seasons and the constellations
> The time of milking and the time of harvest
> The time of the coupling of man and woman
> And that of beasts. Feet rising and falling.
> Eating and drinking. Dung and death.

For us today, listening to the Fantasia does not of course evoke such immediate memories of the seasonal cycle of the earth; but it does remind us of the continuity of social customs inherited from childhood, bringing a warm sense of solidarity, slightly tinged with sorrow for its passing.

In such dehistoricized history there must be artifice since Vaughan Williams, if not a sophisticated cosmopolitan like Eliot, was no peasant but an educated, literate Englishman, as were such consciously rural writers as Jefferies, Hudson and Sturt. None the less, what gives the Fantasia its immediate reality is that Vaughan Williams respects the identity of the tunes, and this is true whether he is making a self-subsistent work like the fantasy on English carols or whether he is making straight arrangements of tunes for use at school or at home. Most harmonizations of British folk songs tend to be or to become chromatic, like the almost enervatingly beautiful version of 'Brigg Fair' which Percy Grainger made shortly after he noted down the Lincolnshire melody in 1905. He handed it on to Delius who, using it as basis for an orchestral rhapsody, submitted it to variants even more harmonically luxuriant. This imparts a plangent nostalgia – not merely an awareness that the old world is gone, but also a romantic sense that the loss is a Fall from Eden. There is nothing reprehensible about such chromaticized modality, for it is natural enough that an urban man of the twentieth century should find in the tunes occasion for regret. In the folk-derived pieces of Bax, and possibly Warlock, there is occasionally an over-indulgence disproportionate to the tunes' simplicity. If Grainger is the most convincing of these folk rhapsodists, this may be because his Australian bumpkin vivacity usually tempers his chromatic pathos – with oddly piquant effect in the 'room music ramble' around the tune 'Robin is to the greenwood gone', scored for small instrumental ensemble; in the wittily as well as sensuously inventive passacaglia for small orchestra on 'Green rushes'; and in the weird apotheosis of the tremolandos of the village pub piano in the version of 'Shallow Brown'.

Even so, Vaughan Williams, in avoiding both irony and regret, is doing something different from any of these composers, and perhaps more significant. In this respect he is closest to his friend Holst, his early partner in the exploration of folk tradition. Delius, loathing industrial society, spurned it; Elgar teetered between his rural Worcestershire and the capital and hub of the Edwardian Empire; Holst and Vaughan Williams, born a generation later and brought up in metropolitan London, found it inimical to the values they cherished, yet stayed there while recognizing that pomp and circumstance were rightly in abeyance. The human spirit, as reflected in English music, seemed weary with consciousness of self and of material power; if we were to live again, imaginatively and musically, we must return to the beginnings of our consciousness, before the Renaissance.

True, Holst's early music includes a measure of the 'good old Wagnerian bawling' he deplored in himself as well as in English oratorio. When he found himself, however, his music often had the melodic-modal chastity of late medieval or early Renaissance English music, notably in that key work, the *Four Songs* for voice and violin, written in 1916. In the setting of the carol 'I sing of a maid that is makeless', for instance, the relation between voice and verse is as intimate as it is in folk song; the tune seems to be born of and borne on the words, though a twist is given to folk modality when a discreet chromatic alteration, throwing the middle section out of focus, gives to the melody's innocence a quality both vulnerable and precarious. Twentieth-century insecurity filters into what might seem medievally, and naïvely, religious. This is what makes the music – inspired by Holst's chance hearing of a woman singing as she fiddled in Thaxted Church – so strangely moving. There is a comparably vulnerable flavour to much of the choral music Holst wrote, mostly to medieval and Renaissance texts, during the dark years of the war. 'This have I done for my true love' is an especially beautiful modification of early Renaissance idiom; and throughout his life Holst's techniques derived more from medieval monody, organum and heterophony, and from early Renaissance homophony, than they did from Tudor polyphony in full flower.

In this he differs from Vaughan Williams, whose technical awakening was centred on Tudor polyphony. Vaughan Williams's response to folk song itself is also more 'positive' than Holst's, both in original works freely related to folk melodies, and in the arrangements of tunes he published as harvest from his field-work. Of course folk song is in essence a monodic music and Vaughan Williams probably agreed with the old Dorset labourer who complained that, while it was 'nice' for a polite singer to have a piano to accompany him, it 'does make it awkward for the listener'. But since Vaughan Williams's purpose in collecting folk songs was to salvage them for 'the people' while there was still time, he had to produce them in a form in which they were likely to be disseminated. In the first two decades of the century the parlour piano was still a household's centre of gravity, while pianos were common even in village schools. So Vaughan Williams published the tunes usually with piano accompaniment, occasionally with violin. Looking back from sixty or seventy years later, we can only marvel at the way in which the arrangments allow the magic of words and tune to shine through.

Folk verse may be great poetry precisely because the experience of 'unaccommodated man' is elemental and universal. The metaphorical language of the verses is, after all, a sublimation of the cadences of rural speech, as we may note in the language of Shakespeare's Old Shepherd in *The Winter's Tale*. The bloom of metaphor and the flow of speech rhythm crystallize into the memorable tune, and on the whole the finest poetry prompts the finest melody: as is testified by the survival value of songs like 'Bushes and briars', 'As I walked out' 'Searching for lambs', 'She's like the swallow' and 'The unquiet grave'. Although the precise date of the songs' origin is usually obscure, since they grow and change through the years, they are still part of the intuitive consciousness even of people like ourselves who have not been brought up singing them. Vaughan Williams sets them for a solo voice – you or me rather than a concert singer – with the support of a piano he would not mind our discarding. On the whole, even today, we are not tempted to relinquish his accompaniments, so subtly supportive are they of the spirit of words and tune.

Sometimes Vaughan Williams presents the first verse monodically, as in the setting of that strangely disturbing tune 'The captain's apprentice'. After the first stanza, unaccompanied except for tenuously preludial fourths and fifths, the later stanzas are punctuated by plain diatonic concords that barely affect the tune's gaunt contours, and preserve its slightly savage melancholy. Similarly, Vaughan Williams begins the wondrous 'Bushes and briars' monodically, later flowing into a thin polyphony with occasional incipient canons in the keyboard figuration. Vaughan Williams probably borrowed this device from the folk song arrangements of the Elizabethan virginalists, especially the more archaic-tempered ones like Gibbons and Farnaby. There is a further link with the virginalists in the setting of 'Geordie', which begins with folk-style pedal drones, and in later stanzas veers between minor-tending modality and major-tinged cadential figures, similar to those in Byrd's and Bull's superb versions of 'Walsingham'. Songs with a religious burden, such as 'The truth sent from above' and 'The Saviour's love', Vaughan Williams tends to harmonize in diatonic concords that respect the melodies' modality and enhance their liturgical flavour. Especially lovely is a set of songs in versions coming from Newfoundland. 'She's like the swallow' uses the piano to nourish the song's latent rhythmic pulse, on which its lyricism soars. 'The maiden's lament' becomes a duet between the voice and single-line, wide-spaced, often pentatonic arabesques on piano. The well-known 'The cuckoo' is artful in a way appropriate to this tricksy bird, for the piano's dotted rhythm comments cheekily on the mortality-obsessed words. The effect of most of the songs is sad, or at least wistful: perhaps more so to self-conscious us than to the 'folk' themselves, though the elemental style of peasant life meant that people could not be impervious to pain.

Indeed folk song, even more than most music, is usually a form of therapy, sometimes, in raucous or bawdy pieces, encouraging escape by way of animal high spirits, but more frequently seeking sublimation by way of lyricism. Although this is most evident if the songs are sung in monody, it is hardly less poignant in the version Vaughan Williams made for voice and a violin handled in a manner not far from a folk fiddle. The linearity of the two melody instruments enhances the tunes' vulnerability, as in the Holst songs previously discussed. 'The lawyer', which is about the (bad) town versus the (good) country, Vaughan Williams sets as a fiddle reel; the therapy is physical but the effect partly metaphysical as fleeting feet promise to take off from the earth. The irregular-rhythmed 'Searching for lambs' begins monodically, using the violin in folk style to hold pedal notes, but turns into modal, often pentatonic duologue, with the violin flowering, for the sacramental experience of marriage, into a foretaste of *The Lark Ascending*. A version of 'The unquiet grave' uses both violin and piano to explore the drama latent in a folk-colloquy between a grieving girl and her dead lover. Whatever it owes to the wondrous traditional tune the piece comes out, as Michael Kennedy has pointed out, as one of the greatest of Vaughan Williams's 'chamber' works, balanced between relatively unconscious folk tradition and relatively conscious art. All the techniques referred to – drones and modal figurations on piano, the fiddle as both an ostinato instrument and as a lyrical complement to the voice – are embraced within the dialogue form. Expressivity becomes drama in the modulating interludes between the verses. The piece thus has beginning, middle and end – as a 'work of art' does and a folk song does not.

The equilibrium here achieved between folk and art music calls for rare talents. Vaughan Williams brings it off too in his arrangements of folk tunes for unaccompanied four-part chorus, mostly made for amateurs and children to sing, rather than for concert performance. We may take 'The lover's ghost' as representative. The dorian tune is harmonized in strict diatonicism, without a single chromatic intrusion except for a couple of cadential major thirds. Not even in later stanzas, when the texture becomes discreetly polyphonic, is dorian integrity threatened, for dissonant or even consonant passing notes are minimal. A more ambitious setting, such as the version of 'The turtle dove' with tenor solo, likewise has no need of chromatics to distil its poetry; the upward flowering of the tune at the end of each third line is never harmonically sentimentalized.

Such works must count as art music, however folk-derived. To understand how Vaughan Williams incorporated folk song into his own evolution we must turn to the second key work in his career, after *A Sea Symphony*. This is the song cycle *On Wenlock Edge*, begun in 1906, finished in 1909, so that its dates overlap with the choral symphony. It contains no folk material, though some of its melodies sound as though they might be of folk provenance. Nor would real folk tunes be appropriate to it, since the poems are from Housman's *A Shropshire Lad*: a slim volume which, appearing in 1896 at the close of the nineteenth century and at the beginning of the end of the Imperial Dream, enjoyed enormous popularity over a surprisingly wide cross-section of the British public. Housman, a crusty academic and Latin disputant 'masochistically practising heroics in the last ditch' (as W.H. Auden put it), created pseudo-folk ballads set in a mythical Shropshire countryside, making a highly artificial deployment of simple ballad forms to deal with universal themes of death, mutability and a world lost. The verses brought home to the guts of thousands of British people not only the loss of the old rural England, but also the tie-up between that loss and a bleak awareness of impermanence in a godless and faithless world. The beauty of Housman's best lyrics is as undeniable as their self-indulgence, compared with Hardy's lyrical confrontation of the same human predicament at the same point in time. Most of us, excusably, need a measure of self-indulgence in circumstances undeniably unpropitious. These haunting lyrics awoke inner disturbances people were racked by, yet not fully conscious of. War and death pervade the poems: both the Boer War in which the Shropshire lads were slaughtered, and the Great War to come, which was to mark the end of their era. The weird fascination exerted by Housman's verse came in part from its equivocal nature. Lovely lyric stanzas as apparently artless as a folk ballad or a threnody of Shakespeare at the same time reveal that the nineteenth century had ravaged innocence once and for all. The beautiful verse is often rent by savagery; sometimes the burden is blasphemous; the very first poem, written as early as 1887, leaves us in doubt whether God will really 'Save the Queen' – or anyone else.

There are close parallels between Housman's literary and Vaughan Williams's musical techniques. Superficially, the composer seems to enclose the cycle in the comfort of an Edwardian parlour in scoring it for tenor with piano and string quartet, a set-up prevalent in parlours as well as concert halls. There is artifice too in Vaughan Williams's meticulous metrics; his concern with the relationship between the contours of an English musical line and the inflexions of speech offers a vernacular parallel to Housman's classical prosody. English folk monody was an intuitive overflow of feeling; the linear shapes blossom both from and into the words. Throughout this cycle Vaughan Williams's folk-like tunes behave comparably; they seem to spring spontaneously from the words as though they were folk songs of the old world, even as his artifice distances that old world from us. But Vaughan Williams's settings, while offering no comfortable panacea for Housman's pessimism, are predictably less dark than the poems. They mollify it – as to a degree does the artifice of Housman's own technique – because experience is presented as illusory; innocence may be recaptured in a state of dream, which is not necessarily a deceit. A technical manifestation of this lies in another aspect of the sophistication with which Vaughan Williams approached his superficially unsophisticated subject. *On Wenlock Edge* was composed as an offshoot of the time Vaughan Williams spent in Paris, studying with Ravel. The artful element in these songs is not German but French; and that Vaughan Williams should have sought out the French composer, who was younger than he, is evidence that genius knows where it is going long before it knows that it knows. For Ravel made a dream world out of his childhood and a *recherche du temps perdu*; the modal, often pentatonic, melodies evoke an antique world of *contes de fées*, seen in a glass darkly or lightly, through the haze of his non-progressive, Debussyan harmonies. Although the influence of Ravel on Vaughan Williams was not deep, the improbable liason between the 'straw-booted' Englishman and the Parisian dandy proves authentic. Their two dreams overlap.

The marvellous poem – it is called 'On Wenlock Edge' – of the first song in the cycle sets the English yeoman in the context of history. He stands on the Shropshire hill during a gale, which is both a physical event in nature and symbol of life's turbulence. So did the wind blow centuries ago when the Roman city of Uricon stood here; ''twas the old wind in the old anger' and the 'thoughts that hurt' the Roman were the same as those that rack the young man wind-buffeted today. Human life is dust, gone with the wind, and that the old agrarian world is gone or going is insignificant in the context of time, in which all passes. Vaughan Williams creates a telling aural image for the wind's imperviousness. Tremolando strings and piano join in whirring pentatonics, sweeping up and down in a phrygian G minor, in organum-like parallel triads; the semitonic A flats of the mode are oppressive. Texture thins as the voice enters with a purely pentatonic (not phrygian) phrase, beginning with a fourth, most primitive of intervals, rocking like the voice of Nature herself:

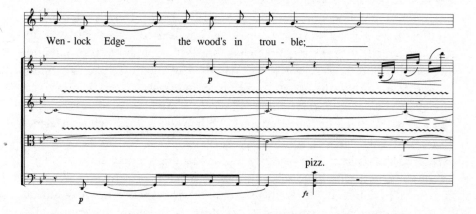

The tenor is echoed by the piano's bass and the cello in unison; flickering octaves on first violin might be lightning or plashing hail. The phrygian A flats are still surly in the bass line, and the chromaticism communicates itself to the vocal melody, which declines from a high G. This, though it generates anguish, is also naturalistic, almost onomatopoeic, emulating the whirling, wind-strewn leaves. Nature is still oblivious of man: as is evident when the instrumental prelude recurs, unchanged.

The second stanza repeats the music of the first, modifying its tail to lead into a coruscation of arpeggios and trills. In the third stanza the remote Roman makes his ghostly appearance in monotone declamation through the trills. The 'heaving hill' suggests chromatics that impart subjective anxiety as the boy on the hill sees himself, in relation to the ancient Roman, as a leaf blown in the wind, yet at the same time humanly sentient and conscious. The 'thoughts that hurt' them both are engulfed in shimmering chromatics. The third stanza begins with the same music as the second but leads to the song's climax at the identification of the two men, across the ages: 'then 'twas the Roman, now 'tis I'. Tremolandos, now shudderingly *sul ponticello*, introduce the final verse wherein the original pentatonic tune murmurs in the bass, beneath the strings' quavering and the voice's monotone. The tenor ends, off-key, on the sharp sixth, E natural. In the instrumental postlude the strings return to undulating chromatics in parallel triads, oscillating between E natural and E flat, declining to D. The piano bass growls the pentatonic theme in its phrygian-tinged form, until the A flats settle on G. The last sounds we hear, in quadruple *piano*, are that rudimentary fourth, D to G, in the bottom reaches of the piano. 'Nature' swallows the tones of vocal innocence with which the song had opened.

The second song, 'From far, from eve and morning', turns from history to the self within coexistent Nature. The poignant poem tells how 'I' was 'blown hither by yon twelve-winded sky'. But its essence is no longer the indifferent collocation of man and the natural world in the context of history, but rather human consciousness itself. I tarry here only 'for a breath'; this being so, 'Take my hand quick' (meaning both 'soon' and 'living')

> ... and tell me,
> What have you in your heart?
> Speak now, and I will answer;
> How shall I help you, say?
> Ere to the wind's twelve quarters
> I take my endless way.

So the poem is about human sentience in both its power and its frailty: for which Vaughan Williams again finds aural images of remarkable precision.

At first, the voice is accompanied by piano only, playing spread diatonic concords, *misterioso* in false relation, E, G, F, G and E majors. The key is E major, the four sharps of which, we have noted, gave it heavenly connotations. Here, however, paradise is paradoxically imperfect, for the mediant false relations between the G sharps of the E major triad and the G naturals of the G major triad, and the dip to phrygian F major and back, make the music float rudderless in time and space. Meanwhile the vocal line, responsive to verbal rhythm, sways between the fifth and the third, the latter sometimes major, sometimes minor. For the second stanza, which turns to the self who tarries only 'for a breath', the 'speaking' strings take over from piano. The vocal line is wide-eyed in pentatonicism, supported by simple diatonic chords on strings. Tonally we move from a pentatonic F sharp to what might be A major with flat seventh: at which point ('Take my hand quick') a chromatic triplet in the viola, echoed by second violin, exquisitely embodies in sound the words' appeal for mutual compassion, within and against eternity's oblivion:

The harmony oscillates between unrelated major triads of A, G and E, until the vocal line breaks off on the unanswered question, 'How can I help you, say?' The final line, carrying the self on its 'endless way', discards the strings and reinstates the piano's wavering concords, modified by a deeply affecting shift to the lower mediant, C sharp. The voice's final cadence stains E major bliss with the flat third. This song is a small miracle, crucial to the Vaughan Williams experience. Nowhere is his equation between words and music – in terms of both prosody and of meaning – more consummate.

If the first song of the cycle is historical and the second elemental, the third, 'Is my team ploughing?', might be called histrionic. The relationship is no longer between man and Nature but between man and man, and it is dramatically presented. The 'I' of the poem is neither legendary nor archetypal, but a specific young man in – or rather out of, since he is dead – a given rural scene. Housman's poem emulates a folk ballad in dialogue form but does so with a grisly humour far from the spirit of real folk poetry. The ghost asks questions of the living man, enquiring whether village life goes on as was its wont: is my team still ploughing, are the lads still playing football, is my girl happy? In each alternate verse the live man proffers an answer, leading to an admission that if the girl is happy, and she is, it is because she lies down with *him* – 'I cheer a dead man's sweetheart, never ask me whose?'

Vaughan Williams begins the song as though its folk dialogue were the real, right thing. Piano and strings (in spectral una corda) undulate in organum-like concords in the dorian mode on D, but sustain a D minor triad when the ghost sings, *quasi da lontano*, perhaps in 'head' voice. His tune could be a genuine folk melody, the simple modality of which is obliterated by the live man's answer, introduced by throbbing triplet chords on the piano, over a chromatic bass reinforced by the cello. The vocal line, compared with the ghost's song, is wide-flung, and incorporates chromatics. The second stanza repeats this pattern unchanged, but the next stanza Vaughan Williams set – he cut out the two verses about the footballers, to the poet's angry disgust – initiates a development with quasi-operatic consequences. On the words 'Is my friend hearty?' tonality is screwed up a third from dorian D minor, and the live man triumphantly yells of his supersession of the dead, starting from a high A flat. The piano's throbbing triplets are now loud as well as chromatic; the strings are fiercely syncopated:

The ultimate climax has the chromatic wail from A natural, drooping to F sharp, while octave unisons on piano grimly enunciate the dotted rhythmed motif that opened the instrumental prelude to the song; it is now a semitone lower. The postlude, on strings only, returns to the organum-like undulations; the 'modern' self-consciousness of the verses is reborn in the ageless folk-world.

The very brief fourth song, 'O when I was in love with you', is an interlude, affording relief between the operatically dramatic, even melodramatic, dialogue of 'Is my team ploughing?' and the inward intensity of the succeeding number, 'Bredon Hill'. The poem consists of two four-lined stanzas, with no word of more than two syllables. But if the guileless simplicity is folk-like, the burden of the words is cynical and perhaps therefore modern, for this is an anti-love song, almost a shrug of the shoulders. Vaughan Williams makes a tune for it so innocent that it may dispense with any instrumental, atmospheric prelude. In the aeolian mode on D, the tune is pervaded by that most vocally instinctual of intervals, the fourth: so we are unprepared for the second stanza, in which the clear modality dissolves in chromatic shifts from F sharp minor, to F major to D major, and 'fancy passes by' in rootless whole-tone progressions. He tells us that since nothing remains of his love, he is 'quite myself again'; but does so in a rallentando, leading to an instrumental postlude repeating the oscillating triads, twinkling to silence. Such illusion and disillusion are uncharacteristic of folk experience, though true to Housman and us.

The fifth song, 'Bredon Hill', is the longest, forming the cycle's centre of gravity. The poem – the very heart of Housman – depicts a pair of lovers lying on a hillside in deep summer, looking over the valley at a distant prospect of the village, from which the church bells 'sound so clear' round 'both the shires'. Earlier (poetic) themes from the cycle are recalled, since this time the girl is dead, and the poem encapsulates past, present and future in a timeless moment. In seven five-line stanzas of six-syllable lines – in which the rhyming last line chimes like a bell – the poem creates trance, as does the music. In this trance-music Vaughan Williams profited from Ravel's example; the almost motionless prelude combines con sordino double-stopped chords on strings with triple piano keyboard chords of 'piled-up' thirds – a sonority typical of Ravel, not to mention white-note Stravinsky:

Apart from a momentary vacillation to a Schubertian sub-mediant there is no tonal movement. The prelude fades out with the seventh chords sustained on strings while the piano wavers in fourths, simulating distant bells.

The piled-up sevenths stay motionless when the voice sings the first stanza, at first pentatonically, and in free rhythm, flowing from the words. The tune extends its range to mixolydian G, momentarily side-stepping to the lower mediant in a way that makes the bells' happiness wistful. The tune is repeated for the second stanza, the instrumental chords shifting, for the 'coloured counties', though the same stepwise descent to the mediant. Slowly, we are hypnotized by the bells, which are pre-conscious: God's instrument, since they resound in Nature's overtones. In stanza 3 they emerge from the summer haze to toll on piano in parallel fourths and fifths, the lowest members of the overtone series. The modality centres on B flat, with a seventh chord on C in the piano's left hand. The strings fall silent; the piano, up to this point una corda, is now tre corde, more reverberant. Though the vocal line does not radically depart from the tune of the previous stanzas, its modality is freer, and the freedom is associated with slow but potent transitions in the harmony. The flat seventh chord on C moves to D minor with added sixth, and that to E flat major against which the bells' fourths chime dissonantly. During this slight animation the bells have called people to church; but the woman ignores them, melting with her lover 'among the springing thyme' – a herb significant in folk poetry, here cannily adopted by Housman. Resonant seventh chords carry us and the lovers back to their bell-haloed trance.

But although the next stanza returns to the static open fifths on both strings and piano, there is a difference: each empty fifth is now punctured by the third A flat to C; the phrygian seconds toll like (rather cracked) bells as they dissonantly pierce the euphony:

Moreover, the thirds in the left hand oscillate in whole tones, wavering through rootless augmented fifths that efface tonality. (We may recall that Elgar, even in large-scale pieces like *Gerontius* and the two symphonies, often allows what we expect to be a progressive development section to dissipate in whole-tone illusion.) And the phrygian contagion spreads to the vocal line, which is darkened with flat seconds and flattened fifth, while the strings float aloft in *parallel* fifths. When the bells become the woman's solitary funeral bell, the phrygian seconds toll more wildly on piano, while the strings realistically imitate the 'one bell', simultaneously arco and pizzicato. The ostinato seventh chord is now dissonant (A flat, C, E flat, G); but it is effaced when the summer haze shimmers again on string harmonics and the key signature changes to G major. The seventh chord is metamorphosed into A, C, E, G, floating in liquid piano arpeggios: through which the tenor opens the last stanza with a literal repeat of its first, folk-like clause. He breaks out and upwards with the second appeal to good people to come to church, encouraged by strings and piano who propel the music through a D minor chord with added seventh. The ultimate climax comes with a dissonant triplet figure hammered over a second inversion E flat major triad, while the voice, high in tessitura, appeals to the 'noisy bells' to cease, allowing the dead to rest. Vaughan Williams tells the players that they need not, should not, metrically coincide with the vocal line. Gradually, the campanological hubbub subsides, and the 'summer haze' sonority again shimmers on strings and piano, leaving us with the piled-up seventh chord at its original pitch. Through the trance the voice intones, 'freely' but on the tonic G, the words 'I will come', welcoming death wherein trance becomes eternity.

The final song, 'Clun', though written first (as early as 1906), is genuinely epilogic, both in succession to 'Bredon Hill' and as the end of the cycle. Based on a folk rune,

> Clunton and Clunbury,
> Clungunford and Clun,
> Are the quietest places
> Under the sun,

it has seven four-line stanzas, but is highly self-conscious within its folk-like innocence. For the timeless quietude of the 'valleys of springs of rivers' shrouds sagas of human disquiet: 'lads knew trouble at Knighton when I was a Knighton lad'. The third stanza brings the rural scene into the context of the industrial world with a reference to 'London, the town built ill'; the blight is such that even in havens of rustic tranquillity a lad must carry his griefs 'on a shoulder That handselled them long before'. In neither town nor country is there abiding refuge: so the poem, and Vaughan Williams's cycle, end elementally, as they began:

> 'Tis a long way further than Knighton,
> A quieter place than Clun,

Where doomsday may thunder and lighten,
And little 'twill matter to one.

The instrumental prelude hints at the stress beneath Clun's quietude, with a soft but urgent descent from C to A, echoed from F sharp to D. The mode may be dorian on A, though the chromatics in the inner parts make it ambiguous. The vocal part, on its entry, seems to efface inner anxiety, for it is at first unambivalently folk-like in a gapped phrygian mode, the flat second being omitted from the vocal line but present in the piano's flowing arpeggios. The extension of the phrase, however, relinquishes folk innocence with a twist to the upper mediant, A flat; pentatonic vacilliations in the voice part become enharmonic as well as chromatic, for the E flats change to D sharps to lead into a luminous F sharp major, evoking boyhood's Knighton as a forgotten Eden:

This brings back the sighs of the prelude, and a second stanza that repeats the music of the first.

But from the next stanza Eden is banished. The declining chromaticized thirds become dissonant appoggiaturas, heavy with the 'luggage I'd lief set down'. This is the most 'harmonic' passage in the work, the one most weighed down by 'the pain of consciousness'; it ends pivoting between triads of B and A majors. The key signature is that of A major, traditionally a key of youth, though the sevenths are sometimes flattened and the fourths usually sharpened. The vocal line, which is pentatonic but in an unorthodox disposition (A, B, C sharp, E, G), could hardly be simpler and its effect, supported by the softly swaying A and B major triads, is curative (as the lydian mode was supposed to be), coming after those wailing appoggiaturas, borne down by the 'luggage' of sorrow and sin. The voice sings its brief eqilogue once only. After it has ceased, the piano repeats its ostinato, while muted first violin, answered by muted cello, echoes the voice's rune-like incantation. The ostinato triads are now in root position; at the end the B major triad, with its sharp fourth in relation to the tonic A, is supended between life and death, before the ultimate, low-spaced A major chord proffers its *requiescat in pace*.

On Wenlock Edge is a key work in Vaughan Williams's life, but one that he had to go through, rather than an end in itself. Through it, he projects outwards, and therefore 'places', the experience of regression, making a work at once sophisticated and naive. In this sense Vaughan Williams's cycle, like Housman's poems, is an exercise in archaism: a world looked back at in (in the strict sense) admiration, since British folk culture, unlike the folk cultures of Bartók and Janáček, was no longer an active force. This is true even though there are moments in the folky dance pieces of Vaughan Williams that remind us, in textural stridency and rhythmic vigour, of Bartók. (Reciprocally, Bartók was enthusiastic about some of Vaughan Williams's music, notably the Piano Concerto, written within a few years of his own first and second concertos.)

Housman, it appears, had never visited the Bredon Hill that became his 'Land of lost content': which gives added point to the valedictory nature of his poems and of Vaughan Williams's settings. For the valediction was irrevocable in that, a few years after the appearance of the song cycle, the catastrophe of the First World War put paid to whatever physical reality the land of lost content might have had. The war had specific musical effects since it destroyed composers, as well as poets, with impartial hand. George Butterworth, born in 1885, and young enough to count as a Vaughan Williams disciple, was killed in the Battle of the Somme, at the age of thirty-one, leaving a small body of music that justifies Vaughan Williams's high hopes of him. Some of these works incorporate real folk tunes – he had assisted Vaughan Williams during his collecting days; all of them are permeated by the spirit of Housman's *A Shropshire Lad*, the best being a small tone poem, written in 1912, which bears the same title. Basically a meditation on the folk-like tune Butterworth had created for his setting, in his own *Shropshire Lad* cycle, of Housman's 'Loveliest of trees', it contains, alongside modal regret, outbursts of passion, even anger, that link it not so much with Stanford and Brahms as with the headier intoxication of Wagner. Wise after the event, we can see how justified both passion and anger were, though artistically the amalgam is uneasy, and would probably have been resolved, as Vaughan Williams resolved it, had Butterworth lived.

Another threnody is pronounced in both the poetry and music of the still more talented Ivor Gurney who, born in 1890, suffered a fate worse than death in the war. He had been a pupil of Stanford, on an open scholarship at the Royal College, before the war overtook him, and on his return in 1919 was briefly a pupil of Vaughan Williams himself. The latter was an appropriate teacher, for Gurney too made his art out of a tension between 'old' England – he was actually born on the Roman walls of the city of Gloucester, and as a boy he was much influenced by his clergyman godfather, Alfred Cheesman – and the exacerbations of the twentieth century, which had climaxed in the Great War. His war experience on the Somme no doubt stimulated an innate tendency to mental instability, which intensified during his years with Vaughan Williams. The last fifteen years of his life were spent in a mental hospital, in deepening silence and incoherence. On the evidence both of his poetry and his music he would seem to have been the most talented of his tragically lost generation.

Although as a poet Gurney ranks among the Georgians, his verse touches, by way of unpredictable metaphor and rhythm, raw nerves of disturbance far from those of the average bucolic poetaster. And although his musical idiom shows little evidence of a desire or need to supersede Stanford, the best of his songs display the same mysteriously disturbing sensibility as does his poetry. Rather oddly, he set his own verses seldom: though in the tiny 'Severn Meadows', sketched out both verbally and musically in the trenches, he encapsulates the heart of his experience. The contrast between 'England's graces' in the peace of Severn meadows and the present reality of the 'wanderer that dwells in shadows' is exquisitely imaged in a gently drooping phrase ballasted by piano sonorities the more poignant for their discretion. On the whole, however, there is little correlation between the quality of the verse he set and that of the music he fashioned for it. Minor versifiers like Edward Shanks and Wilfrid Gibson produce some of his most moving songs (for instance 'The singer' and 'All night under the moon'); and if settings of distinguished poets like Yeats, de la Mare and Edward Thomas result in even subtler songs (for instance 'The folly of being comforted', 'Epitaph' and 'Snow'), the reason is mainly that Gurney's meticulous declamation allows the listener to relish the words along with the tune. Interestingly, what may well be the finest of all his songs eschews contemporary verse to set John Fletcher's 'Sleep'; and is unembarrassed about using a modal–diatonic post-Stanford, early Vaughan Williams song-style to set Elizabethan verse. The comparison with Peter Warlock's famously skilful setting of the same poem is revealing. Warlock makes a sophisticated adaptation of the idiom of a Dowland lute song, authentic in response to verbal inflexion, with a piano part – influenced by van Dieren – that is a modern, chromaticized re-creation of lute polyphony. Gurney has no truck with such revivalism, yet penetrates to the poem's heart no less, perhaps more, deeply. He accepts his tradition, whereas Warlock was intelligently and sensitively rediscovering the past. Gurney also accepted the fact that his tradition was on the way out: as he himself was, incarcerated in the mental hospital from the early twenties until his death in 1937.

Yet if both the dream and the reality of old agrarian England were finished, there was another aspect of Old England that, in the first two decades of the twentieth century, still endured. That was the Anglican Church which for Vaughan Williams, a non-believer, enshrined the mind of England – the more potently because the English Church was itself founded on schism and division. This doubleness was not unrelated to that between traditional folk culture and the more overtly materialistic values of the modern world; and this is why, in musical terms, Tudor ecclesiastical polyphony was to prove of greater significance in Vaughan Williams's self-discovery than the British folk song which, in his blood and bones, he had known all his life.

III

THE DOUBLE MAN

TALLIS, THE ENGLISH REFORMATION AND THE
FANTASIA ON A THEME OF THOMAS TALLIS

It is not possible for a man to rise above himself and his humanity. ... We are, I know not how, double in ourselves, and what we believe we disbelieve, and cannot rid ourselves of what we condemn.

MONTAIGNE

The Church of England, being a Reformed Church that broke from the Universal Church of Rome, was instably founded on intellectual and spiritual bifurcation. God as absolutist, with the king as his earthly lieutenant and the 'new man' as *Protestant* testifying on his own behalf, redefined the relationship between Church and State. The English Prayer Book which, although not subversive, offered a vernacular liturgy for 'all sorts and conditions of men', was but the tip of an iceberg most of which, below the waters of the unconscious, effected a mutation at once exhilarating and disastrous.

For the Catholic and Universal Church was undermined as man substituted individualized human power for what had been thought of as the will of God. Henry VIII quarrelled with the Pope because of sexual as well as pecuniary greed, since his challenge to the Universal Church came to a head over the matter of his divorce. That the Church harboured abuses that called for reform was indubitable; but Henry's motivations, being personal, were suspect, and when once the immense wealth of the Church had been plundered by desperate men, power went to their heads. As reform brought material profit to the reformers, the spiritual impulses that justified reform were obscured. What the Prayer Book called the 'man of good will' found himself marooned in a world which, in the words of F.M. Powicke, 'was not sure of itself and did not much care, because it was conscious of the strength and energy and freedom in itself; a world in which cruelty and cynicism had free play, and indifference did not matter; yet a world in which self-assertiveness was almost indistinguishable from the craving after experience, whether of beauty or adventure or sheer evil. It was an exciting, though very dangerous, time for men with ideas, and a good time for those who wanted to see what would happen.' (*The Reformation in England*, 1941.)

This was not a merely insular state of affairs but a European phenomenon, given its most pungent expression in the words of the great Montaigne quoted at the head of this chapter. One of its most crucial manifestations was none the less at the heart of the Anglican Establishment; and it is exemplified with peculiar force in the life and art of Thomas Tallis who, according to a funeral tribute, 'As he dyd live, so dyd he dy, In myld and quyet Sort (O happy MAN)'. In the original the word man appears thus, in capitals, perhaps testifying to a contemporary hunch that whatever tranquillity of mind Tallis attained was due more to his human stoicism than to divine intervention in terrestrial affairs. Muddled and hazardous those affairs certainly were for Renaissance man who, trying to be responsible for himself, found that he was, in Sir John Davies's words, 'a proud, and yet a wretched, Thing'. Tallis, surviving through eighty years of the sixteenth century and serving the Church under four monarchs with varied creeds, was a seismograph to the century's turbulence, however unruffled the surface of his almost exclusively liturgical music may seem.

During his early years at Canterbury Cathedral and at Waltham Abbey Tallis naturally made music within the Roman rite and in the vocally polyphonic idiom inseparable from it. The traditional music of the Universal Church remained the essence, for the lines move, as in plainsong, smoothly by step; if they leap, it is through the primary consonances of fifth, fourth and pentatonic minor third. The euphony of the consort of voices is stabilized on the triad, to which any passing dissonance is no more than a momentary disturbance. Similarly the pulse of time – the dimension within which mortal men inevitably exist – is only latent; a swing of the pendulum is necessary if the parts are to keep together, yet it may seem effaceable in so far as the plainsong-like lines avoid obvious metrical accent.

At the same time Tallis's early music demonstrates how English composers of the mid sixteenth century unconsciously modified ecclesiastical practice because they worked for a church that was re-forming Roman hegemony. Beneath the apparent calm of Tallis's devotional music we may detect evidence of the religious and political dissensions he lived through. Even his early four-part setting of the Latin Mass, dating from before 1540, could not be mistaken for a High Renaissance Roman Mass. At the outset the monodic plainsong intonation, preserving the old order unsullied, echoes through the church; but the 'new' music of the Kyrie substitutes for monody four-part homophony for voices moving note for note, the rhythms following the inflexions of the words. The human import is thus more readily apprehensible than it is in the labyrinths of

Catholic counterpoint; and although that is hardly necessary with a text as familiar as the Eucharist, we can understand why English Reformation composers favoured this style when they set vernacular rather than Latin texts. Man on his earth is becoming the centre, with God up there, in his heaven. Punningly, we may speak of a transition from plainsong's *mono*phony (representing the *monos* of the One God), by way of *poly*phony (a socially harmonizing concourse of many equal voices, each individually seeking a plainchant-like spirituality), to the *homo*phony of a communal solidarity (wherein homogeneous men and women sing and dance on the earth in consort with their fellow creatures.) Although such English anthems, sung in parish churches throughout the land, were acts of devotion, their perhaps more important function was to affirm fellowship and the durability of tradition.

So in this Mass-setting gentle vocal modality and the euphony of the aptly titled 'common' chord aurally incarnate God in man's harmonic flesh. Vestiges of traditional counterpoint occur in moments of praise such as the hosannas, but they too are becoming man-directed in that they are dominated by the rhythms of dancing bodies. The old techniques may even foster the new, for as Tallis's music grows more contrapuntal so the independence of the parts makes for intenser dissonance, and potentially a deeper human expressivity. This becomes more overt in Tallis's later music, composed for the Chapel Royal after 1540 and Henry VIII's dissolution of the monasteries – a despoliation certainly of their material assets, and probably of much of their spiritual charisma. For evidence we need to look no further than Tallis's best known, and probably best, work, the *Lamentations*. Plainsong-like intonation of letters of the Hebrew alphabet – a ritualistically magical device – alternates with polyphonic settings of the Book of Jeremiah as Tallis calls fallen man to repentance. Though his lament refers in general to the human condition, he gives it specific application to the religious-political dichotomy he lived in.

In Part I the archaically severe phrygian modality is swept from its moorings by the passionate 'Plorans ploravit', attaining climax when the modality reaches B flat, a devilish tritone away from the initial E. In Part II the people's groans and the bursting of the city gates are enacted in grinding dissonances accruing from the simultaneous or near-simultaneous sounding of the minor and major third. This phenomenon, which came to be appropriately termed false relation, sprang from the clash between the two worlds, medieval and Renaissance. Voices nurtured on monodic plainchant (and folk song) naturally favoured the flat sevenths and thirds that are acoustically basic, while lively 'modern' men also relished the sharp leading notes and major thirds that can mark harmonic cadence and, implicitly, the passage of time. The two concepts may literally bump into one another: two or three of the lower parts may define a sonorous cadence with the sharp leading note, while another voice may, in accord with polyphonic tradition, enter with a new phrase descending through the 'natural' flat seventh. An intimation of immortality floats in the traditionally modal, plainsong-like phrase, the minor third of which clashes with the sensuous satisfaction of the cadential major third. A metaphysical and a physical view of the world meet in an equilibrium both precarious and intense.

Even so, Tallis's pain is not insupportable. Out of pain and conflict floats the possibility of evolution and consummation. The repeated note figure on the word 'convertere' does effect conversion, stabilizing what had threatened to disrupt – and does so, moreover, in the accents of a humanly reassuring, speaking voice. The peace this music creates 'passeth understanding' precisely because it is aware of the anguish of fallen man, the more acute the more consciously articulate it has become. In the thick of turmoil, racked by divisiveness, Tallis makes music that, rendering the heart, remains ineffably serene.

Although in Latin, not the vernacular, the *Lamentations* are probably a late work (Tallis died around 1585). They fuse past and present in being riddled with canonic ingenuities that, in accord with late medieval heritage, are as though divinely preordained, yet at the same time they express a pathos profoundly human and humane. Tallis sang of Paradise Lost, which was to be the dominant theme of the next century; in his music contrition and remorse lead – in those radiant cadences in which the justly intoned major thirds sound blissfully *un*fallen, especially after those falsely related triads – to hope. While our ears cannot for obvious reasons be as precisely attuned as were his to his contemporary situation, we cannot but be aware that in his world ours was born.

After the crucial seventeenth century, in which our psychic tensions erupted in Civil War, the religious impulse in Britain tended to be submerged beneath the rampant materialism only too patent in the machinations of the political men of the Reformation, and still insidious in the ever more power-ridden, gradually industrialized institutions of the eighteenth and nineteenth centuries. In particular, English music, as we have noted, was moribund; and there was point in the fact that our musical renaissance, at the turn of the century, should have been closely associated with a man, Ralph Vaughan Williams, who was 'double' as was Thomas Tallis, but more overtly so. Nor is it fortuitious that if we had to cite one work wherein Vaughan Williams first discovered his identify and the direction his life-long exploration must take, it would be his *Fantasia on a*

Theme of Thomas Tallis scored, unsurprisingly, for double string orchestra.

Thomas Tallis, though divided, had no doubt that he was a Christian and a servant of his Church; Vaughan Williams's doubleness is compounded by the fact that, born in rural Gloucestershire but by adoption a Londoner, he was a tradition-loving humanist without a faith but with a social conscience. He revered English institutions, most of all the Anglican Church that had moulded the mind of England; yet he was, like most of the distinguished historians and mathematicians with whom he consorted at home and at Cambridge, an agnostic who in the strict sense did not 'know'. For him the history of the Anglican Church was the story of the nation, with its nerve-centre in the English Reformation and breakaway from Rome. He came to realize this not, one suspects, by a process of conscious cogitation but in an unheralded act of revelation – the work he created in 1909–10 for the Three Choirs Festival, which is itself establishmentarian. This *Fantasia on a Theme of Thomas Tallis* was his first *great* masterpiece, and it is hardly extravagant to say that in it his later symphonic achievement, which defines his crucial position in our musical history, is implicit.

Though the proportion of Tallis's English to his Latin church music is small, it contains deeply affecting examples – such as 'If ye love me' and 'Hear the voice and prayer' – of a genre that is prevailingly homophonic and homogeneous: though not entirely so, since the expressive dissonances accrue from a measure of independence in the inner parts. Most briefly basic of all are the settings Tallis contributed to the 1567 Psalter of Matthew Parker, first Anglican Archbishop of Canterbury, in which the 'togetherness' of Tallis's four vocal parts is attuned to the Archbishop's sweetly rhyming metrics. The Psalter was 'published by John Day, dwelling over Aldersgate beneath St Martin's'; and the homely superscription bears on their being memorably metrical hymn tunes for common men and women who use the new Book of Common Prayer. The tune Vaughan Williams chose is the third of the set, and while it must have been its melodic nobility and harmonic subtlety that attracted him, the words are pertinent to his deepest concerns. Their burden is both religious and social.

> Why fum'th in fight the Gentiles' spite, in fury raging stout?
> Why tak'th in hand the people fond, vain things to bring about?
> The Kings arise, the Lords devise, in counsels met thereto,
> Against the Lord with false accord, against his Christ they go.

Material and spiritual values conflict, producing false relations in the process; repeated notes, speaking in verbal rhythm, generate harmonic pathos. On the words 'The Kings arise' the tune lifts through a minor third, with a lyrical effect the more potent because the basic mode is phrygian, wherein the flat seconds feel cabined, cribbed, confined.

Vaughan Williams had known the hymn for some years, for he had included it, furnished with different words by eighteenth-century John Addison, in the English Hymnal he published in 1906. There is a Tallis-like element in the very concept of a New English Hymnal, in so far as it was a minor Counter-Reformation. For just as the Protestant Reformation had metrically clipped the wings of Tudor polyphony in the interests of verbal communicability, so in the early years of this century Vaughan Williams strove to reanimate communal hymnody with the spirituality it had surrendered. Often he succeeded, himself creating at least half a dozen tunes that are among the finest in Anglican tradition, simple enough to be relished and sung by plain men and women, yet an inspiration to spirit as well as lungs. He offers release from the military harmonic and metrical concordance of Victorian hymnody (which tells us more than it meant to about Victorian religion); and achieves, if not the ecstasy of monodic plainsong or Tudor polyphony, a spiritualized humanism relatable, modally, harmonically and rhythmically, to the metrical psalms set by Tallis and later, in our religiously ambivalent, war-ridden seventeenth century, by the brothers Lawes.

Some of Vaughan Williams's hymn tunes – notably 'Down Ampney' and 'Sine Nomine' ('For all the saints') – leave their mark on his later music, though he did not use one in this seminal Fantasia of 1910. In choosing a melody by his sixteenth-century forefather he rather paid tribute to tradition itself, and to a critical moment in English history. The mind of England *then* is reborn in a modern work for double string orchestra, complementing the Tudor convention of the double vocal choir. The double man is incarnate in two choirs of strings which must if possible be separated, on the analogy of the divided stalls of a cathedral choir. It may be that the partiality which Tudor church music shows for divided choirs testifies to the fact that the devotional music of Christian 'fallen' man seeks a healing of breaches; 'the desire and pursuit of the Whole' implies that the Whole has been sundered. This was still pertinent in the early twentieth century. The miracle of Vaughan Williams's Fantasia is that divided man *is* healed; or at least his duality is transcended.

The piece opens with a two-bar preludial phrase that is a Vaughan Williams fingerprint. It appears in the first years of the century in the Rossetti and Stevenson song cycles, and embryonically in the opening bars of *Toward the Unknown Region*. This motto phrase is a declining pentatonic scale, in a solemn four pulse, the two orchestras playing as one. The falling pentatonic scale in the top line is balanced by a rising diatonic scale in the bass, each note of melody and bass being harmonized with a diatonic triad in itself consonant, though chromatically false in relation to its neighbours. G major in root position is followed by F major first inversion, B flat major root position, A flat major first inversion, G flat major second inversion. No modulation, in the eighteenth-century sense, is in question, though the tonal spectrum has shifted, in two bars, from G to G flat:

The effect is awe-inspiring, as is the similar alternation of diatonic concords that opens the 'elemental' second song of *On Wenlock Edge*; indeed, it is more awesome, given the sonority of stringed instruments in the acoustics of Gloucester Cathedral, for which the piece was composed. Mystery is inherent in the fact that, while the concordant but rootless harmonies are in limbo, the melodic formula is the acoustically 'innocent' pentatonic scale; and since the melody declines it may even affect us, thus harmonized, as a Fall from grace to disgrace. In the next chapter we will have more to say about the philosophical significance of pentatonicism; in introducing the Tallis Fantasia it must suffice to say that in the course of the work some such rite of passage occurs, and has something to tell us about the reasons why the Christian Fall was also a blessing. This is reinforced, as we shall see, by the many reappearances of this 'motto' throughout Vaughan Williams's life.

In this early example ambiguity survives into the third bar, when the time signature changes from $\frac{4}{4}$ to $\frac{3}{4}$ and a high D (the fifth, in the aeolian-phrygian G modality) sounds as an inverted pedal, *pianissimo*. Beneath this the first phrase of Tallis's hymn emerges on pizzicato strings, moving up pentatonically from D to A in octave unisons. The pedal note is then interwoven with undulating parallel triads in syncopated rhythm, the disturbance of the false relations between triads of D, C and E flat major now being palpable:

The ambivalence of the feeling – between belief and disbelief, as Montaigne put it – is of our time though it is latent in Tallis, as our world is the child of his. Belief seems to be fortified when Tallis expands the tune's rising third to a godly fifth, and spreads that into an ascending scale in dotted rhythm ($\frac{6}{8}$ in the prevailing $\frac{3}{4}$). This takes him to the tonic G and to a repetition of the rising third motif, literally more elevated because a fourth higher, on the affirmative tonic. In this passage Vaughan Williams traditionally presents the hymn in tenor register, in cantus firmus style; but to a degree counteracts affirmation because the common triads fluctuate between major and minor, and because the phrygian A flats in the bass are depressive. The A flats seem to get the better of aspiration; the rising dotted rhythmed $\frac{6}{8}$ scale is inverted and subsides to a plagal cadence, returning to the preludial four pulse as the triads shift from VII flat, to IV to I. The final tonic is an alleviating tierce de Picardie:

This concludes the initial statement of the hymn: which Vaughan Williams repeats with re-creative embellishments. The tune now soars on high violins, while the second violins burgeon in arabesques, innocent in pentatonicism yet disturbed in their oscillations between major and minor. The contours of the theme are unchanged but the subsiding coda omits the resolution to the tonic major. Instead, a further repetition is enharmonically transmuted from flats to sharps. A B major (really C flat) triad is cancelled by an E minor triad, C sharp minor by D major. Tonally, we are in Dante's *selva oscura*, the enharmony being a doubleness, like a pun.

Divisiveness now extends to the music's structure, for the two orchestras, which up to this point have played as one, assume twofold identities. And the music develops in a technical sense: though one might more accurately call it anti-development, in so far as it functions by fragmenting aspects of Tallis's theme and discovering within them unpredictable cross-references – to which the Christian connotations of a cross are relevant. The enharmonic codetta triads had ended on F sharp major: from which basis the rising fith of the second half of the tune is strongly sounded by the violins of Orchestra I, answered even more forcefully by a rising octave on cellos and basses. These leaping intervals are physical gestures: which have dramatic consequences when the F sharp major triad is suddenly punctured by a *fortissimo* D *minor* triad, fading back to F sharp major *pianissimo*. The falseness of the relation is emphasized by the dynamics; and is the more pointed because the second orchestra responds with the undulating, syncopated triads (from bars 3 to 5) whispered con sordino, as though by a choir of slightly distraught angels. The ambiguities are subtle; for if the harmonic dislocations of Orchestra I are humanly corporeal and dramatic, the distant false related undulations of Orchestra II are, though seraphic, wistful in their instability. The two orchestras are not equated respectively with the physical and the metaphysical, but change identities as they interact. Thus when the first orchestra repeats its 'gestural' rising fifth and octave, it is punctuated by an E flat major instead of D minor triad, again echoed by the second orchestra's undulating triads, now around E flat. Orchestra I modifies its gesture to rising octave and major sixth, a more emotive interval than the fifth; and guillotines the ripe E flat major sonority with a sudden *pianissimo* triad of A minor, a devil's tritone away from the initial E flat (see the music example on p. 54).

Such startling juxtapositions of chromatically 'altered' chords have their origins in sixteenth-century false relation but are more typical of the seventeenth century – especially of overtly dramatic music in (newly) operatic form. One of the most famous passages in European music is the

moment when, in Monteverdi's *Orfeo* of 1607, the Messenger recounts, in continuo-accompanied recitative, the grim fact of Eurydice's death – a disruption of humanly instigated marriage-concord by the (in this case literal) nip of the serpent's tooth. At the dire news the chords supporting the recitative shift from heavenly E major to tragic G minor, a chromatic alteration inducing panic and fear. Vaughan Williams's sudden chromatic changes of gear between chords in themselves concordant are in the same sense representations of a Fall: which in this particular context encourages Orchestra II to transmute the triads into the preludial 'falling' motif. After so much tonal rootlessness the music is steered from the edge of the abyss; and as the preludial motto is sung in its original shape, tonality blissfully roots itself on E instead of G. (Interestingly enough, this polarity of mediants is the same as that in Monteverdi's famous passage.) Dynamics are soft, *senza espressione*, but Orchestra I answers with the false related undulations, *forte*. Both orchestras join in the oscillations, and dissonant passing notes – C and A against B and G sharp of the E major triads – for the first time lend sinew to the texture. They vanish, leaving the triads vacillating in second inversion on the violas and cellos of Orchestra I, echoed by the cellos and basses of Orchestra II.

At this point there is a further division, for a quartet of solo strings (played by the leaders of each group) initiates an extension from the theme. This is re-creative in a significant way, for the solo string voices are conceived monodically: as though, through the previous fragmentation, the individual spirit has been freed, to flow like a vastly expanded folk song. At first the melody, on solo viola, is long and meandering, in a mode veering between dorian and phrygian E. Beginning with three 'speaking' repeated notes (an augmented version of the opening of Tallis's tune), it flows in flexible rhythm, incorporating triplets in dotted rhythm:

Though this stems from the $\frac{6}{8}$ dotted rhythm in the original hymn, it has become a quintessential Vaughan Williams melody, transforming ecclesiastical devotion into pastoral lyricism. It is to have many metamorphoses in Vaughan Williams's later music, notably in the cantata *The Shepherds of the Delectable Mountains* (1922), which became part of the Bunyan-based 'operatic morality', *The Pilgrim's Progress*. We shall be exploring the obsessive influence of Bunyan on Vaughan Williams in a later chapter. For the moment, we may say that the spirit of Bunyan helps Vaughan Williams to carry Tallis's 'people's prayer' into the open fields. When the 'Bunyan' melody is sung by a high solo violin we cannot but relate the soaring line to Vaughan Williams's ascending and transcending lark in the work which, above all others, contains the heart of his religious sensibility. (This piece, which followed a few years after the Fantasia, will be discussed in the next chapter.) And the winging lark inspires all four members of the solo quartet, for they take up the melody in free canon, firmly rooted or earthed (as contrasted with the oscillating 'ecclesiastical' triads) on a pedal E. Folk song becomes a many-in-oneness like Tudor polyphony in full flight. The music settles into a swinging triple pulse.

Tonally, the two orchestras still fluctuate rapidly, shifting through mediants prompted by the false relations in the tune. Slowly, the soloists merge with the orchestras, flowing through passing dissonances and modifying the undulating triads to accommodate augmented fifths – an effect unexpectedly painful in so consistently diatonic a texture. Tallis's hymn and Vaughan Williams's pastorally Edenic song become one with the marriage of the divided choirs; ripe double stops and leaping arpeggios impart to the music both corporeal energy and spiritual grace. At the climax tonality veers between mixolydian C and its mediant E, the momentum being such that the false relations now enhance, rather than threaten, ecstasy. There is not much music that so comsummately identifies body and spirit; and there is a philosophical, even theological, as well as a musical dimension to this, for the cycle of Vaughan Williams's symphonies is to reveal that innocence and experience are interdependent. This Blakean marriage of heaven and hell reminds us that Blake is to be Vaughan Williams's third literary mentor, succeeding Whitman and Bunyan. The Tallis Fantasia might even be considered as a study for Vaughan Williams's Blake apotheosis, the 'masque for dancing' he created under the inspiration of Blake's illustrations to the Book of Job. In this light we may understand why the preludial phrase of bars 1 and 2, which looks like a Fall, serves in *Job* and in other later works for the descent of God in the whirlwind, and even as a gesture of benediction.

We have noted that, during the exultantly climactic pages, the two orchestras and four soloists increasingly play as one, in ripely polyphonic textures and unbroken triple metre. Gradually the polyphony, still fluctuating between mediants, coalesces in the pre-harmonic (medieval rather than Renaissance) technique of organum, and is again stabilized on the dorian E in which the Bunyan or Delectable Mountains theme had started. Ultimately this theme is chanted *fortissimo* in a cross between organum and monody; though now sturdy, it does not abandon the rhythmic flexibility of its triplets. But at last the $\frac{3}{4}$ pulse stumbles into an erratic $\frac{5}{8}$ as the theme declines scalewise, ending in undulations around E, fading to *pianissimo*. The rhythm of Tallis's tune recurs without the rising third, as the orchestras are again, and more violently, divided. Monteverdi-like triads cancel one another enharmonically, effecting a fall from heaven-storming ecstasy to the heavy earth (see the music example on the facing page). This passage is echoed, often in explicitly dramatic contexts, in later works such as *Job* and the Fifth Symphony. In its original context it ends on the dark F minor triad that had first appeared in the codetta to Tallis's tune. From it there now emerges a coda-recapitulation of the hymn at the original pitch, the undivided orchestras at first playing the lower parts, while solo violin chants the full theme in high register, garlanded by solo viola in melismatic embroideries. The line flows as freely as the Delectable Mountains song, if without the untrammelled lyricism of the ascending lark.

The last statement of the hymn ends with the same level-rhythmed coda phrase, again enharmonically echoed. For the final passage of syncopated triadic undulations the two orchestras duplicate one another, though dissonant passing notes grate more thickly than in any comparable

Molto adagio

passage. The end is a protraction of Tallis's plagal VII flat, IV, I cadence. A lark-like solo violin soars over the muddily earthy F minor triad; solo second violin has the complementary rise to the tierce de Picardie. For the ultimate G major triad the two orchestras and four soloists meet in sonorous double stops, beginning *fortissimo*, fading to quadruple *piano*: which the cathedral's period of reverberation prolongs, so that the music seems to enter timeless eternity and spaceless infinity. The ecclesiastical building is part of the music's acoustic. Vaughan Williams's Fantasia is not a concert piece, though strictly speaking it is not a liturgical piece either.

Its secular-sacral character bears on its modernity: as is evident in so far as the music, despite its affinities with Tudor vocal polyphony and the seventeenth-century string consort, does promulgate a 'symphonic' argument. After the preludial motto, the first section (up to figure E in the score) makes one straight and one varied statement of Tallis's hymn; the second section (letters E to I), extending the technique of false relation, fragments and divides, literally establishing the doubleness of the orchestras. This leads to a further division into two orchestras and a consort of four soloists, who metamorphose the Tallis hymn into a liberated melody of folk-like cast, prophetic of the composer's Bunyan-inspired pieces. In the longest section of the work – though section is a misleading term in relation to music that is in essence evolutionary – pulse stabilizes as the four soloists, whom we may think of as individual spirits within the religious-social community, interact with the orchestras in increasingly ecstatic polyphony. Borne on mediant transitions, the polyphony gells into organum, and that into almost unisonal monody, as division is healed. Only it is not totally healed, for after the organum has simmered down the most violent form of false relation – chromatically and enharmonically altered triads – reinstates our fallen condition. The final da capo of the hymn synthesizes (pentatonic) lyrical innocence with harmonic experience.

From the Tallis Fantasia's discovery of generation and regeneration within techniques basically melodic rather than harmonic springs Vaughan Williams's approach to the 'problem' of the English symphony: a convention which, for reasons already discussed, England had bypassed. The Third (Pastoral) Symphony is to create intense drama out of melodic speech, mostly in slow tempi and unobtrusive dynamics; Symphonies 4, 5 and 6 make dramatic argument overt – aggressively so in the case of No. 4, which is almost a symphony about the doubleness of false relation. Yet these newly symphonic symphonies function mainly by way of techniques latent in the early Fantasia: a work which, moreover, adumbrates many of the literary themes that dominate the composer's life – the link with Bunyan's *Pilgrim's Progress* and an Eden in the Delectable Mountains, the Blakean fusion of innocence and experience, the vision of the Celestial City and of the New Jerusalem. The Fantasia has direct links with the works of Vaughan Williams's maturity, notably *Job* and the middle symphonies, though it does not follow that when he made near-literal quotations from the Fantasia he was consciously aware of what he was doing. It was rather that this work was, in Blake's sense, the smithy of his soul. Henceforth his most personal and significant music flows from a single source.

IV

THE ASCENT OF THE LARK

NATURE AND TRANSCENDENCE IN
THE LARK ASCENDING AND
THE MASS FOR DOUBLE CHOIR

To hoard no boon beyond his wing,
No bauble but his beauty,
His but to be and soar and sing
And wave his dear his duty,

And shout him blest and over-blest
Until the skies reject him,
And hear the while within his breast
No privy woe correct him ...

No burnings for a bygone day,
No bodings of hereafter,
No wounds like them we hide away
Beneath our smiles and laughter ...

Yet are we blest; we know we climb
From darker ways behind us,
That suns will break for us in time,
Too early broke would blind us,

And lit within we'll stand among
The corn at last receiving
The secret of our skylark's song,
And more we go believing.

RALPH HODGSON, 'The Skylark'

Vaughan Williams's long symphonic pilgrimage was, we have suggested, precipitated out of the experience of the *Fantasia on a Theme of Thomas Tallis*: a work that had sprung from a marriage of the traditions of the Anglican Church with those of agrarian Britain. The first two authentic symphonies in the Vaughan Williams canon represent, as their appellations of 'London' and 'Pastoral' indicate, urban and rural states: which are spiritual rather than topographical or geographical. As an approach to them we must first examine two works which, although small, are crucial to Vaughan Williams's development. We have already hinted that the earlier of them, *The Lark Ascending*, for solo violin and small orchestra, takes us to the heart of the composer's religious sensibility, which is not the same as an accredited faith, let alone doctrine. It is rather affiliated to English Nature-mysticism, already mentioned in reference to Delius, and to writers such as Jefferies and Hudson.

Behind those authors is a long literary tradition, with which Vaughan Williams was familiar. It is to the point that this tradition attained its heyday during the sixteenth and still more the seventeenth century: for it was then that England passed through a crisis of faith exemplified in the English Reformation and, more painfully, in the years of Civil War. It is not surprising that in times when men can find little satisfaction in their man-made institutions of Church and State they should seek consolation in the impersonal forces of Nature, wherein God, however mysteriously he may work his wonders, may be presumed to be manifest. A religious poet of the seventeenth century such as the orthodox Anglican priest George Herbert wrote out of conflict with, as well as in worship of, his God; and he is complemented by many poets whose religious sense had no need of conventional devotional practice. The Celtic Henry Vaughan sought salvation in moments of transcendence, since 'there is in God, some say, a deep but dazzling darkness'. He prays for 'that night where I in him Might live invisible and dim'. Nature may offer release from the consequences of the Fall, which bore all too weightily on Englishmen of the seventeenth century, divided against themselves and one another.

This is why the seventeenth-century cult of Nature was allied to a cult of the child and of our prelapsarian state. 'Sure it was so', says Vaughan;

> Man in those early days
> Was not all stone, and Earth;
> He shin'd a little, and by those weak rays
> Had some glimpse of his birth.

In another poem he exclaims:

> Happy those early days! when I
> Shin'd in my Angell-infancy,
> Before I understood this place
> Appointed for my second race,
> Or taught my soul to fancy ought
> But a white, Celestiall thought. . . .
>
> But (ah!) my soul with too much stay
> Is drunk, and staggers in the way.
> Some men a forward motion love,
> But I by backward steps would move,
> And when this dust falls to the urn
> In that state I came return.

Thomas Traherne explores similar themes, both in his verse and, more remarkably, in the prose poems of his *Centuries of Meditation*. The lyrically surging rhythms of Traherne's vision of childhood's Celestial City are prophetic of the free verse of Whitman and the poetic prose of Jefferies, the influence of which on Vaughan Williams was direct. Vaughan 'felt through all this fleshly dresse/Bright Shootes of Everlastingnesse'; such as we surely encounter in Traherne's famous account of the Golden City, wherein

> Boyes and Girles Tumbling in the Street, and Playing, were moving Jewels. I knew not that they were Born, or should Dy. But all things abided eternally as they were in their Proper Places. Eternity was manifest in the Light of the Day. ... The Citie seemed to stand in Eden, or to be built in Heaven. The Streets were mine, the Temple was mine, the People were mine, and their Gold and Silver were mine, and I the only Spectator and Enjoyer of it. I knew no churlish Proprieties, nor Bounds, nor Divisions ... So that with much Ado I was corrupted, and made to learn the Dirty Devices of this World. Which now I undo, and become as it were a little Child again, that I may enter into the Kingdom of God.

Though Christian eschatology and biblical cadences inform this prose, its message needs no specifically religious formulation, any more than does the 'Green thought in a green shade' which transfigured Marvell in his (Edenic) garden.

The mundane cynicism of the Restoration, when the ambiguity of civil war seemed to have been resolved in favour of secularity, stifled this dream, which made only fitful appearances during the rational eighteenth century. It resurfaced, however, at the close of the century in the poetry of Blake, Wordsworth, and 'mad' John Clare. Shelley's skylark and Keats's nightingale are only the most celebrated among many romantic birds who were to haunt the nineteenth century: by the end of which we find that Vaughan Williams's immediate predecessors, Richard Jefferies and W.H. Hudson, deal not only with the social realities of rural life, but also with Nature as a source of mystical experience. Here is Jefferies, motionless in a summer field:

> If a breeze rustled the boughs, if a greenfinch called, if the cart-mare in the meadow shook herself, making the earth and air tremble by her with the mighty convulsion of her muscles, these were not sounds, they were the silence itself. So sensitive to it as I was, in its turn it held me firmly, like the fabled spells of old time.

And here he is, discovering in a brook a sacred fount:

There was a brook, indeed; but this was different, it was the spring; it was taken home as a beautiful flower might be brought. It is not the physical water, it is the sense or feeling it conveys. Nor is it the physical sunshine; it is the sense of inexpressible beauty which it brings with it. Of such I still drink, and hope to do so still deeper.

The spiritually purgatorial motif that an Andrew Marvell had found in fountain or stream may still, it seems, be tapped in direct contemplation of Nature.

Nor is the tradition only literary. Samuel Palmer, contemporary of the romantic poets and friend and colleague of William Blake, painted, in the 'visionary years' of his youth at Shoreham, those magical evocations of an English Eden rediscovered, in sunlight and more especially moonlight, in the corn-fecund, apple-heavy vales. Palmer, like Blake, is peculiarly pertinent to our theme, for his visionary landscapes were havens from an incipiently industrialized world which, as he was well aware, would bring distress alike to the countryside and to the men and women who lived in it. Palmer's social conscience was acute; yet despite his intelligence and moral probity he was a victim of the encroaching industrial malaise, since his genius did not keep pace with his productiveness. The 'visionary gleam' came, and went; he became a good but untranscendent academician, who followed the conventional course of sojourn and study in Italy. Nor did he realize what he had lost; Shelley's Spirit of Delight is indeed elusive, though it is not illusory. Blake, as usual, went to the heart of the matter: 'He who catches a joy as it flies, Lives in Eternity's sun-rise'.

Vaughan Williams loved Palmer's visionary paintings, as he loved those of Blake (and for that matter those of the French Impressionists, which are relevant to the composer's earlier years, especially the Debussyan and Ravellian 'moments of sensation' in *On Wenlock Edge*). If there is a soundscape that offers an aural complement to Palmer's landscapes, it is Vaughan Williams's *The Lark Ascending*, significantly dated 1914 – the year of the war that was to silence English larks of most breeds. The piece is in one continuous movement which is evolutionary, though it has rondo–like characteristics. It is a dialogue between the lark, who is instinctual like the bird in Hodgson's poem, and man, who is 'accommodated' in his agrarian state, yet aspires towards the spirit of delight the lark embodies. Since the work is about the interdependence of a lark and us men and women it is, for all its quietude, a 'symphonic' piece which evolves, even develops. Later we shall see that Vaughan Williams's first real orchestral symphony, the London, completed in the same year as *The Lark Ascending*, touches on this very theme, especially in its slow movement.

The score is prefaced by a quotation from Meredith's poem with the same title, which sees the lark as the liberated spirit, but is less explicit than Hodgson about the blight of industrialism. Nor is there any reference to blight in Vaughan Williams's music, though we are aware of it because we listen in the context of the composer's work as a whole. The orchestra – strings, one oboe, two each of flutes, clarinets, bassoons and horns – opens with a 'piled-up' seventh chord on a pedal E, such as pervades 'Bredon Hill'. Muted violins and horns move up in parallel fifths, from D to F sharp. The rising third – echoing that in Tallis's hymn – is a gentle gesture of aspiration that summons the lark in the guise of a solo violin. *Senza misura*, he launches into a long cadenza – meandering because he does not need to know where he is going. Slowly he elevates himself from his low open-stringed D to the D three octaves above, floating (not progressing) by way of pentatonic roulades. Already the interdependence and at the same time the separation of human and avian aspiration is implicit, for whereas the orchestra's softly harmonized rising third wants to 'go somewhere' even if it does not, the lark is unconscious of past or future.

At this point we must ask what is meant when we call pentatonic formulae – such as the lark carols and such as we have frequently referred to in Vaughan Williams's music – 'innocent'. When we sing or play a given tone we call it, for convenience, a single tone. In fact it is an aggregation of the infinite number of tones contained within the harmonic series, of which the few prime numbers are in some circumstances audible to the human ear. These prime partials are the intervals defined by the ratios of 2 to 1, 3 to 2, and 4 to 5 in that order – the octave, fifth, and fourth (which is the fifth inverted). Since no one can sing a sequence of pitches without being subconsciously aware of these relationships, the reason for their primacy in all so-called primitive musics becomes clear.

A further characteristic of these intervals is that the distance between the fourth and fifth defines the interval of the 'tone' – the norm of conjunct motion in music at least until the unequivocal acceptance of equal temperament and of the Schoenbergian semitone. The natural interval-relationships define the natural norm of progression. That these basic elements of song-speech link up with the spoken word was suggested by Vaughan Williams himself in his book *National Music*, when he pointed out how a public speaker, moved by passion or perhaps merely by a desire to make himself heard, will fluctuate between two adjacent tones, incorporating at points of climax a sudden leap of fourth or fifth or even, exceptionally, an octave. Such 'natural' figures are among the fundamental formulae of folk song as of plainsong or any purely monodic music; they are the seeds of melody, from which song germinates.

Suppose we call our prime tones C, F, G, c. If one takes fourths and fifths from the two interior tones (F and G), one arrives at two new tones (B flat and D), and at a more extended, five-note melodic figure – one of the several permutations of the pentatonic scale. This is the basis of all 'primitive' musics and of most civilized monophonies, over most of the world's space and through centuries of time. Significantly, it is the basis of all musics spontaneously invented by children – as the present writer can testify from experience with his own children, who were brought up in a household dominated by equal-tempered instrumental music, and even by Schoenbergian semitones. The child, even in our complex urban technocracies, is a small savage, aspiring towards consciousness. He sings as the lark sings, while being inevitably more restricted in range.

Vaughan Williams's violin lark is, in this opening cadenza, as untrammelled as the air he floats in, oblivious of any latent harmonic tension such as might accrue in a line embracing intervals other than pentatonic seconds, thirds and fourths. When, however, he reaches the cerulean heights on the D three octaves above the tone he started from, his measureless winging hints at a temporal pulse. This is how he makes the transition:

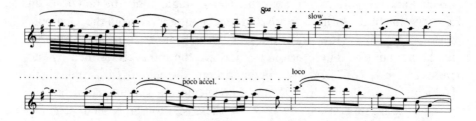

Drooping from the highest D through a pentatonic minor third to B, in level dotted crotchets, he moves up stepwise in pastoral dotted rhythm, as though, high in the sky, he is offering intimations of immortality to earth-bound men and women. But the intimation is momentary; resuming his measureless state, he floats down, still pentatonic in line and yet more flexible in rhythm. When he has alighted on his original low D, and has dipped below that to B and A, he slowly mounts again. This time the orchestra joins him.

The music is now barred, in $\frac{6}{8}$; and the orchestra, over the pedal E that was the first sound we heard, sings the rising third of the prelude, now undulating up and down, not merely pressing up; the mode is dorian E. Above the orchestra, though not *impossibly* high, the lark sings the phrase – beginning with pentatonic minor third from D to B in dotted crotchets – he had hinted at when at his most stratospheric point. His heavenly pentatonic song has come to bless us, like a messenger of the Holy Ghost. But although he at first sings with the orchestra's song-dance, he is not confined by it. Recurrently he breaks into his original roulades, while the woodwind and horns breathe the orchestra's rising third motif in dotted rhythm – as it is in Tallis's hymn:

Imperceptibly, the human song grows stronger and the lark, instead of singing, twitters fragmentarily, *sur la touche*. As though encouraged by the humans, he joins in their song, high in register, while the bird-twitterings are taken over by flute. Breaking the $\frac{6}{8}$ pulse into pentatonic figuration in $\frac{3}{4}$, the lark inaugurates the first climax in a still gentle orchestral tutti; at last the dorian E modality shows signs of movement, if not progression. The music swings through mediant-related triads involving double stops; even the lark harmonically acquires two voices, chanting an upward-thrusting version of the pentatonic motif at first in octaves, then in double stopped chords that form two real parts, notated as such. This modest climax subsides in a freely canonic version of the original rising third, stretching up to the seventh, drooping through the same pentatonic third that the lark had piped in the heights. The canonic polyphony is a human togetherness, perhaps inspired by the spirit of delight. The section ends with an orchestral repetition, triple *piano*, of the preludial rising third. A chord of the ninth is sustained while the lark takes off again, alone, in a more rapidly ecstatic cadenza, rising to the same stratospheric D and B.

This is the end of the first section, which has been lark-propelled, on the base of man and his earth. Now for a while man dominates, for the metre changers from $\frac{6}{8}$ to $\frac{2}{4}$, and an *allegretto* tune is sung by the flutes, supported by other woodwind and horns. Though the tune is still pentatonic on E (with the occasional addition of a flat sixth), its earthy and temporal nature, as compared with the larks's convolutions, is unmistakable. It might be, though it is not, a real folk dance, evoking the 'earth feet, loam feet' of our quotation from Eliot's 'East Coker' (p.28). It is not long before the lark joins the men and women with a pentatonic figure that is a horizontalized version of the 'piled-up' earth-chord at the beginning. The effect of this solo song is, however, different from the lark's earlier airy cascades, for it is metrical, with each note bowed separately. What happens then – this is what the work is about – is that the man-music and the lark-music gradually coalesce. The bird loosens the shackles of metre, coruscating into trills, triplets and septuplets; and though the earthy dance continues, its rhythms are freed. The 'folk' dance had begun in something close to diatonic C major. Now the lark steers the music back to dorian E, ready to take off again, transforming us men and women in the process.

For the third section, marked *allegro tranquillo*, opens with the lark gliding from dorian E to what seems to be aeolian A, though there is a B flat in the key signature which is always cancelled. Chains of trills from the soloist whirl into pentatonic roulades, while the woodwind evolves a melody beginning with the lark's descending third, and fusing the triple pulse of the first melody with the duple pulse of the folky dance. The orchestral melodies, encouraged by the lark, grow gradually more airborne, until the soloist sings *their* transmuted melody in uninhibited glee, accompanied by tremolandos. The lark adds tipsy chirrups, consistently pentatonic, while the orchestra arrives at a mating of heaven-seeking lark and earth-dancing humans. The music fades as the bird descends to the earth, his line low but still trill-garlanded.

The modality is now clearly a pentatonic-inflected aeolian A. The one sharp returns to the key signature and, over an E minor triad with an additional C as bass, the original piled-up chord murmurs, without its low A. The soloist embroiders an infinitely soft E minor triad with eerie double stops beginning in parallel fifths; with an inversion of the falling pentatonic third in dotted crotchets, linked to the rising-third scale, we reach the coda. This is a recapitulation of the first $\frac{6}{8}$ theme, modified to embrace its later permutations. The lark attains his earthiest climax in octaves and double stops, while the orchestral harmony descends flatly through a phrygian F major triad. The dialogue between lark and orchestra ends with the soloist singing, low in register, the full version of the marvellous melody that has emerged from the marriage of earth and heaven. Flutes and oboes flood a shaft of light into the lark's falling third figure. The pedal E falls to C but returns to E with the added seventh chord, which is sustained while the lark is airborne on his last flight, barless, pentatonic as at the start, though more rapid in figuration. This time the string chord dims to silence. The lark is left solitary in the empty sky, soaring to the same altitudinous D and B, the latter so long sustained that one hardly knows whether one hears sound or silence.

The ramifications of this magical piece haunted Vaughan Williams throughout the rest of his creative life, and its presence is at least latent in the finest music of some of his successors, notably in Finzi's settings of Traherne. But by no other composer is the interdependence of man and Nature more movingly expressed; and we should note that Vaughan Williams's lark is at once an instinctual voice of Nature and a man-made artefact. For larks do not really sing pentatonically but microtonally, though if they listen to their own song (and it seems some birds do), they might light on basic pentatonic formulae in acceding to the acoustical properties of Nature herself. The real lark whose song Vaughan Williams rejoiced in as he tramped the downs, may know nothing of 'privy woe' or 'burnings for a bygone day' or 'bodings of hereafter', but he became, in Vaughan Williams's music, part of the warp and woof of our tangled natures. We should be grateful for him; he offers a rare glimpse of eternity's sunrise.

Vaughan Williams described *The Lark Ascending* as a 'romance for solo violin and small orchestra'. That sounds modest, though it is significant that he applied the term romance to some of his deepest music – for instance the slow movements of the Piano Concerto and of the Fifth Symphony. One suspects that for him 'romantic' had little if anything to do with the popular sense of the word; a romance was not a love story nor did it have any connection with the romance languages. It might, however, have links with the medieval tales of chivalry that indirectly derived from Romance tradition; certainly the pilgrim latent in the Fifth Symphony's slow movement is on a quest. *The Lark Ascending* does not tell a story, though it does, as we have seen, imply dramatic evolution: which is why, despite its unassuming nature, it is a 'symphonic' work, related to the Second Symphony on which the composer was working more or less simultaneously. The exact chronology is obscure. The London Symphony was first performed in 1914, which was also the date of the *Lark*'s composition; but Vaughan Williams tidied the romance into a drawer, and made no attempt to get it performed until 1921, when the turmoil of the war was over. Perhaps he felt it was, in those circumstances, anachronistic, whereas his first true symphony, being a symphony, was *ipso facto* a work about conflict. However this may be, *The Lark Ascending* is very far from being an escapist piece; and there is appropriateness in the fact that the date of its first performance should more or less coincide with that of his Third Symphony, the Pastoral: in which he first revealed what an 'English' symphony might be. Contemporary with this, moreover, is another small work which, like the Tallis Fantasia, might superficially be mistaken for an exercise in archaism. Vaughan Williams's *a cappella* Mass is as intimately associated with his Third Symphony as *The Lark Ascending* is with his Second. In between the 1914–15 and the 1919–21 pieces was the catastrophe of war.

Vaughan Williams's Mass was composed for the Whitsuntide Singers directed by his friend Gustav Holst; the pre-Tudor flavour of much of the music may pay homage to Holst's predilections, though no doubt Vaughan Williams himself, after the war, needed to make music that looked back at the English heritage in purity, even chastity, of spirit. In any case he did something he had not done before, even in the Tallis Fantasia, which is simultaneously sacred music and concert music. He wrote a Mass conceived uncompromisingly in liturgical terms; it was performed by Sir Richard Terry's choir at Westminster Cathedral, and was considered by that fine musician and devout Catholic to be conducive to worship. Its polyphony is comparable with that of Tallis and his contemporaries – and sometimes his predecessors; even so, starting from the religious-social solidarity of modal polyphony, Vaughan Williams extends the technique of false relation so far that what might have been a Tudor Mass becomes modern music: such it seemed when it was performed at the 1922 International Festival of Contemporary Music. That liturgically devotional music has acquired something one might call dramatic evolution is supported by the fact that its most 'modern' movement is its last: a cry for God's mercy, uttered in the aftermath of 1918. For that, one did not need to be an orthodox Christian.

Doubleness is patent in the Mass's being scored for double choir, as was much of the music of Tallis himself, as well as Vaughan Williams's Fantasia on Tallis's theme, in which the vocal choirs are translated into strings. The parallel between the Mass and the Fantasia extends further: for as the latter turns doubleness into tripleness by the addition of a solo string quartet to the two string orchestras, so the Mass introduces a third dimension in the form of a quartet of vocal soloists. And the functions of the solo quartets are the same: they introduce into the 'mystical' impersonality of the tutti an element of individualized human expressivity, and extract incipient drama from the interaction and, on occasion, the confrontation. For the most part the Mass is as consistently modal as is a real sixteenth-century liturgical work, and although the Mass is said on the score to be 'in G minor', no section is in fact in G minor and only short passages are in G major (which, in context, would be more properly called the ionian mode on G). Even so, Vaughan Williams's Mass is, within its G-orientation, polymodal, as a real Tudor Mass could not be. If its root tonality is G, it has a complementary pole in E, and its latent drama is usually related to the contrast between the G naturals of the G chords and the G sharps of E major. It is worth recalling that for Bach, especially in the so-called B minor Mass, G major is a key of benediction, E minor (its relative) a complementary key of crucifixion, with E major (rarely touched on) as the light of heaven. Vaughan Williams's handling of tonality, or rather modality, in his Mass is not schematic; but we cannot question that the climactic effect of the soloists' entrance, in the Agnus Dei, in a phrygian E minor is attributable to long-range tonal architecture. Still more powerful is the effect of the movement's oscillations between E (phrygian) minor-major and G minor-major – precisely the same oppositions, incidentally, as those commented on in reference to the Messenger's narration in Monteverdi's *Orfeo* (see p.53–4).

In the first Kyrie the two choirs initially sing as one – as do the two string choirs at the beginning of the Tallis Fantasia. The mode is dorian on G (with sharp sixth but flat seventh), and the theme is almost a cliché of ecclesiastical polyphony, floating either by step or through a rising fourth which then droops down the scale. Each line, individually considered, could be plainchant, and the rhythm is, or seems to be, non-metrical. The effect of the music is thus time-effacing and non-, even anti-dramatic. This remains true as the four voices enter in tranquil fugato, each entry traditionally at the fifth, and closer than its predecessor. The polyphonic texture is concordant, without even passing dissonances. This, with the prevalence of organum-like parallel triads in first inversion, enhances the spiritual, and in a sense archaic, flavour.

The 'Christe' changes the key signature from two flats to one sharp, though the F sharps are often cancelled since the mode is mixolydian. When the sevenths *are* sharp, they often create false relations between mixolydian and straight diatonic G major. The music is personalized by being sung by the four soloists instead of the two choirs together. The prominence of mixolydian major thirds gives the texture a luminosity appropriate to the incarnation of the Godhead in Christ the man; while the pulse, which has so far been no more than an implicit duple pendulum, is now triple. In Renaissance music triple rhythms were usually associated with the physical momentum of dance – further evidence of the Christe's 'humanization'. Moreover, contrapuntal treatment of the theme – a decorated decline from the dominant through a fifth – is soon abandoned in favour of note-for-note movement, lightly dancing, even hinting at sharpwards modulation to the dominant. The soloists are silenced when the duple pulse is re-established, along with the mixolydian mode, in which the second choir recapitulates the Kyrie. The modality is devoid of chromatic alteration, let alone passing dissonances. Indeed, the organum-like texture is so pure that it recalls not only its ostensible model in early Renaissance church music, but also the 'folk' re-creation of this idiom in American shape-note hymnody; the Kyrie theme gradually dissolves into its pentatonic source, and finally into measureless undulation around the fifth. At that date it is unlikely that Vaughan Williams would have heard any shape-note hymnody, though he might have consulted more orthodox American hymn books in connection with the New English Hymnal.

In traditional style, the Gloria is prefaced by its plainsong intonation; also traditionally, it is at first scored in resonant homophony for the two choirs, both together and in antiphony. Whereas the Kyrie is a summoning of the Godhead, the Gloria concerns peace on earth, attainable by men of good will. The earthiness is inherent in the massive triadic homophony, in speech rhythm, in eight parts; but that our fallen state is divisive is manifest because the concordant triads are in false relation. G major shifts to E major, which acts as dominant to A, though both the sixth and seventh are flattened. At 'Laudamus te' the choirs divide, answering one another in jubilant antiphony. Each choir moves note for note, riddled with tingling mediant false relations, but the Glorificamus becomes traditionally canonic, launched by a rising fourth. 'Gratias agimus' and 'Rex coelistis' divide the choirs antiphonally again, the motif being almost identical with the 'fingerprint' that opens the Tallis Fantasia. False relations occur more rapidly than they would in a real sixteenth-century motet, but are similar in spirit: men of the Reformation lived – as our quotation from Powicke indicated – dangerously as well as joyously. Excitement simmers down, however, at the invocation to the 'Filius Patris', ending calmly on a G major triad.

The 'Qui tollis' looks back to the spirituality of medieval monody, while at the same time the false relations are more acute. Soloists vocalize the words in tender pentatonicism, answered with 'misereres' from the boys of both choirs, rocking in parallel triads. In a piercing sweetness the major F sharps of the soloists clash with the minor thirds of the undulating triads; at 'Tu solus sanctus' the burden of the words prompts a *senze misura* soprano solo very close to the Pastoral Symphony. Pace quickens at 'Cum Sancto Spiritu', again in accord with tradition. The eight voices of the double choir overlap in canon, the mode being pentatonic on D, veering to aeolian and mixolydian G. Since the voices overlap in range as well as canonically, doubleness is momentarily healed; we float in or on the interlacing voices, which toll like bells. In the Amens even the false relations enthrall, and perhaps assuage. They make a gateway into the Credo's affirmation of faith, again introduced by the plainchant intonation.

The choral theme begins with the pentatonic descent inverted, making the Father sound omnipotent indeed. Grandeur is inherent too in the hemiola rhythm at the top of the ascent, this being one of Vaughan Williams's fingerprints in its most overt form. The catalogue of God's attributes ('Et invisibilium' and so on) is bandied between the two choirs, each moving homophonically around a pentatonic figure. The word 'consubstantialem' provokes a tellingly 'substantial' shift to duplets within the triplet pulse. Soloists naturally sing the 'Incarnatus', since it brings God 'down' to man through flatward shifts in the modality from mixolydian G to lydian and dorian F, the voices moving in canon at the fifth. Simple though the music is, it subtly symbolizes the descent from spirit to flesh; and the subtlety is enhanced at the moment wherein God is actually 'made man' – in a return from the soloists to the two choirs singing long sustained, falsely related triads of C, B flat, A flat and F majors. Even texturally, man-music becomes god-music, or at least god-like music, in these awesome chords, whispered in quadruple *piano* (see the music example on p.72). It is typical of Vaughan Williams that he should thus stress the moment at which God is translated into man, achieving a dramatic event without destroying devotional serenity. The crucifixion and burial, on the other hand, drain the music of intensity, as Christ's martyred body was drained of life. The soloists tell of his death in or around a dorian F wherein traditionally lugubrious F minor is mollified: $^6_3$ organum chords rock in piquant false relation at the reference to Pontius Pilate. Christ is sepulchrally buried by the two choruses, triple *piano*, in enveloping A flat major triads (F minor's relative), rounding to F minor-major.

The 'Et resurrexit' is antiphonal between the choirs and quicker in pace, as was traditional. Tonality sharpens to a modalized D, the theme being the familiar pentatonic rise: which may make a point, its familiarity signalizing that rebirth is perennial. The hemiola rhythm is again

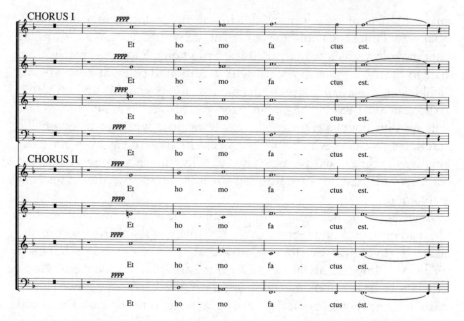

prominent; false relations are grandly spaced, reinforced by the intermit-tent duplets, and climax in a falsely related triad of E major. 'Spiritum Sanctum Dominum' is given to the soloists, in the dorian mode on E, with aeolian and phrygian excursions. The two choruses take up the theme antiphonally, merging for the Amens and returning to dorian G, with the clangour of wild bells. The final G major chord, after many reverberating B flat, C and F major triads, spendidly shines.

The Sanctus is the most solemn moment in the Mass: at once the most archaic and also the most modern music thus far. It begins with an undulation rocking in parallel fifths or thirds between adjacent tones, in overlapping canons between the two choirs. The effect is again bell-like, but these bells are not clamorous but distant. They float, always double *piano*, from beyond the horizon, without pulse, directionless, because they are as 'pre-conscious' as Nature herself, or God. The basses, chanting 'Sanctus' on their bottom D, make a holy humming such as so-called primitive peoples associate with the stirring of creation within the void. The second 'Sanctus' also begins on D but ends on a G major triad; this time the canons are by contrary motion, though motion is hardly a concept relevant to this music, which is as nearly outside time as man could make it. For the third cry of 'Sanctus' the canons fall pentatonically from a high G, chiming in close stretto. The invocation of 'Sanctus Dominus' is elevated from G to A. The sonority, both luminous and numinous, has in its spiritual purity something in common with 'folk' polyphony and heterophony. This we will understand better when we consider the Pastoral Symphony which, as we have seen, coincides in date with the Mass.

According to custom, which Vaughan Williams approved of, the 'Pleni sunt coeli' is quicker and more conventionally contrapuntal. It is in double canon, with mixolydian themes on G, veering to its mediant E. The first Osanna also behaves conventionally in moving sturdily in triple rhythmed homophony, the choirs in antiphony. The music dances earthily, though the final 'In excelsis' chants the pentatonic motto-phrase, first heard for the 'Gratias agimus', in octave unisons. The earthiness of the Osanna does not long survive, though its 'humanism' affects the Benedictus which is *molto tranquillo*, but also for the first time in a radiant G major, more correctly called the ionian mode. The theme, opening with a godly falling fifth, is given to the solo voices, answered by the trebles and altos of both choirs in swaying $^6_3$ organum. The 'Qui venit' is enacted in close canonic entries, which are combined with the soloists' chanting of their serene, fifth-founded fugato. The brief second Osanna does not return to the folk dance of the first. Opening with solemn, unrelated diatonic triads for divided choirs, it then immediately heals breaches with the pentatonic motto phrase, descending from the high G in unison octaves. The two choirs end as one, though this affirmation leads into an Agnus Dei that is the most disturbingly 'modern' music in the score, at the opposite but complementary pole to the mystical, and perhaps folk-affiliated, Sanctus.

Four solo voices open the Agnus, singing homophonically, in rhythms springing from the natural declamation of the text. They therefore suggest, more vividly than any previous section of the Mass, individual human beings addressing God in 'fear and trembling' – the more so because the mode is phrygian on E, often associated with both suffering and healing. The flat F naturals waft up to G, only to cadence in false relation on an E major triad: which both choruses, together, answer with a repetition of the clause a third higher, in phrygian G minor. The soloists' balm-dispensing 'misereres', however, are traditionally canonic, returning to the theme of the first Kyrie, with its traditional rising fourth followed by falling scale. The four entries are at the fifth, as fugal entries should be, but the modality tinges the Kyrie's original dorian with hints of aeolian and phrygian around a tonic E. Both choruses interject appeals to the Lamb who taketh away the sins of the world, returning, *agitato*, to the phrygian homophony in declamatory rhythm, this time echoed by soloists a third higher:

The 'Dona nobis pacem' balances the 'misereres' by recapitulating the mixolydian G theme of the 'Christe' in the first movement, as the Son returns to anneal our suffering. The chorus deflates the mode from mixolydian (with sharp third) to dorian (with flat third); solo voices inject the declamatory cry of 'Agnus Dei', segregating the 'I' from the congregation, so that the solo parts, although monodic and quasi-medieval, are moments of dramatic intensity, even exacerbation. The final 'Donas' begin in simple canon, floating up and down the mixolydian scale through a fourth. They rise to a modest *forte* in wide-spaced triads of F, G, B flat and C major, without the perturbation of a single passing note; and end with a *pianissimo* phrygian cadence from D minor to F major to G. In the last three bars the alto unusually embraces a dissonant passing note as, recapitulating the opening phrase of the first Kyrie, it rises through a fourth from C, to droop from F through E to D. In the concordant context the dissonant E natural sounds – in the Greek sense – infinitely pathetic. It consummates the effect of the Mass as whole, which is wondrously beautiful and wondrously sad: as is to be expected, since it was created by a 'Christian agnostic'. This is why it is a Mass for our time and is, although liturgical, hardly less initmately related to Vaughan Williams's twentieth-century symphonic pilgrimage than is the Tallis Fantasia. It is pertinent to note that, while the Mass is effective as liturgical ritual, it is elaborately structured in musical terms. The recurrences of the rising pentatonic theme, the recapitulation of material from the Kyrie and Christe in the Agnus Dei, the echo of the work's first bar in its last – these are only the most obvious means whereby the Mass is given a tighter musical unity than would be necessary for its purely liturgical function.

Houseman's 'blue rembered hills' had shrouded, it would seem, a personal agony he dared not bring to light, and Vaughan Williams more discreetly echoed that pain in *On Wenlock Edge*. But the experience of the war left nothing to hide, as is evident in the lives and deaths of poets such as Gurney, Owen, Sassoon and Rosenberg, and vicariously in the work of Americans such as Eliot and Pound. In British music after the war there were no such direct stirrings of modernism since, as we have seen, the task of English composers, when once Elgar and Delius had reanimated our music within conventions basically European and specifically German, was to rediscover a national identity. For Holst and Vaughan Williams it was progressive to be regressive: to seek the sources of British musical inspiration in forgotten folk song, in medieval organum, and especially in Tudor polyphony. Yet this archaism turns out, in Vaughan Williams's Tallis Fantasia and his Mass, to be also a rebirth. In creating, from the premises of English monody, organum and polyphony, an English symphony that compensated for our failure to establish one during the nineteenth century, Vaughan William was also saying something about the nature and quality of English life. He offers, through the cycle of his nine symphonies, a vision of Albion – of the making of an Englishman (himself), and of the making of twentieth-century Britain. We shall not be surprised to discover that the process is difficult, and its progress chequered.

V

SOLIDARITY AND SOLITUDE, TOWN AND COUNTRY

THE DOUBLE MAN IN THE LONDON SYMPHONY AND THE PASTORAL SYMPHONY

How these two shame this shallow and frail town!
How ring right out our sordid turbid time,
Being pure! We, life's pride and cared-for crown

Have lost that cheer and charm of earth's past prime:
Our make and making break, are breaking, down
To man's last dust, drain fast towards man's first slime.

GERARD MANLEY HOPKINS,
'The Sea and the Skylark'

No flame we saw, the noise and dread alone
Was battle to us; men were enduring there such
And such things, in wire tangled, to shatters blown.

Courage kept, but ready to vanish at first touch.
Fear, but just held. Poets were luckier once
In the hot fray swallowed and some magnificence.

IVOR GURNEY, 'On Somme'

Vaughan Williams's Second – which is his first purely orchestral – Symphony has features that behave like a post-Beethovenian symphony in nineteenth-century tradition, but also contains elements that anticipate the 'English' symphony he is to explore in his Third. That the second is called the London Symphony would seem to indicate that it is concerned with modern life. Yet it is London seen in the context of the mind of England and, composed at the outset of the war, it simultaneously concerns a death and a birth. The death was both specific and general: specific because the Symphony is dedicated to the memory of George Butterworth, Vaughan Williams's disciple who was killed in the Battle of the Somme; general because Butterworth stands for the lost generation, and possibly for Old England herself. But if the Symphony celebrates death, it opens with a birth, for the slow introduction to the first movement allegro stems from the religious sensibility – and the pentatonic

77

and modal formulae – of *The Lark Ascending* and, behind that, of the *Fantasia on a Theme of Thomas Tallis*.

Over a deep pedal D, muted cellos and basses murmur a rising fourth, expanding to fifth, then to the upper octave. This motif is latent in acoustical phenomena since (as was noted in our account of the genesis of pentatonicism) the fourth and fifth are the prime members of the harmonic series, embedded in our aural consciousness. Naturally enough, this sequence of pitches became identified with the voice of Nature and with the well-springs of being. At the opening of this symphony it is certainly a seed of creation, and sounds, too, like a gesture of prayer as the ascent merges into undulating whole tones on D and C, hummed by violas and clarinets, with pedal notes on horns. The rising fourths and fifths, repeated, extend to embrace the higher D and E, so the open intervals become a pentatonic pattern prevalent in all the key works we have examined:

When this 'aspiration' is repeated by cellos and basses, it is balanced by a violin scale falling from D through a fifth, in a hemiola cross-rhythm ($\frac{3}{1}$ equalling $\frac{6}{2}$) that further effaces the temporal sense. The pattern of this opening clause is repeated a tone lower, still triple *piano*, but hinting at inner agitation with chromatic passing notes. With the bass root back on D, the rising fourth and fifth unfold in lyrical melody, not merely in pentatonic gestures. After the singing strings have been pierced by acute suspensions on woodwind, the violins translate the fourth-fifth motif into an ascending lark. Upper strings sustain a chord telescoping the fourths and fifths, while cellos and basses undulate in whole tones. Solo harp harmonics pick out the 'Westminster Chimes' motif which, though derived from Nature's pentatonics, reminds us that we are in London, here and now. The juxtaposition of London and Nature is the point, a harbinger of what is to be the central theme of Vaughan Williams's life's work. Is

London the biblical City of Destruction or the New Jerusalem, or both? Woodwind flutter in whole tones, brass chant the fourth-fifth motif loudly, in canon. Life has evolved from Nature's void and bursts on us in the allegro.

If the introduction has harked back, the start of the allegro risoluto – making the Good Life in the city calls for resolution! – is startlingly prophetic of later works, especially of *Job* and the Fourth and Sixth Symphonies. In triple *forte*, *molto pesante*, full orchestra asserts doubleness in roaring a G major triad against an E flat bass; the melodic motives are shattering descending chromatics:

The bitonality, the chromatics and the metrical dislocations prophesy the music of the Fallen Angel in *Job*; at this moment the industrial city seems baleful. The chromatic 'Fall' – which obliterates the introduction's pentatonic flowering – leads into a tramping march built on pounding thirds in E flat, against the strings' tremolando G major triad. Flatness seems to triumph as the basic key of the march establishes itself as G minor, instead of the G major latent in the introduction. Even so the march, despite its violence, is also potentially affirmative, as a march, banding people together, might be expected to be. It becomes an aural synonym for building as well as destroying; chromatic descents are fused into lyrical lines stemming from the preludial undulations, while the chugging thirds become a supportive, rather than minatory, ostinato. Modalized G minor, C minor and E flat major and minor still incorporate pentatonic figures, pierced by an occasional chromatic wail on brass, recalling the initial outburst. But lyricism prevails the more freely tonality flows, especially when triplets set the lines winging. The second subject, generated from the first, begins in B flat major, G minor's relative, and could almost be described as jaunty.

Since the tune is jolly, the rhythm symmetrical and duple, it would seem that the conventional function of first and second subjects is reversed. The pentatonicism of the tune sounds bucolic, though the brilliant scoring and regular pulse bring its simplicity within the province of the city. As it evolves, so it imbues social conformity with martial insouciance; perky syncopations and piping piccolos hint at the 'low' world of Elgar's *Cockaigne*, the scoring having near-Elgarian virtuosity. But when the brass reintroduce the prelude's rising fourths and fifths their effect is paradoxically a negation – perhaps because the City is by nature un-natural. The original chromatic scream sounds yet more exacerbated; and the development begins with a return of the rocking thirds in the bass. For some time dynamics are quiet, as development transforms the rising fourths and undulating steps into a polyphonic texture in incessant modulation. Fragments of the jaunty second subject are tossed around by flute and bassoon, sounding pathetic rather than comical. Development is also anti-development, for it reveals London as Eliot's 'unreal city' in a waste land. Texture thins and disintegrates into a harp cadenza, leading into *espressivo* string harmonies in six parts, based on the undulations, shifting through mediant sequences; the effect recalls the 'benediction' phrase in the Tallis Fantasia (see the music example on p.51). Out of these intimations of immortality pentatonic lyricism is reborn, and the murky bitonal G minor of the allegro's opening becomes a radiant lydian G major, with sharp third and fourth. But resolution is only apparent, because temporary. The woodwind's echoes of the bouncy second subject are banished with a bitonal snarl on the mediant opposition of G and E flat majors, which had been the movement's original impetus.

This starts off the recapitulation, which has much in common with the nineteenth-century model, though it is more morphological – like a growing plant – in that recapitulation is still development. Thus the jaunty second subject reappears in the tonic major, as it conventionally should, but leads into a positive refashioning of the march. Indeed, its falling scale proves to be a descendant of the original chromatic Fall, rendered affirmative. Modulation is often by mediants, involving implicit or explicit false relations. And that recapitulation is still development is indicated when the coda proves more substantial, and certainly more assertive, than the development itself. All the thematic elements coalesce: the undulations on low strings and bassoons, the declining scale in cross-rhythm on violins, the full version of the pentatonic 'aspiration' on upper woodwind. In a swinging triple pulse and in a mixolydian-flavoured G major, full orchestra bounds into a jovial version of the downward scale, now in dotted rhythm and yanked up sequentially by thirds to end in a blaze of pentatonics. Trumpets chant the fourth–fifth–octave motif which, far from being mysterious, is now affirmative. Trombones and tuba echo it in thunderous minims, the orchestral hubbub reinforced by clattering percussion and tinkling glockenspiel and harp. This is far from being a conventionally triumphant apotheosis, however, for its affirmation is not far from aggression; and at the ultimate climax the bitonal E flat again thrusts into G major clarity, and the satanic chromatics of the opening howl venomously on woodwind and shuddering tremolando strings. Even though G major soon effaces threat, the effect remains ambiguous. The movement ends with brazen brass in G major, with tremolandos on woodwind, arpeggios on strings, and glissandos on harps, but its jubilation is oddly abrupt. Man may be a 'maker' in his urban metropolis, but his task seems to be both arduous and hazardous. The remaining three movements are more hopeful of a rapprochement between the poles of innocence and experience, even good and evil, though the coda to the finale introduces another, and very mysterious, dimension.

The slow movement, one of Vaughan Williams's most inspired utterances, reveals the relationship between the London Symphony and *The Lark Ascending*, which we have seen to be contemporary. It opens with the same gesture of scalewise rising third on strings, now harmonized in parallel minor triads, triple *piano, con sordini*. Since the third is major, from E to G sharp, it entails tension between the G natural of the E minor triad, and the G sharp of the G sharp minor triad; and this is enhanced when the passage is repeated a third higher, the G sharp having been enharmoically transmuted to A flat. Through these organum chords solo cor anglais sings a melody beginning with one of those opening gambits which, being instinctive acoustical behaviour, often initiate a folk tune. This melody, beginning with the rise up a fourth from E flat to A flat, sets one humming several possible continuations derived from real folk songs; Vaughan Williams mentions 'Lavender city', though it is not a direct quotation, and its effect – as the composer's directive tells us – is mysterious. For the tune's tail subsides from its A flat minorish start on to the fifth G to C, from whence it droops pentatonically to the low G:

The A flats thus function as extended appoggiaturas to G; or at least the harmonic root remains ambiguous, even when muted strings take up the 'folk' tune, while wind instruments sway in the rising thirds. The 'tail', expanding the rising fourth to fifth, floats in a pentatonic C minor over a D flat bass.

As the melody fades on a solo horn, triplets throb on resonantly spaced C major triads on strings. Woodwind and brass interject fragments of the folk-like melody, until it is transformed into more lyrically spacious form over a pedal E. Acquiring something of the false-related major triads that support it on harp and woodwind, the tune wings to a high A. Its chromaticized descent is again prophetic of the 'Fall' motif in *Job*, though oboe, clarinet and horn chant the opening gambit of the folk song in echo, capped again by the strings' muted concords and throbbing triplets.

After a moment's silence and a double bar, we are transported from whatever tranquil corner of the city we have been in (Bloomsbury Square has been suggested) into the heart of the country – which, as the composer pointed out, needs no geographical location. Solo viola murmurs a measureless pentatonic arabesque in a phrygian-tinged mode on E; we recall the 'Bunyan' theme from the Tallis Fantasia, and more directly the melismata of the ascending lark. *This* lark, answered by harp-accompanied woodwind, extends his melody through a triplet rising in dotted rhythm – again recalling the Bunyan theme and the lark's 'humanized' version of his song. Flutes and clarinets interject chirrupings; darker creatures gibber or grunt on *misterioso* bassoons and cellos. Gradually the orchestra burgeons into 'the Chime and Symphony of Nature', in Henry Vaughan's phrase, though the lovely cantabile melody continues to affirm a human songfulness. Since this theme is the pentatonic 'aspiration' of the first movement turned upside-down, this may suggest that man, in a state of Nature, does not need to seek, but may simply be. Certainly the climax, in which the throbbing triplets return, is of extraordinary spiritual exultation, flowing through harp-garlanded mediant sequences, falling pentatonically from B flat to D flat. A rising third to F flat, notated as E natural, triggers a brief recapitulation of the opening of the movement, at the original pitch. After the organum-like rising third, however, with the folk song again on cor anglais, the bass subsides to A flat and then D flat, supporting a C minor triad. The throbbing C major triplets recur but disperse as solo viola distantly chants the lark-like melody, pentatonically on A, dissipating into empty air.

The scherzo, being called Nocturne, presumably evokes sights and sounds of the city at night. Since the thematic material is mostly pentatonic, as was the jolly second subject of the first movement, it would seem that Vaughan Williams's 'common men' are vulgar – of the people – in a fundamental sense, rather than through social conditioning. The first, flickering $\frac{6}{8}$ tune is pentatonic veering to dorian on D. Bandied between violins and woodwind, tinged with harp and pizzicato strings, it is scored with an exquisite fantasticality, belying the composer's reputation for orchestral gaucherie. Dynamics are dreamy, unreal, as merriment at night often seems to be; links with previous movements – a precipitous pentatonic descent, rising fourth followed by stepwise wriggle – barely register at conscious level, and are not meant to. The phantasmagoric quality is enhanced by the modulations or modal shifts, as well as by the hemiola cross-rhythms that are the only noisy moments. The first section, which is repeated, ends with a familiar mediant modulation to a pentatonicized B flat minor. After the double bar the figuration of chattering quavers does not cease, though its $\frac{6}{8}$ is expanded to $\frac{9}{8}$, and the mood is modified by a savage cantus firmus in pentatonics, blasted by horns and *marcato* strings, each note marked *fffz*. This dissipates in a recapitulation of the first section, fused with the second, ending around D major with flat seventh. A gawky, music-hall-style tune in duple rhythm, similar to those in the first movement, intrudes near the end. Pentatonics on strings evaporate in a subterranean murmur; the scherzo dances out on solo bassoon.

The trio, taking up the duple rhythm of the 'music-hall' tune, begins with the famous imitation of a street organ-grinder, scored with Petrouchka-like relish. His tune is pentatonic on C, often harmonized with Stravinskian telescopings of tonic and dominant. Both orchestrally and structurally this music is of considerable sophistication, and becomes the more so when the da capo of the scherzo turns out to be itself development. Unity from duality is achieved as the $\frac{6}{8}$ scherzo tunes and the organ-grinder's duple tune are metamorphosed into the seminal rising fourth to fifth to octave that has pervaded the Symphony; in a bright D major, the motif is pointed by trumpet, squealing piccolo and flutes. The organ-grinder tune pops in grotesquely on bass trombone and tuba, but texture disintegrates into snatches of the rising-fourth/undulating-second formula. Pentatonic fragments flit through solemn triads on low strings, their D minor modality grating against the strings' B minor triads. A more gently undulating scale, one tone to a bar, distantly recalls the 'cantus firmus', now bland rather than savage. But this is not a consummation; indeed the fade-out, again on solo bassoon supported by D minor string triads, is oddly non-resolutive, as though the noises of the nocturnal city continue oblivious of human joys or sorrows – as they do.

The finale is in true post-Beethovenian tradition in that it is fully intelligible only in relation to the previous movements. Like the first movement it has an introduction, in this case slowish but not slow. The key signature has two flats but the tonality is at first obscure, in the same way as is that of the first movement allegro since it begins with a grinding dissonance between a G major triad and a second inversion of E flat major. Melodically, the fingerprint of rising third falling down the scale is here imbued with painful passion; the effect is similar to, if less ferocious than, the notorious opening of Symphony No. 4. Before tonality is established, the orchestra tutti utters a grander form of the chromatic 'wail' that had triggered the allegro of the first movement. Unexpectedly, the wail tails off in interwoven polyphonies in the dorian mode on G – thematically anticipating the Kyrie theme of the Mass. A pedal E flat, however, tugs against the E naturals of the mode.

The violence of this introduction, recalling that of the first allegro, suggests that the big city contains an incipient frenzy. The work, like Elgar's two magnificent symphonies written a few years previously, is an elegy on, as well as a celebration of, the urban metropolis; which is why the marvellous slow movement evokes a mode of life not ostensibly urban. Certainly elegy is an appropriate concept in reference to the main theme of the finale, since it is a funeral march: in a vein comparable with, if less grandly impassioned than the funeral march that in Elgar's Second Symphony was a tribute to the dead king. The two flats in the signature suggest G minor, basic key of the first movement allegro, though the tonality has a plagally flat, C minorish feel to it. The tune, though grandly solemn, is without Elgar's *nobilmente* expansiveness, while the harmony lacks his opulence. Nor does Vaughan Williams's soberer grandeur remain impervious to threat, for its dotted-rhythmed march is interrupted by oscillating triads in false related concords.

With a change to *allegro* and a key signature of one sharp the oscillations take charge, at first *pianissimo*, on fluttering strings and woodwind. An upward-thrusting pentatonic G major motif in the bass, taken up by full brass, launches into what is both a development of the march and an episode in sonata-rondo fashion. The tune, precipitated out of the upward-stabbing, dotted-rhythmed syncopations on brass, is aggressive, for its repeated crotchets transmute the march from funereal gravity into brazenness. Woodwind and brass chatter in parallel thirds, oompah basses swagger. It would seem that the city is vulgar in the colloquial as well as in the literal sense, though not to the point of obliterating authentic vulgarity and grandeur. The assertive pentatonic march, now on D, is undermined by chromatic and whole-tone wails on woodwind; dissolves in undulating parallel triads; and leads to a modified restatement of the funeral march, with the nastily martial march interlinked with it! This collocation of two disparate worlds – whether they be town and country, or present and past – generates the Symphony's ultimate climax: noble lyricism, martial aggression, chromatic frenzy coexist in raucously scored, almost hallucinatory music that recalls the later symphonic Mahler. The Ninth Symphony of Mahler, dating from 1911, records the disintegration of Europe, while hinting at new birth. Although Vaughan Williams's English environment was less socially and politically distraught, this climax demonstrates that he was intuitively aware of the anguish latent within his ostensibly stable, even complacent, Edwardian world. Michael Kennedy tells us that, in response to enquiries about the 'meaning' of the London Symphony, Vaughan Williams referred to the end of H.G. Wells's *Tono-Bungay*, published a few years before the Symphony's first performance. In the light of that it is palpable that the work is not merely or even mainly a celebration of the present city, but is also a threnody on the passing of Old England: 'Light after light goes down. England and the Kingdom, Britain and the Empire, the old prides and the old devotions, glide abeam, astern, sink down under the horizon, pass – pass. The river passes, London passes, England passes.' The Elgarian flavour of much of the last movement is more than skin-deep, though Vaughan Williams is less valetudinarian, tempering regret with hope.

In this context the ultimate climax is that the chromatic wail produces a direct reference back to the wails that had initiated the first movement, and to the rocking thirds of the original march. If this suggests that that first outburst had been the dire reality from which the slow movement and scherzo had been momentary and illusory escapes, there proves, in the epilogue, to be another and deeper reality. The bitonal telescoping of G and E flat majors, quoted from the first movement, launches the final descent of the chromatic phrase prophetic of Satan's curse in *Job*; the hurly-burly simmers down; and we are left with the bitonal chord almost inaudible on strings. Solo harp harmonics again ring in the distant chimes of Big Ben which, in the first movement, had emerged as a derivative of the 'embryonic' pentatonic figures. This is, of course, naturalistic – a reminder that we are in a real London, audible, visible and tactile; but its deeper effect is to reveal the illusory nature of barriers between matter and spirit. This becomes manifest when the music merges into the first, and one of the most marvellous, of the movements Vaughan Williams designated as Epilogue.

It opens with a disembodied pastoral sonority of tremolando B flat minor thirds on flutes and strings. Cellos and basses almost imperceptibly rise through the original, acoustically fundamental fourth and fifth, echoed by low brass in triple *piano*. Gradually, the rising pentatonic 'aspiration' or 'prayer' shifts sequentially, completing its pentatonic elevation to the octave. The music sounds like a dawn chorus, in a spiritual rather than naturalistic sense, though Ravel's (then recent) aubade in *Daphnis et Chloe* may have been seminal to Vaughan Williams's discreeter muse. Certainly, there is an irresistible burgeoning of life within Nature's void, transcending the city's sorrows and excitations. Through many tonal meanderings, dynamics remain soft: until Nature's shimmerings are banished by a distant return of the chromatic wail on woodwinds and horns. For a moment, the string choir chants a liberated version of the pentatonic ascent from a pedal D, beginning in radiant octave unisons. Brass remotely moan the chromatic ululation, piercing a solo violin's *con sordino* singing of the lyrical theme:

The solo violin is now a lark ascending whose spirit of delight is unbroken by chromatic cries from the distant brass. The Symphony ends, after so many tonal ambiguities and contradictions, on a protracted chord of G major, gradually thinning to silence. The end of the Symphony is peace, but this peace, like that of *The Lark Ascending*, is ultimately a metaphysical act. So although this is in many ways a traditional symphony, its apotheosis is not traditional, for it marks the beginning of Vaughan Williams's attempt to create large-scale symphonic works evolving from, not against, the principles inherent in 'religious' vocal monody.

The London Symphony goes much further than *A Sea Symphony* in purging Vaughan Williams's language of the vestiges of Victorianism and Edwardianism that had proved incompatible with its nature. His authentic 'new man' was, however, born of the cataclysm of the First World War that swept away so much more than the bodies of young men. On its publication in 1920 the Second Symphony was dedicated to the memory of George Butterworth; the Third was written in the war's immediate aftermath, and was first performed in 1922, shortly after the Mass for double choir. As a war symphony it seems improbable, being usually quiet and often serene, as well as pastoral. This impression is superficial, for the essence of the piece is that it confronts the problem of the English symphony head on, becoming a key work no less crucial than the *Fantasia on a Theme of Thomas Trallis*. The London Symphony is a presumptively urban work that turns out to be a religious, even mystical, experience. The Pastoral Symphony is a presumptively rural piece that, since it is also a religious experience, has no specific topical and local ambience. Although its four movements are prevailingly quiet and slow, its pastoralism is far from being peace, as opposed to the turbulent city of No. 2.

Its pastoral elements have nothing to do with cows looking over gates, as jibers used to suggest; or at least if an English rural landscape is implicit, so – according to the composer, more directly – are the desolate battle-fields of Flanders, where the piece was first embryonically conceived. Until its last pages the London Symphony is concerned, if not always with the city, with social solidarity. The Pastoral Symphony, on the other hand, is mostly concerned with solitariness: wherein it finds an experience of transcendence.

The main thematic material of the Third Symphony consists of precisely those pentatonic patterns which we have seen to be seeds of such key works as the Tallis Fantasia, *The Lark Ascending* and the London Symphony. The tempo directive for the first movement is *molto moderato*, and its opening sounds are oscillating triads in level quavers, scored for two flutes and bassoon. The mode is mixolydian on G, the germ of the passage being in the Sanctus of the Mass, composed in the same year as the end of the Great War. In both instances the sonority sounds like a murmur of Nature before consciousness impinges: an effect only slightly compromised by the fact that the triads shift from G and F to B flat and back, creating unobtrusive false relations between the naturals in the G and the flats in the B flat triads. The theme that emerges on cellos and basses, triadically doubled by harp, is God's or Nature's rising fifth that then lifts a further tone. But the 'pain of consciousness' shyly intrudes as a solo violin floats aloft, bitonally accompanied by tremolando $^6_4$ chords descending from G flat to C flat. Orchestral violins join the soloist, whose relation to the ascending lark is patent. Serene though the pentatonic melody is, harmonic pain increases as the violins float from the heights while horns and trumpets distantly murmur the $^6_4$ undulations. With a sudden shift to the mediant – B flat minor in relation to mixolydian G – woodwind sigh a melisma in semiquavers, swaying between two false-related triads sustained, organum-like (see the music example on p.88).

Within the triads, cor anglais sings a new theme: an arabesque in the lydian mode on G. Its tritonal fourth gives it an energy not found in the

previous pentatonics. Whether or not one regards it as a second subject, it promotes evolution, if not development. As in the middle section of the Tallis Fantasia, pastoral melody – the 'Bunyan' theme – begins as monody, but quickens to harmonic life in a kind of folk polyphony. The texture is spare, yet luminous, and the flowering of the melodies effects a tonal shift from G up to A, from whence the triads move to their radiant lower mediant, F sharp. Momentarily, Nature's undulating quavers are exacerbated by chromatics. Polyphony in parallel triads makes for tension, though all the component elements of the music are calm. The scrunchy sonority resulting from telescoped concords hints faintly at neo-classic Stravinsky.

But a symphonic and un-Stravinskian development accrues from the interaction of pentatonic lyricism, woodwind arabesques, and parallel triads. Though all the melodies sing and flow, tension between them and the falling chromatics increases. The pentatonic phrases themselves decline on violins, their B flat minor and G major triads clashing with the low strings sul ponticello tremolandos on the second inversion of E flat, dropping to D flat. The strings' alternation between B flat minor and G major triads is repeated, triggering further extensions from the cor anglais's lydian melisma. If the movement has no sonata-style development, this is because it is all evolution. The quaver-undulating voice of Nature seems to be acquiring human attributes as strings sing the fourth-fifth-octave motif in inversion, ripely concordant; the suspiration of quavers is still present on low strings and clarinets. Climactically, chiming bell-sonorities, with organum chords on harp, induce timelessness, so that a distant echo of the B flat minor-G major semiquaver figure is no longer a threat. Multi-divided strings play motionless G major triads.

The cor anglais's lydian arabesque fades, leaving God's rising fifth singing, if con sordino, on cellos and basses.

Although this movement may seem naïve as a symphonic argument that is because its innocence, in conflict with experience, is profound. The two states of being are associated mainly, though not of course exclusively, with pentatonicism and with false relation: which between them generate a symphonic movement not strictly in sonata form, but of considerable inner intensity. And if the first movement concerns the process of life within Nature's continuum, the slow movement presents the dichotomy between 'unconscious' joy and 'the pain of consciousness'. Duality is immediately evident, for muted strings play a sustained triad of 'infernal' F minor, while solo horn chants a pentatonic incantation around G or possibly E. The bitonality is dichotomous, and its negative effect is manifest when the strings, in undulating whole tone chords and false related triads, float wispily upwards, to end in vacillations between $\frac{6}{3}$ chords of F and D minor:

This weird sonority will bear strange fruit in the elemental seascapes of *Riders to the Sea* and the *Sinfonia Antartica* – and, still more mysteriously, in the epilogue to Symphony No. 6. Meanwhile, the cavernous F minor triad persists; but is effaced as the woodwinds' pentatonic arabesques, and then an extended melody on solo viola, wrest lyrical life out of pain.

Dichotomy is spelt out when the appoggiatura sighs turn into undulating second inversion chords, wavering between E flat, F and D flat: out of which floats a pentatonic trumpet solo. Vaughan Williams specifies that the instrument must be a natural trumpet in E flat, so that the partials may be justly intoned; acoustically, as well as spiritually, innocence is truth. Tonally, the trumpet is not at odds with the sustained E flat chord on strings, as was the solo horn at the beginning; and woodwind and strings, in passionate outbursts of E flat pentatonics, seem to yearn for the trumpet's wholeness. They do not find it, for their outcries dissipate in wavery alternations of $\frac{6}{3}$ triads of F and D minors, now with D as bass. Nor is doubleness healed, for low strings come to roost on an F major concord, but then slide down to E flat and D flat, while a natural horn distantly sings the pentatonic incantation, staying on F as the string harmonies subside.

Simultaneously, clarinet solo has the original horn melody. High strings float into the stratosphere in those unrelated $^6_3$ chords. The parallel with the epilogue to No. 6 is unmistakable; we begin to understand how Vaughan Williams's symphonies define a life-long pilgrimage.

The slow movement is, to put it crudely, about the spiritual state and our separation therefrom. The scherzo brings us to earth, beginning as a peasant dance – Vaughan Williams's most potent evocation of Eliot's 'earth feet, loam feet'. Its energy is generated from a triplet rising (yet again) from fourth to fifth, then down to the tonic G. Since the effect is mainly rhythmic, even percussive, we do not immediately recognize this as thematic; that it is not strongly melodic is part of its earth-bound nature. The tune nags around itself, its rhythm hesitant, hiccuping. Parallel $^6_4$ chords on brass are lumpish rather than bouncy, so this is far from being a nostalgic retrospect of the old rural order. The earth-dance rather seeks liberation, as the strings carry their G-pentatonic tune aloft, in their swinging triple rhythm. Solo flute melismatically extends their lyrical flight in a winging dotted rhythm, aerated with harp arpeggios, and the flute is joined by a lark-like solo violin. Yet the tug of the earth-dance is not effaced; and wins hands down in the trio, a triple-rhythmed dance basically in mixolydian G. Flickering folk-like 'snaps' in demisemiquaver triplets point the stomping accents, and it is perhaps through them that earthiness does not, after all, finally triumph. At least when the scherzo is repeated da capo it is not so much recapitulation as development, for the cloddish dance is now pervaded by graceful woodwind arabesques, as though flesh and spirit were seeking reconciliation.

It seems they will not achieve it, for at the climax two bars of $^5_4$ time, scored for brass and woodwind, break even the earthbound progression. The coda, however, is unexpected, and magical. Over a pedal drone on G, outside time, the strings are airborne in *pianissomo* fugato, bounding in cross rhythms between $^6_8$ and $^3_4$, very fast (*presto*) and flickering. The modality is pentatonic or dorian G, the texture wraith-like:

The dancing peasants have become ghosts: not surprisingly, since they are long dead. Another quotation from Eliot's 'East Coker' is relevant:

> In that open field
> If you do not come too close, if you do not come too close,
> On a summer midnight, you can hear the music
> Of the weak pipe and the little drum
> And see them dancing around the bonfire.

Vaughan Williams's symphony predates Eliot's poem by twenty years, but the parallel is exact; we can see as well as hear the dancers as the strings flicker, while woodwind and muted brass pick out pentatonic fragments, creating incipient tunes, which fade into thin air. The strings' pentatonics glitter on flutes and celesta; finally, twiddles on low strings become wisps of smoke floating through a *pianissimo* chord on horns. Distant echoes of the origianl earth-dance tinkle on magic celesta, alternating with harp harmonics. The ghostly scherzo of the Fifth Symphony, though twenty years off, is also just over the hill.

The finale of the Third Symphony, like that of the Second, is a true symphonic finale in that it is dependent on the previous movements. Over a scarcely audible timpani roll on A, a distant soprano sings a wordless vocalise: a cantillation that is basically pentatonic on A veering to E, though it garners an occasional extra tone from the aeolian mode. It begins with four repeated notes which of their nature suggest syllabic declamation, though there is no text. The latently human expressivity of this, however, fades into an impersonally, bird-like, slowly arching song; and with the entry of the strings we discover that the movement will render aurally incarnate precisely such an equation between the human and the divine – or at least the other-than-human. For the violins unfold in a prayer-like pentatonic ascent centred on E, while the lower strings descend in diatonic triads from F to E flat to D flat majors. This bitonality recapitulates that of the slow movement, but now leads into a song–dance that is also a hymn, scored for woodwind and harp, soon joined by *pianissimo* brass. The mode is aeolian, veering to dorian, D; overlapping concords create a rich but luminous, scrunchy yet glowing, sonority, comparable with that of Ravel's 'antique' fairy-tale melodies. The Pastoral Symphony opens with a passage remarkably similar to the prelude to Ravel's parable of childhood's awakening from innocence to experience, *L'Enfant et les Sortilèges* – a work yet to be written: we have noted parallels between Vaughan Williams and Ravel in 'Bredon Hill' and in the epilogue to the London Symphony. Both composers evoke a dream-world, whether it be a French *conte de fées* or an English Eden. Vaughan

Williams's dream is less a matter of artifice, more a re-vision of an idealized heritage. Here there is no simple consummation of the equation between the physical and the metaphysical; the pentatonics are subject to agitated tremolandos, pulled towards the mediant B flat minor triad that had been 'enemy' to G major in both the first and second movements. The London Symphony's dichotomy of G and E flat majors also returns, as does its chromatic snarl. In this movement the hymn, which is a man-made affirmation, seems to be threatened by the perturbation of Nature herself, as well as by man's inner dubieties. The music becomes potently dramatic, the repeated notes that had neutrally opened the soprano's cantillation now sounding declamatory, in 'speaking' accents.

The dramatic and chromatic climax, phrophetic of *Job* and the slow movement of the Fifth Symphony, merges into an ostinato on arpeggiated harp, telescoping C sharp minor and D major. Solo violin, lark-like, sustains a high C sharp, while cello sings a vocal-style pentatonic melody, routing the powers of darkness. Though the tonality has four sharps, it is not heavenly E major, but rather a modal compromise between E major and C sharp minor. The 'natural' modality may be more 'innocent' than any diatonic key, as becomes obvious when solo flute wings aloft, without a single chromatic alteration. The chromatic wail, softly intruding, is no more than a memory. Harp arpeggios flow more fluidly; false-related triads on horn thrust up now almost in triumph, until all the woodwind and strings jubilantly chant the soprano's original pentatonic melody in *fortissimo* octave unisons – an effect recalling the octave unison climax of the Tallis Fantasia. This movement climaxes in an expanded statement of the 'prayer' theme in modal polyphony – a ripely sensuous sonority, stemming perhaps from a Blakean marriage of heaven and hell, or at least earth. The bass line is as lyrical as the violins and flutes; a long scalewise ascent on strings and horns culminates on a chord of D major, in false relation with F and B flat majors (see the music example on the facing page). From that point song subsides, literally falling through the thematic fourths and fifths, to silence; muted first violins hymn the prayer, rising to the heights while the bitonal triads sink. Yet duality becomes unity, for at the end the violins, on a high A, are 'the still point of the turning world', while the yet more distant soprano sings a shortened version of her purely pentatonic monody. This time there is no timpani pedal to earth her; she, even more than the ascending lark, is an angelic messenger as well as the spirit of delight.

If, taking Vaughan Williams's clue, we think of her disembodied song as ringing over the ravaged fields of Flanders we may understand why this symphony has so poignant an effect. Innocence survives horror, and the

angel-lark promises a birth. In its unassertiveness, the Pastoral stands with the Tallis Fantasia, *Job* and the Fifth Symphony as one of its composer's master-works, and as one of the great symphonies of the twentieth century. The moment of being, recollected in tranquillity, becomes a moment of truth. What Siegfried Sassoon in his autobiography called 'the old century' becomes, in Vaughan Williams's symphony, a moment eternally present.

VI

THE ENGLISH EDEN

PAN-CHRIST IN ARCADIA: *FIVE TUDOR PORTRAITS,* *FLOS CAMPI,* THE *MAGNIFICAT* AND *SERENADE TO MUSIC*

The corn was orient and immortal wheat, which should never be reaped nor was ever sown. I thought it had stood from everlasting to everlasting. ... O what venerable Creatures did the aged seem! Immortal Cherubims! And the young men glittering and sparkling Angels, and maids strange seraphic Pieces of life and beauty! I knew not that they were born and should die; but all things bided eternally. I knew not that there were sin or complaints or laws. I dream'd not of poverties, contentions or vices. All tears and quarrels were hidden from my eyes. I saw all in the peace of Eden.

THOMAS TRAHERNE, *Centuries of Meditation*

In the first two chapters of this book we discussed Vaughan Williams in relation to his background in Edwardian England, including his reaction from and against it. The next two chapters charted his relationship to the past in wider historical contexts: in that of the English agrarian tradition and of the Anglican Church, which was simultaneously past and present. The following two chapters dealt with the inner life of the spirit latent in history – with Vaughan Williams's response to English Nature-mysticism, and with the threats offered to such transcendence, as well as to agrarian society, by the urban-industrial world. Both the London Symphony's urbanism and the Pastoral Symphony's pastoralism imply not so much a physical place as a spiritual state. But the pastoral Arcadia had, if not outward manifestations, at least places that might be envisaged as material equivalents to the Kingdom of God, the Celestial City and the New Jerusalem – a mythology which was to inform Vaughan Williams's later music with increasing vigour. We will approach these psychological-social states by way of writers and visual artists (rather than composers) who were of peculiar import to Vaughan Williams. Chief among them are Skelton, Bunyan, Milton and Blake.

The earliest in date is John Skelton who, born in 1460 and dying in 1529, was of the generation just preceding that of Thomas Tallis. Skelton too was a 'double man'; but whereas Tallis's doubleness was manifest almost exclusively under the aegis of the Church, Skelton, though himself a priest, was involved in secular politics and the machinations of the Court.

Court politics were not, of course, separate from Church affairs, and Skelton's invective was levelled at undeniable abuses in ecclesiastical polity. Yet although brave in the virulence of his attacks on Cardinal Wolsey – who more than any man brought to fruition the identification of Church and State (*ego et rex meus*) – Skelton was not a revolutionary; he approved of the status quo, though he would have liked it to operate with more humane efficiency. In any case neither his rhetoric nor his invective was inspired by spiritual fervour. Poised between the Middle Ages and the Renaissance, between country and town, Church and State, spirit and (often rather dirty) flesh, he was a complementary opposite to Tallis, since his feet were planted on the muddy earth. Regarded by his contemporaries as a slightly scandalous joke, he was, without conscious intent, socially, politically, and perhaps religiously subversive.

So was his verse, in relation to English poetic traditions. He used his talents both as agent for and as enemy of the State, regarding the title of laureate as political rather than poetic, as indeed it was. The era that had made it possible for Chaucer to make great poetry out of an idealized vision of feudal society was past. Gower and Lydgate were respectable poets in more senses than one, substituting a pedestrian gait for Chaucer's rhythmic variety, and a schematic allegory for his vivacity of image and symbol. In literature – though not, as we have seen, in music – the letter had superseded spirit, replacing psychological insight with pious moralism. The legacy of medieval theocracy was moribund.

Skelton's historical importance – it may even be his greatness – lay in his refusing to accept the sloth of contemporary literature. Though the conventions of rhetoric and invective in which he excelled were not invented by him, he gave them unprecedented energy. The kind of versification that came to be known as Skeltonics was at the opposite extreme to the ornate artifice favoured by Court poets; it was rather a species of popular verse, in short lines that skip in unabashed corporeality. If its origins were in the low, goliardic Latin verse of the declining Middle Ages, Skelton, using the vernacular, was directly in the orbit of contemporary life, high and low. His virtuosity serves the ends of humanity, if not of spirit, offering exuberance aplenty, irony, wit, farce, bawdy and bathos: but also pathos, a lovely vivacity and tenderness, especially in dealing with woman – to whom the Middle Ages, unless she were disguised as the Virgin Mary, had given a raw deal. All this makes Skelton a peculiarly modern poet, for us as well as his own contemporaries, and he has been a presence behind English verse ever since Robert Graves rediscovered him in the 1920s. He was also a 'natural' for Vaughan Williams; and it is to the point that the composer lighted on Skelton when, with the Pastoral Symphony a decade behind him, he had recently finished his Fourth Symphony – a radical though not illogical change of front in which forces of energy and aggression seemed to be taking over from spirit. In fact there was no contradiction: or rather, Vaughan Williams knew, like Blake, that 'without Contraries there can be no Progression' – and provided evidence for that throughout the rest of his life's work.

Oddly enough, Vaughan Williams had been introduced to Skelton by Elgar, who had considered doing a setting of *The Tunnyng of Elynour Rummyng* himself. What that would have been like is difficult to imagine; but it was astute of Elgar to see that Skelton's broad humanity and jazzy metrics would strike answering chords in Vaughan Williams. They prompted him to what now seems one of his finest as well as biggest secular works: a zestful companion to the newly completed Fourth Symphony and a prophecy of religious-social works, such as *Dona Nobis Pacem*, which were already in gestation. Vaughan Williams's Skelton piece, the humanity of which he stressed by calling it *Five Tudor Portraits*, was first performed at the Norwich Festival in 1936, in company with another première, that of the young Britten's *Our Hunting Fathers*, which also earned a measure of notoriety. The reasons for the slight scandals occasioned by the old man's and the young man's works were very similar. The suite of Vaughan Williams, then in his sixties, brought breaths of rank as well as fresh air into the polite purlieus of the English Establishment, while Auden and Britten compounded that with a consciously anti-Establishment political stance. Both works were carried through with an exuberance and technical virtuosity that could not be gainsaid. The parallel is worth making in view of the once passively accepted account of the older composer's technical limitations.

Five Tudor Portraits, like the early *A Sea Symphony*, is a cross between a symphony and an English oratorio, albeit one of a pronounced secular character. Vaughan Williams unpretentiously called it a 'choral suite', which is accurate, though there are analogies with symphony in that it has a first movement allegro, a Burlesca which is patently a scherzo, a Romanza as slow movement, and an Intermezzo comparable with the 'light' movements introduced into the symphonic scheme by Mahler. The finale is called Scherzo but serves, relatively slight though it is, as a symphonic last movement also. Although the work displays less evidence of symphonic argument than does *A Sea Symphony*, it is more than a suite, for the movements complement one another, even if they do not progress.

The first movement, 'The Tunning of Elinor Running', sets part of a long 'flyting' which Skelton adapts from a medieval convention of theological and political disputation. He turns it into a roistering portrait of a blowsy trollop of an ale-house keeper and her clients, dancing the verse at a lick through four or five-syllabled rhyming couplets, low in jargon, prattling in puns and bubbling with scatological jokes. Vaughan Williams's musicking of it, called Ballad in reference to its narrative content, matches Skelton's pace and punch, beginning with a ferociously scored, dotted triple-rhythmed phrase based on the devil's interval of tritone:

Tritones often recur after the voices have entered in what is basically the 'adolescent' key of A major, though it is pervaded by intermittent lydian sharp fourths and phrygian flat seconds. The men of the chorus at first sing in unison, followed by the women; then men and women are in canon at one bar's distance, the phrygian B flats obtrusive. Restless modulations start with the portrait of Elinor, 'comely crinkled, wondrously wrinkled, like a roast pig's ear'. Rhythms bounce across the bar-lines – a legacy from real Tudor music – and since the pulse is metrical, these rhythms acquire a jazzy animation. The modulations, as is typical of Vaughan Williams, are frequently by mediants. When we reach 'happy' G major, rhythmic vivacity is complemented by lyricism: which turns, with a further mediant shift to E flat major, into a corny waltz, with tipsy tootles from a pentatonic piccolo. This opening section climaxes in a return of the tritonal figure, which gets ironed out into a pentatonic canon. Briefly, the original A major is re-established in the orchestra, only to be shifted up a tone. Dynamically, the music is gentler, though it patters busily as the patrons tumble into the inn.

Bassoons and piccolo predominate in this clatter which, after incessant modulation, returns to A major and transmutes a jig into a triple-metred march. But it lasts only through an eight-bar orchestral interlude: after which mediant (and other) modulations again sweep us off our feet. This section climaxes, after Skelton has compared the drinkers to sundry low beasts, in a canonic outburst on brass, alternating tritonal with perfect fourths. Cross rhythms, in syncopation, are savage. Solo bassoon plays a cadenza (*andante doloroso*) that sounds stupefiedly drunk, punning on augmented seconds and diminished thirds: intervals which, in works such as *Job* and the Fourth Symphony, are powerful synonyms for disruption, guilt and pain. They carry similar implication here, though the surface effect is comic. The cadenza introduces an aria by Alice, a 'slightly nasal' contralto affected by bibulous indulgence, so that her vocal line is syncopated into hiccups, in dialogue with solo bassoon, while the padding bass of the orchestra trundles in a slow march; intermittently, the solo bassoon burps in sympathy. Chromatic cantus firmus-like figures ironically pervade the inner parts, on viola, horn or muted trumpet. The aria is thus far from being a music-hall turn portraying a bedraggled female drunk; or if it is that, it is at the same time a testament to the pathos of failure, mingling not entirely besotted tears with mirth.

Chorus re-enters to depict folk cramming into the alehouse; their tune, based on a fourth, is appropriately trite. Irony is here more patent, for the men sing, at first softly, a palpable parody of a liturgical cantus firmus hinting at the Dies Irae, while the women continue the bouncy fourths and the orchestra flickers in an insouciant boogie rhythm. Modulation is less frantic, perhaps because the tipplers are by now comatose; but there is a literally uplifting shift from B flat to its upper mediant, climaxing in a triple *forte* yell on a D major triad. A briefly dismissive coda brings back the initial tritone, becoming both tonally and metrically chaotic. Skelton's text tells us that he has babbled on long enough about this idiotic orgy and it is time to call a halt. Vaughan Williams does so with a hammering of the tritones, and a curt return to lydian A major. Here the lydian sharp fourths are far from being curative!

This large-scale movement is not in sonata form though it is in effect a mini-symphony, whose five sections are 'trailers' for the five movements of the suite. Roughly, it encapsulates in one movement a riotous allegro, a $\frac{9}{8}$ scherzo, a comic-pathetic slow movement, a fast fugato and a coda-finale. It is followed by an intermezzo setting one of Skelton's tenderly playful eulogies of a woman, this one called Pretty Bess. The verses derive distantly from troubadour convention, for the woman seems to be spurning her lover as though she were an eternal beloved. Yet Skelton's tripping rhythms and chiming rhymes, as well as the catalogue of flowers he conventionally but freshly compares her to, make her a creature of flesh and blood, inspiring love, generous in loving. Vaughan Williams's music catches this precisely. The mode is aeolian on E, which sometimes sounds like G major; the syncopated rhythm lilts in $\frac{2}{4}$; the tune, originally on oboe, mingles a cheeky dotted rhythm with flowing triplets. The vocal line for solo baritone, as sensivively moulded by the words as a melody of Dowland, floats over a gentle pizzicato bass:

Bess, My pret-ty Bess, Turn once a-gain to me, to me!

Four-part chorus answers the soloist with a heart-easing, mostly stepwise-moving refrain. In the middle section the baritone sings his catalogue of flowers in the dorian mode on D – a brighter, sharper tonality – while the chorus croons the refrain inviting Pretty Bess to 'turn again' to her lover. When he confesses to his distress because it seems that she will not respond, the chorus sings the refrain (which rises like outstretched arms) in canon at the fourth or fifth. This tenderly affecting passage carries us into a da capo, ending in radiant homophony with the words 'Mine heart is with thee', sung by both soloist and chorus; so it looks as though Bess's obduracy was only a teasing game, like that of the troubadour's beloved. The final cadence is an unambiguous G major, with harp arpeggio. It sounds benedictory.

The third movement, 'Epitaph on John Jayberd of Diss', is called Burlesca and is a palpable scherzo. The text, in dog Latin with snatches of English, is goliardic: an anti-eulogy of a clerk of the Church who had riotously died in 1506. He was apparently turbulent, violent and disreputable, and Vaughan Williams's music, scored for men's voices only with orchestra, lives up (or rather down) to him. The orchestra begins with a nagging ostinato pattern of quavers, in an ambiguous modality. The key signature is three flats; the key might be phrygian C minor or aeolian-cum-dorian F minor with, of course, F minor's traditionally malign connotations. The first appearance of a vernacular text ('God forgive him his misdeeds') introduces a new section: a pendulum-swinging andante in $\frac{6}{8}$, over an ostinato in the bass consisting of an A major arpeggio, though the key of the vocal melody seems to be aeolian C sharp, with intermittent, tritonally 'altered' fifths. The two themes alternate rondo-wise, the duple nagging growing increasingly spiky and tonally volatile. The dismissive coda ('hey ho, rumbelow!') is yelled over an oompah bass rocking in thirds. Satirical, even parodistic, juxtapositions dominate the end, with the liturgical 'Per omnia secula seculorum' from the Office for the Dead chanted *maestoso*, but brushed aside by the dissonantly nagging quaver ostinato. Hammered dominants four times repeated are curtailed by a triplet descent to the tonic, through lydian B natural. This abrupt end suggests that a modal F minor *was* the basic tonality, never clearly defined. Certainly the nasty negation of this none the less comic scherzo makes a perfect foil for the penultimate Romanza, which is the longest and deepest movement in the suite.

The goliardic aspects of the Epitaph on Jon Jayberd, as well as its percussive rhythms and ostinato patterns, remind us that Carl Orff's *Carmina Burana* was to appear a couple of years later. Goliardic denunciation as well as exuberance was in the air, though both the Vaughan Williams and the Orff cantatas had earlier precendents in neo-primitive pieces by Stravinsky and Bartók. Orff's work, though often scoffed at by the sophisticated, has become a best-seller with the general public who, at least over a time span of fifty years, may be trusted to know. The cantata has survived because it combines corporeal energy with a vein of lyricism that, related to the composer's music for children, distils a *premier matin du monde* atmosphere, linking the dawn of the Renaissance with a potential rebirth for our jaded century. Vaughan Williams's Burlesca, being a denunciatory scherzo, does not embrace these positive aspects; but they are present in the child-like lyricism of the next movement, the work's centre of gravity, and one of its composer's most poignant inspirations.

The text is extracted from Skelton's poem *Phyllypp Sparowe*, Jane Scroupe's lament for her pet bird slain by a nefarious cat. Just as John Jayberd was a real man whose story is attested to, so Jane was a real girl, whom Skelton knew personally. She was a teenager being educated at Carrow Abbey, near Norwich, and she is personified by mezzo-soprano solo, accompanied by the orchestra and by female chorus, balancing the men's chorus of the burlesca. The chorus represent young nuns, or more probably school-friend novices who do not intend to enter the cloister. Ironic parallels are drawn between the religious life and the tender humanity of young girls in a world increasingly secularized. Neither Skelton nor Vaughan Williams treats the situation jokily. Jane's anguish over the loss of her pet tugs at our heart-strings as well as hers, since it involves the cognition of mortality by a person young enough to have been no more than half-conscious of it. So the piece is about growing up, as is suggested by the opening bars: an aspiring cello solo, *lento doloroso*, which rises from the open fourth string (C) through an arpeggio, and descends, with wailing chromatic passing notes, in tenor register. The modality is dorian on C, modified by more chromatic descents as the orchestra takes up the chant.

The vocal music begins with the young nuns or pseudo-nuns intoning a

Placebo. Jane nervously qustions them as to what they are doing. With a bird-chirruping reference to the plainsong Dies Irae, the solo cello pushes the orchestra up to aeolian E, drooping chromatically to E flat, and thence back to dorian C as the girls' intonation tells Jane and us that they are singing a Mass for 'the soul of Philip Sparrow That was late slain at Carrow'. The little chromatic wail invades the orchestral fabric, and intrudes into the altos' intonation:

The yearning cello solo reappears on G instead of C, the chromatic sighs on woodwind garnering dissonant suspensions. This orchestral interlude prefaces a little air wherein Jane piteously recalls the tragedy – for such it is, in the context of her guileless youth. Her vocal line teeters between G and B flat, her word rhythms delicately contradicting the $\frac{2}{4}$ metre. Modal incantation itself absorbs the chromatic descent, echoed by woodwind and by the girls' chorus in undulating triads. The orchestra is silenced at the naming of the arch-fiend, Gib the cat, Gib being one of the Devil's many names, and a cat the consort of witches. Unsurprisingly, this momently provokes a transition to the darkness of E flat minor, and then infernal F minor, in which Jane and her friends vow vengeance on the feline tribe. The climax is in chromatically declining $\frac{6}{3}$ chords. Antiphony peters out in the rocking thirds of the 'vengeance' motif, ending quietly but sepulchrally on bassoons, in lugubrious F minor.

Jane's solo, following, preserves the gentle duple pulse and also the sighs, enhanced by a silent hiccup at the beginning of each phrase. But the mood is different, as is the mode, now a radiant G major. Jane sings reminiscently of her pleasure in her pet, her melody being unobtrusive, mostly by step, ignorant of bar-lines, scrupulously attentive to the way one would speak the heart-felt words. The music diatonically smiles, though the little wails are not entirely banished from the orchestra. For a moment, Jane forgets her sorrow in reliving the gamesomeness of the bird, who has his own perkily fourth-founded, dotted-rhythmed tune. The music offers comic, exquisitely scored description of Philip's way with wasp, fly or ant, and although the onomatopoeic music is funny, it is also pathetic – and catastrophic, from the insects' point of view! Probably

Skelton inteded no irony about the arbitrariness of death and fate since that was accepted as part of his medieval heritage. What matters to Jane is her own grief, though everyone knows that death and destruction are handed out impartially. To us, however, the irony registers: especially when Philip's death-dealing games ('Lord, how he would pry After a butterfly!') occur in fluttery triplets in paradisal E major. It seems that Vaughan Williams was aware of the irony, for the E major episode is abruptly succeeded by a return, on the exclamation 'Alas', to the chromatic wails, centred around a dorian G minor – the same negation, in relation to E major, as we have commented on in the Messanger's famous arioso in Monteverdi's *Orfeo*. Here the oscillating triads are close to those in *Job* and the Fourth Symphony, and although this may be in context a tragic irony, it is not parodistic. A girl like Jane may be less 'experienced' than a middle-aged man like Skelton, let alone an old one like Vaughan Williams, but her humanity and pain are real:

Returned to dorian E minor, the solo cello sings the original arpeggiated phrase, to which the chorus intone a Pater noster, summoning birds of all species to attend the funeral.

With a sudden dip from E natural to E flat in its dorian mode, Jane, playing priest, declaims an ornately stylized, quasi-liturgical Latin incantation. Woodwind, with intermittent horn and muted trumpet, leap into a birds' chorus, hardly less realistic than Messiaen's, and with comparable point, for the birds are angelic messengers whose carollings remind mortally sinful humans of Nature's innocence – as Ralph Hodgson has put it, in distinctly Skeltonic verse:

> Of Nature write ... tell
> That all's Eden and well;
> No sniggers or smirks
> At sight, sound and smell
> Affront her chaste works:
> She never fell.

We did, however: as we are reminded by the intrusion of the Dies Irae in parallel thirds on bassoon and muted tuba. When the girls resume their funereal chant they are introduced by oscillating triads of B flat minor and G minor, those same false related triads that had launched Vaughan Williams's first venture into the unknown region. While the girls chant, in the aeolian mode on C, the birds continue their blithe babbling as they are 'named' in a roll-call. It is appropriate that this section should be at once naïvely illustrative and expressive: for although, in Hodgson's words, Nature has nothing 'to foul the pen of an innocent Muse: She keeps no stews', her innocence is apprehensible only through our fallen humanity. This long section is Edenic yet cumulative, if not developmental. The music lyrically flowers in a swaying $\frac{12}{8}$ dance that depicts swan, drake, owl and heron in a grave aeolian mode on F; jollier creatures like pheasants and turtles lilt the music into E flat major. For the proud peacock we move to the upper mediant G, which turns into a phrygian fugato around E. Magical indeed is the music for the phoenix, 'rarest bird of loudest lay', whose whirling woodwind arabesques act his self-consuming flames. Most of his music is rooted on a pentatonic ostinato on E or A, the static nature of which, allied with the swirling arabesques, enhances the exoticism.

The legendary bird has, of course, led us into realms of fancy; from which we return to the convent school by way of Jane's Latin intonation – startlingly in a pentatonic B flat minor, after the phoenix's A ostinato. The chorus join her with homophonic 'Libera me's, falling still more darkly to E flat minor, with a pizzicato ostinato of rocking thirds, like muffled bells. This is an apotheosis of the birds' non-humanity. The flute, descending from the heights by fifths, must be a dove, another holy messenger; with E flat minor illuminated to major, the girls sing an unaccompanied blessing on the sparrow's soul – music so tender that we do not query their belief that he has one. For the first time the tonality is plain diatonic major, though an occasional passing note reminds us distantly of the wail that has pervaded the movement. During this luminous blessing Jane, still playing priest, intermittently murmurs 'Dominus vobiscum' and other Latin tags, again without suspicion of parody. The passage is musically as well as liturgically consummatory, for it absorbs reminiscences not only of the chromatic lament, but also of Philip's dotted rhythmed fourths. The coda returns to the lovely, hesitant lyricism in which Jane had first recalled Philip's sitting, 'in his velvet cap', in her lap, and also returns to that episode's key, G major. Although the little chromatic wail still moans, *teneramente*, in the orchestra, it dissolves as the girls sing adieu, the theme a rising fourth that slips down the scale.

Their almost unaccompanied diatonic harmony sounds Ravellian: similar to the unaccompanied closing chorus of *L'Enfant et les Sortilèges*, wherein birds and beasts sing a benediction on the small boy who, like Jane, has experienced a first revelation of mortality and guilt. Ravel's marvellous chorus is in G major; when in the final six bars of Vaughan Williams's lament modality clears from aeolian E to radiant G major triads, blessedness is unalloyed:

Jane Scroop's lament, despite its ostensibly slight theme, is so extended and so subtle a piece that it is difficult to imagine what could follow it. Vaughan Williams hardly tries to face up to this, though he found no problem – as many composers have done – in creating adequate finales to his symphonies. Still, the *Tudor Portraits* do not claim to form a symphonic whole, so Vaughan Williams may be justified in making the work's last movement another scherzo, briefer and more insouciant than the burlesca. It is a portrait of Jolly Rutterkin, a gypsyish outcast who makes forays into town, setting cat among pigeons, but puckishly bringing good luck. Skelton versifies him in virtuoso metrics and rhyming, to which Vaughan Williams responds in the spirit in which it was intended, making the jazziest movement in the work, riddled with Gershwin-style pentatonics on brass and woodwind, propelled by the rumba rhythm of 2 plus 3 plus 3 quavers a bar, or permutations thereon. The modality is dorian on B, sometimes turning into D major; but the whole score is so obsessively pentatonic that tonality, let alone modulation, matters little. The music

creates an eternally present fiesta, a secular complement to the timelessness he seeks in his spiritually orientated works. Probably in order to
extend the piece a bit, Vaughan Williams incorporates as middle section
a setting of a lyric from Skelton's court-morality play, *The Bowge of Courte*.
In this Rutterkin projects himself theatrically into a Court fancy-man,
whose tune, sung by the baritone soloist, is rudimentarily fourth-founded,
ornamented with tinkling flute scales, in a bouncing $\frac{3}{8}$. The song is in E flat
major, virtually without tonal movement, cockily mindless, but the
chorus bring Rutterkin back to grimy earth by combining the original
Rutterkin music with his new song. Primitive fugato carries them into a
sudden wrench back from E flat major to D, and a truncated
recapitulation of the 2 plus 2 plus 3 pentatonics. Briefly this is disrupted by
another tonal lurch, through a tone to C, but bounces back to D for the
final cadence. The non-developmental nature of the music is what it is
about: a state of fiesta on the edge of chaos. Subconsciously, that may have
been why Vaughan Williams found Skelton congenial, and relevant to our
times. More significantly, he also found in Jane Scroop's lament a parable
of innocence and experience that reaches to the heart of his and our
humanity, at any time and place.

The *Five Tudor Portraits* are poised between the Middle Ages and the
Renaissance and owe their twentieth-century relevance to this doubleness. The savagery that counteracted the spirituality of the declining
Middle Ages was mollified by Renaissance humanism; gradually, hard
angles were smoothed and dark corners irradiated. Italian sun suffused us
vicariously, and the Arcadian paradises evoked in Italian Renaissance
poetry and painting were translated into those bibles of English
Renaissance courtiers, the *Arcadia* and the *Astrophel and Stella* of the 'flower
of England', Sir Philip Sidney. Rhetoric and wit, wondrously refined as
compared with Skelton's ribaldries, distance experience, which at the
same time exists physically, in the moment. Italianate versification
promotes an exquisite sensuality: which became a central tradition in
English pastoral poetry, stretching through the sixteenth and seventeenth
centuries, from the Platonic Spenser, through Milton and Marvell, to the
Nature-mystics, Vaughan and Traherne. A key work is John Fletcher's
The Faithful Shepherdess which, published in 1611, and thereafter immensely
influential, was a free translation of Tasso. Fletcher's *Shepherdess* was a
favourite poem of Samuel Palmer who, living at the dawn of the Industrial
Revolution, found visual inspiration in its bosky nooks, moonlit glades and
Miltonic 'tufted trees' and 'sable clouds'. We have already noted the
affinity between Vaughan Williams's Nature-mysticism and that of
Palmer; and although we have no evidence as to whether Vaughan

Williams knew Fletcher's poem, he probably did, since he was certainly familiar with Milton's early verse, Marvell's garden, and of course the many passages in Shakespeare that evoke Arcadias.

In such verse the worship of Pan, god of sensual instinct, coexists with a cult of spiritual purity and, as a consequence of this, sexual chastity. Here is another doubleness inherent in Renaissance society: for if these men and women, less dependent than medieval people on a law adumbrated by Church and State, attempted to live in their agile minds and subtle senses, it was inevitable that they would become aware that their pride was counterbalanced by their frailty. In social terms sex and death merge into the no less inevitable tie-up between love and war, both with their precarious, because man-made, codes of honour. The Petrarchan convention of the wailing lover, harking back to the medieval troubadours, admits that, while love is all we have, it is for ever unappeasable. Desire and abnegation are thus interdependent: a paradox which English artists of the seventeenth century relished with peculiar intensity. Ambiguity is the warp and woof of English Anglo-Catholicism and Calvinistic Puritanism. Poetically a Renaissance Platonist, Milton was theologically a Puritan; the Anglo-Catholic erotic-mystical poet Richard Crashaw was reared as a Puritan but partly educated in Italy and Spain; even the Anglican priest George Herbert employed erotically mystical imagery in his devotional verse. The same duality typifies Vaughan Williams, especially, though not only, when he is setting words by poets such as Milton, Spenser and Herbert.

One of his earliest representative works was a setting of Herbert, with whose family the Vaughan Williamses were distantly connected. The *Five Mystical Songs* were begun in the same year as *On Wenlock Edge* (1906), and finished in the year of the Tallis Fantasia (1910). The poems' equilibrium between faith and dubiety, austerity and tenderness, clearly appealed to Vaughan Williams, whose vocal lines are as sensitive to Herbert's rhythms and metaphors as the melodies of *On Wenlock Edge* were responsive to Housman's. But whereas survivals of Edwardianism in the Houseman settings are not antipathetic to the verses, traces of Elgarian exultation, if not Parryan afflatus, are at odds with the sober precision, tough wit, and humane fervour of Herbert's poetry. The cycle, though full of premonitions of later Vaughan Williams, is not a masterpiece, as is *On Wenlock Edge*. Five years after the Herbert cycle Vaughan Williams set seventeenth-century devotional verse by Crashaw and by Bishop Taylor in two of the *Four Hymns* for baritone and orchestra. The English compromise between spirit and flesh is evident, though the songs do not directly evoke the English Eden. That most powerfully occurs in four works composed during the twenties and thirties: *Flos Campi* for solo viola, wordless chorus and small orchestra, which dates from 1925; the *Magnificat* for contralto solo, chorus and orchestra of 1932; the *Epithalamium* conceived in 1938 as a masque for speaker, singers, flute, viola and piano, but later redone as a choral cantata; and the *Serenade to Music*, an occasional piece of more distinguished origin, since it was written in 1938 for sixteen celebrated solo singers, as a tribute to Sir Henry Wood. Perhaps the quintessential 'English Eden' piece is none of these, but the cantata or scena of 1922, *The Shepherd of the Delectable Mountains*. Since this, however, was incorporated into the 'operatic morality' *The Pilgrim's Progress*, it will be discussed in the next chapter.

The Crashaw setting from the *Four Hymns* of 1914 has an obbligato part for solo viola: an instrument which Vaughan Williams enjoyed playing, and for which he had a deep affection, not unconnected with its being at once the most ethereal and the most voluptuous of the string family. In 1925 he produced a masterpiece in direct homage to the viola and in indirect homage to England's seventeenth-century Eden, in that the work was inspired by that wondrously physical-metaphysical hymn, the Song of Songs, in the Latin Vulgate, though with the superb translation from the Authorized Version appended. The prose of the Authorized Version is probably the only great poetry widely familiar to many 'sorts and conditions' of English people; certainly its imagery and cadences animate Vaughan Williams's music here as so often, though the words of the Song of Songs are not sung, but merely printed on score (and programme) as signposts to the music. The magical potency of the viola informs every moment of this work, even when the soloist is silent. His identity is obscure; he might be the voice of Pan, or Nature, or of human lover and beloved, or he might be all of these simultaneously. The small mixed chorus wordlessly ululates: so they, too, are of ambiguous identity – ghosts or fairies, spirits from beyond, or man and womankind, generically rather than specifically. In this they resemble the wordless chorus in Ravel's superb *Daphnis et Chloe*, a work already mentioned in connection with Vaughan Williams's Pastoral Symphony. The unlikely consanguinity between the young Englishman and the French composer is evident in the fact that Ravel's Ballet, though set in a French Arcadia and dedicated to the worship of Pan, fuses sensuality with the numinous, as does Samuel Palmer's English Eden.

The first of the six movements has a famous opening that was once slightly infamous: the solo viola sings with solo oboe (a pastoral instrument) in arabesques that are innocently pentatonic yet in relationship to one another sharply bitonal:

Vaughan Williams's hymn to Eros ('Stay me with flagons, comfort me with apples') begins with this stark admission of the doubleness inherent in sex and love; and it seems to be the laceration that arouses both the music's physical voluptuousness and its metaphysical exultation. This is psychologically and physiologically on the mark: as becomes evident when the viola and solo flute sing the emergent theme not doubly, but in low unison – a most mysterious, erotic-ethereal sonority. Strings fluctuate in false related triads, similar to those in the Pastoral Symphony. They might be sighing winds or supernatural creatures, though we also hear them anthropomorphically, as though they were equivalents to human longing or despair – as they must be, since a man invented them. In a very different piece, composed in the same year as *Flos Campi* – the one-act opera *Riders to the Sea* – Vaughan Williams used similar techniques to emulate wild wind and surging sea; they were to crop up again many times, climactically in the *Sinfonia Antartica*. Here the climax sounds as natural as Nature herself; and subsides into the second movement: 'For lo, the winter is past and the voice of the turtle is heard in the land'. Chorus and strings murmur Nature-music again reminiscent of the Pastoral Symphony: into which steals the solo viola with a pentatonic vocalise that aspires to the blessedness of G major. The chorus take up the melody more lyrically, though their humanity soon dissolves into undulating triads, picked out by waterdrops on celesta. This is prophetic of the fairy-wood music in Britten's *A Midsummer Night's Dream* – and perhaps, more darkly, of the nocturnal garden in *The Turn of the Screw*. The magic dimension, in Vaughan Williams as in Britten, may involve a 'retreat from the West': which is one of the ways whereby modern man's sundered spirit and flesh may hope to be reunited.

A melismatic cadenza for the viola carries us into the third movement, scored mainly for women's voices with the viola: appropriately enough, since the unsung text is about the beloved's yearning for a lover lost: 'Whither is thy beloved gone, O fairest among women?'. This is the most voluptuous section in the score; the women's oscillating triads whip themselves to near-frenzy. The theological symbolism with which the Church somewhat desperately interpreted this book of the Old Testament is not – on Vaughan Williams's own testimony – pertinent to *Flos Campi*, though it might be called a religious work in that it is concerned with the incarnation of spirit in flesh and with the spirit's liberation from this 'mortal coil'. This two-way traffic becomes manifest as the impassioned yearning promotes a radical change of mood and manner. Up to this point the music has been in the spiritual province, springing from female instinct and intuition. Now this matriarchal concept is banished by a patriarchal march describing Solomon and his 'three score valiant men' who 'all hold swords, being expert in war'. Although the theme is pentatonic, like so many non-Western melodies, it is also metrically rigid, marshalling spontaneity: so if it is erotic as well as exotic it points, in macho patriarchalism, to the link between sex and death, love and war. Even the solo viola is affected by the change, for its counter-tune is at first rather gawky, square in metre. None the less the viola manages to inspire the chorus to reassert their sensory rights, and the substantial fifth movement becomes a ceremonial dance to the beat of an antique as well as exotic tabor. Themes from the first movement reinstate pristine magic; voice and dance fuse, in the process creating the theme of the last movement, first heard on the solo viola, then on solo oboe – the original initiators of the work.

This D major tune is one of Vaughan Williams's miracles: simple enough to be a hymn of common men and women, yet potently a part of the marriage of sense and spirit which the piece has consummated. Imperceptibly and inevitably, the tune has been derived from the song of the turtle in the second movement: which contains both the tune itself and its counter-melody which is not far from the alleluyas in Vaughan Williams's great hymn, *Sine Nomine* – which in its turn is to be echoed at the end of the Fifth Symphony. Flowing levelly in stepwise-moving lines, the music creates in its sensuous diatonic euphony a potential New Jerusalem for society in the modern world. The bass is earthed on a long tonic pedal; and although the peace that passes understanding is momentarily ruffled by a reminiscence of the original bitonal arabesques on solo viola and oboe, this only reminds us that the precondition of peace is division. Man and Nature, 'for the time being', attain at-one-ment; and do so in a final D major triad that is almost as blissful as the end of the Fifth Symphony. The word miracle, used at the beginning of this paragraph, is pertinent, for it is difficult to think of any music, apart from Bach's, that seems so strongly to affirm the certitude of a faith; yet it was created not by a German Lutheran with centuries of religious tradition behind him, but by a Christian agnostic in secularized, industrialized Britain.

It is not surprising that Vaughan William's protest against the more mechanized aspects of modern civilisation should involve a rebirth of the female principle, for Western technocracy had been nurtured on patriarchal aggression. *Flos Campi* associates its magic with matriarchy; the *Magnificat* of 1932 is explicitly an act of homage to the female principle, in that Vaughan Williams said he conceived it not as liturgy for the Established Church, but as the drama of Mary's human response, which is that of a woman to her lover, to the miracle of the Annunciation. The act of praise is, in the composer's view, sensual in its very *ecstasis*, and is thus a counterpart of *Flos Campi*, inspired by the universal love song of the Song of Songs. Seven years later in date, however, the *Magnificat* differs from *Flos Campi* in that the mysticism inherent in its eroticism is more developed. This is a matter that calls for further enquiry into the relationship between Vaughan Williams and Holst, previously referred to only in the context of folk tradition.

Holst's partiality for early and pre-Renaissance music is linked with his being, although even less of an orthodox believer than Vaughan Williams, as much interested in oriental as in occidental religions. Of their nature these offered values alternative to those of Western technocracy, and in this spirit Holst conceived his major religious work, *The Hymn of Jesus*, dating from 1917. Taking his texts from the Gnostic Acts of St John, Holst scores the hymn for chorus, semi-chorus and orchestra in an idiom that abandons not only the harmonic opulence and tension of German romantic music such as had dominated British music during Holst's and Vaughan Williams's apprenticeship, but even the interrelation of line and harmony that had been the core of European music since the Renaissance. Monodic plainchant is the source of the prelude, for the stressless, near-pentatonic line is accompanied by swaying parallel fourths and fifths, having affinities both with medieval organum and with the ritualistic musics of the East. When a Hymn of Glory unfolds it is more metrically conceived; but since it is built on a falling scale ostinato and has no harmonic movement, it too creates a hypnotic obliviousness of time. All these elements occur, as we have seen, in Vaughan Williams's music, but never in such isolation from post-Renaissance interplay between 'horizontal' line and 'vertical' harmony.

When the words speak of the self's mystical relation to the godhead ('Fain would I be pierced') there is, at last, a kind of harmonic progression, as brief contrapuntal entries create stabbing dissonances. Yet supernatural

Amens continue unruffled on the semi-chorus, and personal excitation is subsumed in 'the Mind of All' when the swaying organa return. As the soul seeks a resting place, the music flows into a cosmic dance in a metrical ostinato in $\frac{5}{4}$ time, later alternating with $\frac{5}{2}$. The ostinato, being unremitting, suggests eternity, while its irregularity may hint at an inner agitation. The climax comes with the vision of the lamp. One choir moves chromatically in parallel triads while the other stays still, so that we hear simultaneously the triads of F and F sharp major: a 'piercing' intensity that 'blinds the gazers' until it is resolved into the light of D major on the word lamp. The music is of startling originality, if naïve in comparison with 'anti-Western' Stravinsky, from whom Holst learned much. Interestingly enough, a reference to human suffering triggers the only passage in the score that carries a whiff of oratorio-style rhetoric; Parryan or even Elgarian sequences do not convince in the context, but are readily forgotten as the ground bass sinks to silence while the Amens of the semi-chorus float upwards into space.

There are comparable 'visionary' moments, attained by way of similar techniques, in other choral and orchestral works by Holst, such as the *Choral Symphony* and the *Choral Fantasia*, which take their texts from romantic poetry – Keats and Bridges. Though the visionary moments are remarkable, the works are not totally convincing, and, significantly, have worn less well than *Egdon Heath*, a symphonic poem inspired by Hardy's solitudinous landscape, or the harsh, wry, abrupt orchestral scherzo which was all Holst wrote of a projected symphony. If Vaughan Williams fulfils Holst's thwarted aspirations it is because he is the greater – more technically adept as well as deeply humane – composer. None the less he profited from Holst's flashes of originality, especially during the thirties, his creative heyday. The presence of Holst behind the opening bars of the *Magnificat* is unmistakable, for the orchestra oscillates in tritonal and whole-tone chords, swaying like a pendulum whose duple pulse contradicts the notated $\frac{3}{2}$. There are links not only with the religiously mystical aspects of Holst but also with the stellar music of *The Planets*, by far his most popular work, probably because of its powerful momentum and the virtuosity of its scoring. Vaughan Williams borrows from it what he needs, relinquishes the theatrical panache, and adapts Holst's stratospheric devices to the service of spirit. The stellar orchestra becomes the medium through which a natural woman, Mary, communicates with a chorus of women's voices that is, or rather represents, a supernatural dimension.

Through the swaying ostinato the chorus chants an invocation to Mary, moving by step or pentatonic third, with an occasional chromatic wriggle that is in effect disembodying. As the ostinato shifts to parallel $^6_4$ chords undulating chromatically, a solo flute utters a cry descending from B through B flat to G: an alternation of major and minor thirds such as we have frequently commented on in earlier works, and which will increasingly dominate the music of Vaughan Williams's later years:

In this work the flute is a magic instrument, intermediary between the human and the divine, as is the viola in *Flos Campi*. Magic is indeed potent when the flute melody turns into a cadenza, wherein the alternating thirds reveal their identity with the 'blue' notes of Negro jazz. The affinity is understandable, for if the false relations in Tudor music sprang from tension between the monody of the old medieval (spiritual) world and the harmonic homophony of the new (secular) world, we can see that black African melody and rhythm played a similar role in the context of white American military metre and hymn book harmony.

The swaying ostinato chords return, more chromaticized so that they sound like early Messiaen as well as planetary Holst. The flute solo expires as the chorus evokes the Holy Ghost by whom the human woman has been impregnated. Thirds and sevenths are recurrent in the pentatonic chant, during which strings take over the 'blue' motif. With a quickening of tempo, tonality becomes G major, oscillating to minor; the choric phrase lifts from D through E and G, but flattens the B above that, only to clear again to the major third for the naming of the Son of God. The chiming ostinato patterns are still pronouncedly Holstian, but the music Mary sings in response to the divine visitation is essential Vaughan Williams. Through its impassioned fervour, G major, a blessed key, is arrived at by way of an ecstatic melisma. The 'lowliness' of God's handmaiden calls for flat blue notes, which this time lead to a real modulation for the blessing of 'all generations'. The melody now begins with a scale falling through a fourth from E flat, the soloist being canonically imitated by both chorus and orchestra. The modality is aeolian on C, occasionally merging into E flat major. God does 'great things' by way of an upward lift to C major, over another Holstian ostinato derived from the swaying minims.

When the text refers to God's holiness, the pendulum swings again, in very remote chords built from piled-up thirds. They sound immaterial: as do the vocal melismata, hovering between dorian and lydian F. The static nature of the orchestra's swaying seventh chords and the self-rotating, F-centred introversion of the vocal arabesques wondrously evoke the numinous, creating an oasis in the 'planetary' movement of the ostinatos. A hushed return to G major takes us to the section of the text that deals with God's power in relation to Mary, his 'vessel', and to the world at large. The soloist begins with a stepwise rising third followed by its blue flattening: from which – over an ostinato that is passacaglia-like without being strictly a ground – the music modulates by mediants, the triple beat reinforced by organum-like parallel fifths, fully scored. The exalted are 'put down' in vehement music riddled with ambiguous thirds; while those of low degree are 'exalted' in extended melismata, in pentatonic G flat major or E flat minor. The roulades that fill the hungry with good things carry ecstasy to the point of hilarity. Vaughan Williams's Mary is a warm-blooded human animal, and the physicality of her music is here emphasized by the tramping minor thirds in the bass. When God helps his servant 'in remembrance of his mercy' the soloist's line quietens over the orchestral chords of piled-up thirds, which turn once more into a swinging ostinato. The climax of the work comes in Mary's vision of the durability of God's benediction: the melody on 'for ever', back in G major, is a thrillingly expanded version of the descending scale theme first heard in reference to the 'generations that shall call me blessed'. The recapitulation has point, therefore; and again the bass moves like a passacaglia in $\frac{3}{2}$, though it is not one. Moreover, this leads into a recapitulation of the opening chords in their original form, in scoring which tingles like timeless bells.

When the angel-chorus tells Mary that she has conceived a son by God, astonishment effects a chromatic lurch to E flat. The ostinato bass, once more Holstian, moves up two minor thirds separated by a tritone. But the identification of her son with God returns to G major, with a pentatonic ostinato bass that intermittently shifts from major to minor. The final song of triumph is sung by chorus mostly in unison, but divided when the sopranos attain their high G. The tune derives from Mary's melisma on the words 'for ever'; and concludes in an orchestral tutti jubilant in pentatonics. Only momentarily, however: for the solo flute's lamenting descent in 'blue' thirds – perhaps the most evident of all Vaughan Williams's fingerprints – returns over sustained orchestral triads, in a bitonality as piquant as the opening of *Flos Campi*. The coda returns to the original swaying chromatics, interlaced with the blue lament. The work ends with luminous G major triads in second inversion for the chorus, with an orchestral ostinato also in G major: $^6_3$ chords float in high register, while in middle register a scale rises through a major third from D. This is at the same pitch as the rising third that had initiated the lark's ascent, nearly twenty years earlier. Added sixths glow in the chorus's diaphanously spaced G major chords – as they do in the quasi-oriental coda to Delius's *Requiem*.

The third of these English Eden pieces of Vaughan Williams's middle years is not a masterpiece like *Flos Campi* or, to a lesser degree the *Magnificat*, but calls for comment because it is the composer's only setting of the major epic poet of our late Renaissance. Spenser wrote his superb *Epithalamion* for the young second wife he married in 1594. It is a passionate celebration of sexual love, as a marriage piece ought to be; no longer is love something to be transcended into worship of a presumptive Virgin Mary, or to be resisted as a temptation of the Devil. At the same time Spenser's poem is a neo-Platonic hymn to marriage as a sacrament, for Renaissance man hoped to have his cake and eat it. Vaughan Williams, loving the poem and its companion *Prothalamion* deeply, found that its duality was mirrored in the idiom he had evolved from the Tallis Fantasia through the Second and Third Symphonies; and decided he could make use of it for an *ad hoc* occasion, when in 1937 he was invited to produce a masque for amateur performance by the English Folk Song and Dance Society. Originally Ursula Wood, later to be the composer's second wife, had devised a masque on the subject of the ballad of Clerk Saunders. On the felicitous spur of the moment the Spenser *Epithalamion* was substituted for it. Ursula Wood arranged a text from sections of the poem, under the title of *The Bridal Day*: which Vaughan Williams set for baritone voice, small chorus, flute, string quartet and piano, with a speaker, dancers and rudimentary choreography. A private run-through was given late in 1938, with the composer as singer (and turner-over), and with the Leighton string quartet, Eve Kisch on flute, and Joseph Cooper on piano; the audience consisted of Douglas Kennedy, who was to have been the choreographer, Maud Karpeles and Ursula Wood. A public performance, with Ursula Wood as the Bride, was planned for autumn 1939, but was a casualty of the Second World War. A television performance, with Cecil

Day Lewis as reader, materialized in 1953; and may have persuaded the composer that the music deserved concert presentation also. In 1957, the year before his death, he made the version in which the work is usually heard – for the original baritone, flute and piano solo, but with the string quartet transformed into a normal orchestra and the chamber choir into a full-sized chorus. The octogenarian composer wrote some additional music to give the chorus more to do.

The music has considerable corporeal energy, as befits a masque; the solo flute is another Pan, rhapsodically embroidering pentatonics; a solo viola is erotically mysterious, as it is in *Flos Campi*. Yet the piece is 'double' in a somewhat unsatisfactory way, as well as in the sense Vaughan Williams meant it to be, for it falls between the stools of a full-sized choral and orchestral work and the amateur activity it started from. The transitions to and from orchestral accompaniment to piano are uneasy, the piano part being neither a virtuoso display piece nor a continuo part in seventeenth and eighteenth century tradition. None the less, the *Epithalamium* has a place in the canon if its luxuriant choral writing is regarded as a study for the work that immediately succeeded its 1938 performance. That was the *Serenade to Music* composed for a more august occasion, Sir Henry Wood's Golden Jubilee concert at the Albert Hall. It is not strictly a choral work, being scored for the solo voices of sixteen illustrious British singers who wished also to pay homage to Sir Henry. The original remains the best version, though the work is often performed in an arrangement for four soloists, chorus and orchestra.

The text is the most wondrous passage in English verse concerned with the equation between love sacred and profane – Lorenzo's speech about music, from the last Act of Shakespeare's *The Merchant of Venice*:

> How sweet the moonlight sleeps upon this bank!
> Here will we sit, and let the sounds of music
> Creep in our ears . . .

The scene is nocturnal; we submit to the sensuous delight of love which, in the unconscious night, both fulfils and, with the help of music, liberates us from the flesh. The ecstasy of love may put us in communion with the Music of the Spheres; it may even be that only by way of sexual love may we attain an intimation of the 'harmony of immortal souls', which we cannot hear whilst enclosed in this 'muddy vesture of decay'. Nowhere else does Vaughan Williams make so explicit an identification of spirit with flesh; nowhere does he create from a symphony orchestra and choric voices a sonority of such sensuous ravishment. The use of the sixteen famous voices was appropriate, for the calibre of the voices and their technical skill ensure maximum beauty of sonority, as the soloists come and go within the interlacings of their homophony. From that voluptuous solidarity each individual spirit soars, intimately responsive to Shakespeare's verbal imagery and spoken rhythms.

The nocturne begins with an orchestral prelude wherein woodwind luxuriantly twine, like the flowers on the moonlit bank. A harp liquidly twangs, suggesting at once natural phenomena like plashing water and lutes or guitars stroked by Renaissance courtiers. A solo violin floats aloft, a lyrically pentatonic offspring of the ascending lark. This is one of the few passages in Vaughan Williams's music that recalls, though it could not be mistaken for, Delius – especially in the chromatics which, on 'the sounds of music', creep into the stepwise undulations. When the voices enter they sound like Nature's half-conscious breathing; they homophonically extend the Nature-noises, from which a single soloist intermittently springs free. The very high first soprano is a child of the wordless soprano at the end of the Pastoral Symphony, and she in turn had been a progeny of the lark. Here her phrases are often pure pentatonic monody, for she 'like an angel sings,/Still quiring to the young-eyed cherubims'. The consort-music for voices and orchestra also merges Vaughan Williams's Nature-music into Delius's, the individual lines being often pentatonic but the consequent harmony chromatic. Pentatonic birds chirrup on woodwind. Nature embraces more of our 'muddy vesture of decay' than is usual in Vaughan Williams, though Delian passion and will never threaten to take over.

The text's reference to Diana, who is to be wakened with a hymn, promotes a more animated middle section, beginning with hunting fanfares. This again suggests that our human sensuality may, in consort with music, work in the interests of spirit; the homophonic evoking of the music of the spheres is itself passionately humane, reminiscent more of the ecstatic Elgar of *Gerontius* than of Delius. Lower voices dispose of unmusical men and women, 'fit for treasons, strategems and spoils', in music that is declamatory, almost operatic. But in invoking 'the music of the house' Vaughan Williams returns to the Nature-music of the opening, subtly enhanced with chromatics on the word 'sweeter', with a flute-piping Pan for 'right praise and true perfection', and with sensual contralto solo for Endymion. At the end solo soprano newly essays the heights in consort with the solo violin lark: an exquisite image for the marriage of the human with the super-, or at least other than, human. The orchestra envelops us in moonlit night; the final harp-garlanded D major triads have an infinite quietude though they are the essence of finite human concord.

The key is D major, the same as that of the end of *Flos Campi* and of the Fifth Symphony. Traditionally the tonality of baroque power and glory, D major becomes for Vaughan Williams a key associated with sensuous fulfilment: which in his world is not likely to occur without the incidence of spirit. The *Serenade to Music*, if Vaughan Williams's most uncompromising statement of this equation, is also his least characteristic. He wrote no more 'beautiful' music; but this is the piece's limitation, which bears on its unwonted, slightly enervating, affinity with Delius. In Vaughan Williams's greatest works the equation between flesh and spirit must fuse tougher disparities – as is patent in *Job* and the middle symphonies.

VII

A PASSIONATE PILGRIM

VAUGHAN WILLIAMS AND BUNYAN: *THE PILGRIM'S PROGRESS* AND *SANCTA CIVITAS*

Now I saw in my Dream, that by this time the Pilgrims were got over the Inchanted Ground, and entering into the Countery of *Buelah*, whose air was very sweet and pleasant, the Way lying directly through it, they solaced themselves there for a season. Yes, here they heard continually the singing of Birds, and saw every day the Flowers appear in the earth: and heard the voice of the Turtle in the land. In this Countery the Sun shineth night and day; wherefore this was beyond the Valley of the *Shadow of Death*, and also out of the reach of the Giant *Despair*; neither could they from this place so much as see *Doubting Castle*. Here they were within sight of the City they were going to; also here they met some of the inhabitants thereof. For in this land the Shining Ones commonly walked, because it was on the Borders of Heaven.

JOHN BUNYAN, *The Pilgrim's Progress*

The Serenade to Music is, if ever there was such, a vision of a humanist's, even a Christian agnostic's, paradise. We may find parallels to it in Spenser, Sidney and Shakespeare; but both Shakespeare and, later, Milton were to be preoccupied not so much with Paradise as with the Fall. The major long poem of England's seventeenth century is called *Paradise Lost*.

According to medieval cosmology and to Milton's epic the world, having been made by God, appeared, 'in prospect from His Throne', to be 'good and faire, According to his great Idea'. Music was the most direct manifestation of this Idea, being the 'undisturbed song of pure Concent' such as is sung in heaven, and was sung on earth in our prelapsarian state. In 'At a Solemn Musick' Milton says that we have to be reminded of the music of the spheres in order

> That we on earth with undiscording voyce
> May rightly answer that melodious Noyse;
> As once we did, till disproportion'd sin
> Jarred against Nature's chime, and with harsh din
> Broke the fair musick that all creatures made
> To their great Lord, whose love their motion sway'd
> In perfect Diapason, whilst they stood
> In first obedience, and their state of good.

He ends with a prayer:

> O may we soon again renew that Song,
> And keep in tune with Heav'n, till God ere long
> To his celestial Consort us unite
> To live with him, and sing in endless morn of light.

The lingering rhythm of the final line reinforces the wistfulness of the passage – which remains, whether we think of the lines in personal terms (we shall be fulfilled only when dead), or whether we think of them as a prophecy about the destiny of the human race. The whole of Milton's life and work proves that he knew that, if every prophecy were to become fact, it could not be in the form of a return to the past. Paradise, once lost, can be regained only by becoming something different – a New Jerusalem.

Milton's dubiety, as epic poet of the seventeenth century, balances the optimism of Spenser, epic bard of the first Elizabeth; and the relationship between the poets is paralleled, in a smaller way, by that between the two finest miniaturists of the day. The age's rage for portraiture is itself evidence of an encroaching humanist bias; but Nicholas Hilliard's 'limning' is pristine, the 'likeness' merging into Platonically symbolic aspects, whereas the portraiture of Isaac Oliver, only a little later, is more naturalistic, his colours soberer, any symbolic dimension being dissolved into what we would call psychological insight. His God, like Milton's, works in a mysterious way to perform whatever wonders may be feasible. Increasingly, it became evident that man's prideful ambition might, *in extremis*, threaten traditional religious sanctions. Christopher Marlowe's career, in the late sixteenth century, as intrepid spiritual adventurer and probable atheist set a pattern confirmed by the melancholic Jacobean dramatists such as Tourneur and Webster, whose heroes, attempting to play God in taking the law into their own hands, die 'in a mist', their souls driven they 'know not whither'. Shakespeare's pre-eminence may lie in the fact that he alone achieved a reintegration of Christian ideas of order with the psychologically humanist impulses that were moulding the modern world.

As the seventeenth century unfolded, spiritual and intellectual bifurcation – already evident, as we saw, in the English Reformation – became materially manifest in the Civil War, which Lady Lucy Hutchinson, in her noble memoir of her colonel husband, John, called 'the Dishonour of the Kingdom'. He, although of high birth and a graduate of the Arminian college of Peterhouse, Cambridge, espoused the Parliamentarian cause and died, after the restoration of the monarchy, in prison. At bottom the Civil War was not a war of religion; at least the struggle between

Catholicism and Protestantism was only one strand of a deeper tension between absolutism and democratic government, king and parliament, Court and Country, religion and science. Charles I, adhering to his father's tenet that 'the state of Monarchy is the supremest Thing on earth', had no doubt that his Divine Right overrode Bishop Selden's utilitarian view that 'A King is a Thing men make for their own sakes, for quietness' sake: just as in a family one man is appointed to buy the Meate'. But although Charles's Church was the Anglican institution of his father, when he married a French Catholic queen his monarchical obsession went rampant. Religion then encouraged an absolutist view of the State; rich favourites acquired disproportionate power as the King's minions at Court; Archbishop Laud steered the Church towards monarchical oligarchy, claiming that his calling came 'immediately from the Lord Jesus Christ'; which, as his opponents were quick to point out, 'is against the Laws of this Kingdom'.

Gradually the Court of Charles and Henrietta Maria became a bastion remote not merely from 'the people' but also from the Country of the landed gentry, notwithstanding their innate conservatism. Paradox was the heart of the matter. Henrietta's French, Catholic, hyper-sophisticated court attracted to it men of learning and culture as well as social climbers; but the instigation of a Court as distinct from the Country itself carried a threat. Living on their estates, upholding the agrarian values of Old England and adhering to Parliamentary democracy rather than absolutism, the gentry justifiably regarded themselves as the country's backbone. Charles's error lay in failing to see how impotent he was, without either their support or a standing army. Ironically, the gentry became a sturdier opposition party than the Dissenters who, under economic pressure, allied themselves ambiguously with the Country, City and Crown. In a society in the melting pot, aristocratic tradition had to come to terms with puritan ethical fervour, with the commercial interests of the City, and with the encroaching strength of the common man.

There could be no clearly defined sides. We have noted how the Laudian High Church embraced the near-Puritan quietism of a George Herbert, and how the Arminian Crashaw came of middle-class stock and of Puritan upbringing. Milton himself, a Puritan reared as a Renaissance Platonist and Latinist, saw that the paradoxical problem of the century was that 'liberty hath a double edge, fit only to be handled by just and virtuous men' who were, and perhaps always had been, in short supply. When Milton supported Cromwell it was because he thought that absolutist monarchy threatened freedom, the more crucial option. But he believed that Cromwell's cause was 'too good to have been fought for';

and at bottom this was the view of Cromwell himself.

Descending from the small gentry but with affiliations to 'trade', he may be interpreted in many contradictory guises: as regicide, revolutionary, Christian zealot, hypocritical man of ambition and, most persuasively, as moulder and preserver of middle-class values in a middle-class state. Yet at least in his early years his ideal was a revivification of the golden age of Elizabeth I: a Protestant queen who governed through a democratically elected parliament, in harness with the 'sweet and noble' ecclesiastical 'politie' of Hooker. Charles had to fall because he usurped parliamentary rights; Cromwell's attempts to re-establish them foundered because, in contrast to Elizabeth whose genius was for parliamentary accommodation, he was both gullible and politically inept. Cromwell's successive parliaments all sold out, and for Milton the restoration of Charles II as a king modelled on the Stuarts rather than Tudors was the beginning of the end. After 1660 Milton abnegated politics in favour of 'a Paradise within thee, happier far'.

Yet morally Milton still hoped for a new, international world in which patriotism was an acknowledgement of the rights of all sorts and conditions of men – if not women! And although Cromwell lost the peace, the causes it espoused did, in time, win through to mould 'a Nation not slow and dull, but of a Quick, Ingenious, and Piercing spirit: a noble and puissant Nation rousing herself like a strong man after sleep, and shaking his invincible locks'. Donne, brooding over contemporary alienation in the first *Anniversarie*, of 1611, had deplored that 'every man hath got To be a Phoenix', arrogant in the belief that there could be 'none of his kind, but Hee'. Milton, after the purgation of war, renovates the phoenix in the guise of his Samson Agonistes, a destroyer who is also a symbol of resurrection. Modern England has been fashioned out of the *mêlée* of these contending forces, which find a latter-day representative in Ralph Vaughan Williams, whose legacy embraced the landed gentry, the army, the Church – and the lost agrarian England. He owed a general debt, we have seen, to Spenser, Shakespeare, Milton, Herbert, Crashaw, Vaughan, Traherne and the like. A more specific and life-long debt was to another figure who strode our turbulent seventeenth century, and may still claim to be part of popular consciousness.

John Bunyan reinterpreted Coverdale's Bible in the light and dark of the religious turmoil thrown up by the Civil War. He was a common man, by trade a tinker, as was his father before him; and a tinker was an outcast from civilized society – sometimes genetically, usually temperamentally, a gypsy. The 'moderate divines' of Bedfordshire naturally regarded Bunyan as 'a pestilential fellow' likely to promote 'the subversion of all government'. When the war broke out Bunyan enlisted – at the age of sixteen – on the Puritan side because it seemed to be the people's party, against monarchical and ecclesiastical privilege. In a sense the war did foster what the burghers called licentiousness since, with censorship and church courts nullified, free discussion became possible among the plebeian populace, not excluding disreputable tinkers. And Bunyan proved to be no ordinary tinker but a speaker and preacher of genius who was also, in the strict sense of the word, a Calvinist – remembering that Richard Hooker, whose *Ecclesiastical Politie* defined the Anglican Church's nature and purpose, revered Calvin for his 'exceeding pains in composing the Institutions of the Christian Religion and for his no less industrious travail for exposition of the Scriptures according to the same Institutions'.

We are apt to forget, because Calvinism became so intolerant and blighting a doctrine, that Calvin himself, born of the demise of the Middle Ages, lived in human fear and trembling. Augustinian in his belief that the world, created out of nothing, was suspended above nothingness, he found in the Abyss an image for the horror of chaos, the unintelligibility of things, and the disintegration of the self. Although rigorous constraints could and must be sought as a bulwark against the Abyss, they brought their own terror – the constrictions of institutionalism, religious, social and political, which Calvin encapsulated in another image, that of the Labyrinth. Ultimately, post-Renaissance, post-Reformation man had nothing to rely on but his own courage and the will to endure.

Because fallen man was incorrigibly corrupt, his salvation depended on the grace of God, which was oblivious of the ranks, titles, honours and social gradations man had evolved to bolster his fallible self-esteem. A king might be damned, a beggar among the elect. Man could not hope to understand the apparently arbitrary distribution of God's grace; but as a mere man, living on the mere earth, he could not help hoping that God's justice might have some reference to social justice, here and now. Certainly Bunyan, imbued with Calvinistic doctrine, had no difficulty in arbitrating between good people and bad. The Prayer Book's Magnificat told him that the poor would be filled with good things, the rich sent empty away: or, in his own words, 'God's people are most commonly of the poorer sort; the great ones of the world will build their houses for dogs … while the godly poor must be glad to wander and lodge in the dens and caves of the earth'.

When the bishops were reinstated by Charles II after the Restoration, it is hardly surprising that they and the gentry thought that Bunyan and his like – such as the communistically Christian Diggers and Levellers –

would be safer behind bars. That Bunyan spent twelve years in gaol did not, however, ultimately serve the interests of his adversaries, for with time on his hands Bunyan discovered that he was not only a preacher, but also a polemicist, of genius. The allegory that he wrote while incarcerated proved to be, after the Bible, the most influential book ever written in English. *The Pilgrim's Progress* describes the journey of a Christian Everyman towards the Celestial City, which is not so far from the English Eden, but carries the social and political implications of a New Jerusalem. This is why Bunyan's characters, despite their allegorical names, are the burghers and peasants of Bedford and its environs, vividly present in the biblical language which they as well as he habitually spoke. Bunyan's baddies, such as Lord Time-Server, Mr Worldly Wiseman and Madame Bubble, are recognizable flesh and blood, as are most of his goodies, such as Mr Great-Heart, Mr Stand-fast, Mr Valiant-for-Truth; and if his blacks and whites allow of no mollifying tincture of grey, the human vitality of his creatures validifies them. Nor are his supernatural beings merely such; the giants who oppose Christian are also enclosing landlords, protecting the rights of property against the poor, monstrous because they are inhuman. Whatever spiritual overtones might be latent in the story, *The Pilgrim's Progress* was an earthy book, an appeal for the people's deliverance. 'Who knows', says Hopeful as the Pilgrim awaits death in Giant Despair's dungeon, 'but that God that made the world may cause that Giant Despair may die?'.

Small wonder that *The Pilgrim's Progress* should have had so obsessive a hold over many social levels of mankind during more than three centuries. The gentry could not ignore it, if only because they were afraid; in middle–and working-class homes it became, during the eighteenth and nineteenth centuries, the most favoured book after the closely related Bible. As a personal testament about the salvation of Tom, Dick or Harry, even Jane or Joan, and also as a vision of a redeemable Promised Land, it struck to the hearts of common men and women – including some uncommon ones, such as Vaughan Williams, who approached it as a traditionalist who loved fairy tales. His first major work, *A Sea Symphony*, had concerned a pilgrimage; the journey of his progressive Pilgrim is more specifically tied to English traditions, though it is no less elemental in range. Significantly, despite the Christian eschatology of the book, Vaughan Williams does not call his hero Christian, but simply the, or a, Pilgrim.

We have mentioned that *The Pilgrim's Progress* was for Vaughan Williams literally the labour of a life-time. Its inception dates back to 1906, or even to 1904 in so far as in that year he composed, or arranged from a folk melody, his sturdily Bunyan-like setting of the hymn 'He who would valiant be', for his English Hymnal. The opera's initiation is thus contemporary with Vaughan Williams's earliest published works. The cantata *The Shepherd of the Delectable Mountains* was published and performed in 1922, and other fragments of the 'work in progress' appeared sporadically over the years – including a substantial score of incidental music for a BBC dramatization of the book. By the 1940s Vaughan Williams seemed to have abandoned the idea of making a totality out of the fragments, and much Pilgrim music found its way into non-theatrical works of his vintage years, notably the Fifth Symphony, begun in 1938 but not finished until 1943. Yet ultimately the opera was finished, and produced for the Festival of Britain in 1951. It was not accounted a success, and has always been regarded as problematical. Its long period of gestation has been held against it: could the bits of a large-scale work conceived over so many years be expected to cohere? To this the answer may be that Bach's Mass in B minor was also a summation of a life-time's experience, put together towards the end of its composer's working days. Another reason for dubiety about *The Pilgrim's Progress* was its ambiguous status. Is it an opera? Vaughan Williams did not claim that it was, but called it an 'operatic morality' – a concept fusing several ancient traditions, notably the medieval morality play (which involved music), and the church dramas of a Renaissance poet-priest like Skelton, whose *Magnyfycence* was half-way between a miracle play and a court masque. Of course, church drama and court masque are conventions distant from, perhaps alien to, us; and one cannot deny that *The Pilgrim's Progress* entails tricky problems in production. None the less one suspects that Vaughan Williams, who was deeply depressed by the inadequacies of the first production, was justified in believing the piece to be viable in the theatre, given the eye and ear of faith. Medieval Church and Renaissance Court drama were often highly spectacular, with brilliant costumes and a cast of thousands – or at least with the entire town or village community. They did not, however, call for the sophisticated technology of a Broadway musical, nor would that be appropriate to Vaughan Williams's opera, though the composer was passionate in his demand for proper scenery and lighting, and resolutely opposed to compromise performances in, as it were, the village hall. Dennis Arundell's stunning production showed the way; and today the eye and ear of faith might be still more readily available, since much avant-garde opera overlaps with religious drama – as practised in the East, if not the West. However this may be, the ambiguous status of *The Pilgrim's Progress*, at once sacred and secular and never sanctimonius, accords with the doubleness of Vaughan Williams's Christian agnosticism. The piece is central to his creative life: the trunk of the tree from which sprang his most verdant leaves and branches. These leaves and branches are the key works in which the composer's sensibility is most manifest; but for the trunk, however, they could not exist.

Because the characters' humanity is palpable, they may be projected into music theatre, and Vaughan Williams can make Bunyan's story his own, and potentially that of Everyman in his (post-) Christian society. Except for a few psalms and the Vanity Fair scene, the words of the libretto, devised by the composer, are all Bunyan's, and therefore closely allied to the English Bible. The work opens with a prologue, establishing a dream within a dream, for Bunyan is presented, in prison, in the act of writing the final chapter of his book. The first sounds we hear are a hymn, scored for brass in an ostensibly seventeenth-century idiom. As Bunyan tells us, in speech-rhythmed recitative, about his dream, the orchestra takes up the hymn, surging into agitated music strikingly similar to, and presumably contemporary in date with, passages in the composer's vintage works, notably *Job* and the Fourth and Fifth Symphonies. Heroic brass fanfares anticipatory of a pilgrimage interweave into the dream, riddled with Vaughan Williams's alternating thirds and false relations. Momentarily, the dream becomes reality; Bunyan's figure, blacked out, is metamorphosed into Pilgrim, who utters a despairing cry, very close to a motif in the (later) Sixth Symphony: 'What shall I *do*?' He asks for a recipe for action; as Bunyan put it, 'the soul of religion is the practic part; God will ask at Judgment not only did you believe, but were you doers or talkers only?'

So the prologue merges into the first scene of the first act, which deals, with dramatic immediacy, with the meeting between Pilgrim and Evangelist. Pilgrim's recitative, so lyrical that it is better described as arioso, is humanly impassioned music racked with terror and despair because of the burden of sin on his back, which will sink him 'lower than the grave'. At 'the thought of these things makes me cry' the music does so, reminding us not only of Vaughan Williams's symphonic agitations, but also of *Riders to the Sea*, wherein the forces of negation, being the blind hostility of the elements, have no Christian associations. Evangelist, being half-way between the human and the divine, sings a vocal line less responsive to human passions, and is often accompanied by sober-rhythmed hymnic brass. His dignity is not, however, impervious to suffering; and his line blossoms in melismata when he sings of the shining light beyond the wicket gate. With Evangelist at his side, Pilgrim is able to rebuff the 'real' world in the shape of Four Neighbours – Pliable, Obstinate, Mistrust and Timorous – who clamorously advise him to flee

Danger, turning 'Back! Back!' Already we see how Bunyan's allegorical beings are presented in total humanity, warts and all: Vaughan Williams's busily fussy music characterizes, without caricaturing, them. Evangelist speeds Pilgrim on his way with a marvel-making transmutation of minor to major triad; but when he has gone, we are left in no doubt that Pilgrim's journey will be hard. An instrumental postlude whirls in a contrary-motion labyrinth such as terrified Calvin. This intensely concentrated music leads, in the prelude to the next scene, into reminiscences of the Tallis Fantasia, and into the most extensive passage to be incorporated into the Fifth Symphony.

At the start of his journey Pilgrim, entering the House Beautiful, is greeted by Three Shining Ones – supernatural beings. The Fifth Symphony music, which auralizes inner conflict, is momentarily resolved into modal bliss, scored for high strings and woodwind. The Shining Ones remove the burden from Pilgrim's back and prepare a room for him to rest in, its window facing the rising sun. An Interpreter indulges in a question and answer session to confirm Pilgrim's resolve. Celestial flutes and oboes are reinforced by brass as a pilgrim's march establishes itself, freely based on the Bunyan hymn of the prologue; the passacaglia theme of the Fifth Symphony's finale is also embryonic throughout this scene. After the Shining Ones have set a seal on Pilgrim's forehead and have robed him in white, he is led into the house; and Vaughan Williams pragmatically inserts an interlude to cover both his sleep and a scene change. The music of the interlude is darkly scored, and dominated by a motif of a wailing semitone that will feature in the Fifth Symphony. Against these night-murmurings Watchful – a choric watchman and spiritul guardian – sings a speech-inflected monody close to the contours of speech and of plainchant. Monody grows into an aria-like psalm-setting, 'I will lift up mine eyes unto the hills', the words being, of course, not Bunyan's but biblical. Lyrical song subsides, however, into the orchestra's semitonic wail as we return, for Act II, to Pilgrim himself.

Morning has followed night and an open road, with Herald and Trumpeter watching over it, stretches into the distance. Trumpet fanfares, soberly pentatonic, sound as Pilgrim sets out, encouraged by the chorus with verses from Bunyan's hymn 'He who would valiant be', in Vaughan Williams's sturdy setting. We experience the hymn not as we might sing it in a modern church, but in its original context, for its call to 'stand fast', whatever dangers beset one, was no idle expression of good intent. In Bunyan's world the dangers were real; those who 'fear not what men say' were socially ostracized and were probably law-breakers guilty of punishable, if to us trivial, offences. The Herald arms Pilgrim so that he

may confront danger and adversity, the scene being conceived symphon-
ically as a fight between Bunyan's briskly triple-rhythmed march-hymn,
and the forces of Chaos. Scene 2 presents the most dangerous variety, since
the monster Apollyon whom Pilgrim confronts, along with a rout of
Doleful Creatures ('Lyons, Hobgoblins, Satyrs, Owles, Dragons, Whis-
perers of Blasphemies, all with Blazing Eyes') may represent social-
political evil in the shape of an enclosing landlord, but is also the grisly
horrors we hide in the depths of the psyche. Whether or not Bunyan was
familiar with the aristocratic entertainment of the Court masque, his
Doleful Creatures exactly parallel the grotesques of the masque's anti-
masque: who, since they represent our fallen selves, must be literally
laughed out of court if our pretence of having created paradise on earth is
to withstand the light of day. The anti-masque grotesques are thus both
farcical and trivial: which Bunyan's Doleful Creatures, given his
Christian-Calvinist eschatology, are not. Nor is Vaughan Williams's
musicking of them. The creatures themselves are not allowed to sing but
only to howl and bellow at indeterminate pitches. Apollyon does have a
pitched voice, a cavernous bass, but can manage no more than intonation
on a single, fearsomely reverberating tone. This is his inhuman monstrous-
ness, which Pilgrim counters by speaking to him in distinctively human
recitative. This is the quality that separates him from brute creation and
makes his purgatorial pilgrimage feasible. He wins the desperate fight,
with the help of heraldic trumpet fanfares. Apollyon is slain, or 'the vision
fades', for he is really nothing, represented in the original production by
a shadow. The Doleful Creatures slink off in a rackety rout, and Heavenly
Beings – Branchbearer and Cupbearer – offer Pilgrim the tree and the
water of life. Introduced by upward glissandos on harps, the high
soprano's melody is near-pentatonic, at the furthest extreme from the
brutish ululations of the anti-masque. Evangelist returns to guide Pilgrim
on the next stage of his journey – not to unspeakable horrors within the
mind, but to the hollow lure of the world, which is all too loudly
loquacious.

Bunyan portrays his materially-minded baddies with sharp immediacy
without expunging their broad humanity; Vaughan Williams follows suit,
not being afraid to make trivial music for trivial people. At the same time
Vanity Fair seethes with raw life, not unrelated to the low-life music of
the *Tudor Portraits*. The beginning of the scene, however, is not only low
but horrendous: which is not surprising, since the theme is the medieval sin
of usury. A savagely jagged, syncopated motif on brass sets the mood, and
dominates the scene. Most of the words are not Bunyan's but the
composer's, with additions by Ursula Vaughan Williams. At first, the

hubbub of the brazen music is interwoven with human crowd-noises as chaotic as those of the non-human Doleful Creatures in the previous act; even in a performance without stage presentation, the illusion of being engulfed in the crowd's vacuity is startling. Lord Lechery is depicted as a snake in the grass who mollifies violence by singing a rhyming music-hall song over an oompah bass; both the savagery and the unctuousness of the music link it with several of the symphonic scherzos. He extols price against value, offering wares for sale, including whores from the brothel. The price of any creature 'is measured in gold'; living is material aggrandizement. Various historical characters such as Judas Iscariot make fleeting appearances to underline the theme. Madame Bubble and Madame Wanton attempt to seduce Pilgrim in a bubbly fairground sonority that vividly simulates a giant calliope. Pilgrim scorns them, saying – prissily, unless one enters the spirit of the Morality – that he buys truth only. (What *is* truth? Pilate historically and cannily interpolates.) The scene builds to a superb theatrical climax when Pilgrim is judicially tried by Lord Hate-Good in a parody of the trial of Christ. Envy, Superstitition, Malice and Pickthank – all sharply etched by both Bunyan and Vaughan Williams – bear false witness against the man who has blasphemed against their Prince Beelzebub, whose sung name is usually smeared with grandiloquent melismata. The ferocious syncopated motif that had launched the scene is transformed into the subject of a fugue: a brilliant device to express the pettifogger's subservience to self-made, self-promoting Law. Counterpoint, become a labyrinth, generates frenzy, as it may in the crowd scenes of Bach and Handel. Entries chase one another in hysterical stretti, until polyphonic order is reduced to disordered noise. The climax, when Lord Hate-Good and the chorus sentence Pilgrim to death, is the syncopated motto-theme in ferocious unison.

For scene 2 we return to Bunyan's words and to a transformed retrospect of the opening of the opera. For Pilgrim in prison is equated with the gaoled Bunyan in the prologue; and Pilgrim's monologue has analogies with Bunyan's preludial music. As he piteously asks God why he has been forsaken, his line again resembles the 'guilt' music in *Job*, though its liturgical manner makes it less distraught, since hope is at hand. Although his arioso threatens to panic as he recalls the crowd's mindless bestiality, he remembers the Key of Promise the Evangelist has given him, for use on a rainy day. There could hardly be a more rainy one: so the effect, when the doors of the prison 'fly open', is proportionate. A trumpet fanfare, derived from the Herald's, speeds Pilgrim on his way, and gently undulating Nature-music, similar to that of the Pastoral Symphony, makes stars glimmer in the night sky. The light of the stars becomes the light of life; 'for a long time' we watch Pilgrim as he walks up the Way. That light is a prelude to rebirth for imprisoned pilgrims: for at the edge of the dark wood, where the Way stretches into the Delectable Mountains, a boy sings, as he chops firewood, a monodic setting of Bunyan's 'He that is down need fear no fall'. For the innocent of heart that Fall may be spelt with a capital and make no odds; the music sounds simultaneously like a child's rune, a rural folk song, and an urban Puritan hymn, anticipating the music of Vaughan Williams's 'second childhood'. The part has usually been sung by a virginal-voiced woman, but a genuine boy treble is the sonority called for; especially since the human boy sings in dialogue with pentatonic flute, oboe and clarinet, simulating the innocent birds of the fields. Pilgrim remarks that the Boy must be happier than 'he who is clad in silk and velvet': thereby making a dramatic point, since his progress to the Delectable Mountains is interrupted by the appearance of Mister and Madam Byends, sycophantic upwardly mobile types who sing, in inanely affected accents, of their distrust of and disgust with religious extremists. In their view compromise with the Way of the World is sensible, even humane. Their music, a corny cocktail-lounge jazz in idiot boogie rhythm, is cunningly placed in relation to the Boy's vernal monody, for nothing could be more worldly-wise and world-weary. The exaggerated courtesy of their exit is pitiful, even piteous, as well as ludicrous. Though the pity is probably not in Bunyan, it is audible in Vaughan Williams's music, which again proves itself sharply dramatic and theatre-worthy. After the Byendses have minced out, the Boy brings Pilgrim back from vanity to the eternal mountains, 'where thou may'st see the gates of the Celestial City'. As Pilgrim trudges towards them, the Boy resumes his wood-carting and his hymnic folk song. A pentatonic bird-clarinet warbles with him.

The Delectable Mountains scene, already referred to as the supreme example of Vaughan Williams's English Eden, opens with undulating strings and woodwind that create a sonority at once sensual and spiritual. A Samuel Palmer landscape, with corn-stocked dell, immense moon, nibbling sheep and balmy air is magically auralized: a night-piece more richly complementing the Palmer-like morning landscape of *The Lark Ascending*. Whether the scene is actually nocturnal is not altogether clear, though Pilgrim's journey physically ends in total darkness. But whatever the time of day, a parallel with Palmer is not fortuitous, since Geoffrey Grigson tells us that passages such as that quoted at the head of this chapter were direct sources of inspiration to the painter. In some such landscape, three shepherds (a traditional magic number) greet Pilgrim at the Delectable Mountains, offering him rest in lyrically flowing modality again presaging the alleluya-tinged passacaglia of the Fifth Symphony. A pentatonic lark carols on solo violin, though the strings still oscillate in false relation as the Shepherds make ambiguous answers to Pilgrim's questions about the safety or danger of the Way: they would seem to share the common view that God's way, whatever else it may be, is mysterious. But Nature, at least, is not: for as the Shepherds describe the delectability of the mountains a bird-chorus chirrups on pentatonic woodwind, floating even more seraphically than the funereal bird-chorus in Jane Scroop's lament for her sparrow. And the Voice of a Bird acquires human language to carol the 23rd Psalm.

The singing bird introduces, or perhaps is metamorphosed into, an angelic Messenger who comes to escort Pilgrim over the river of death. False relations and ambivalent triads increasingly pervade the texture as the Messenger pierces Pilgrim's heart with an arrow, 'the point sharpened with love' – so that the seventeenth-century equation between sexual ecstasy and death is not evaded in the Calvinistic morality of Bunyan. Indeed the music here is close to the most voluptuous of all Vaughan Williams's works, Flos Campi, as, to ornate melismata on woodwind, the Shepherds anoint Pilgrim with spices. Yet when Pilgrim, taking the Messenger's hand, enters the river, there is no emotive consummation and no hint of sentimentality. A violin-lark may soar aloft (or may be it is a nightingale, for darkness is descending), but immersion in the waters is an agony, with tenebrously scored, bitonally descending triads. Death is at once terror and redemption – out of darkness a distant trumpet annunciates the magic fanfare, and heavenly voices chime in alleluyas. Momentarily, splendour shines as Pilgrim, trumpet-haloed, enters the Golden Gates. The celestial alleluyas are bells, tolling through the man-made, time-measured Puritan hymn: a miraculous moment which, the vision spent, fades to silence. For the ultimate apotheosis of the vision is not here but at the end of the Fifth Symphony, which will be discussed in a later chapter. It is as though Vaughan Williams needed the abstraction of instrumental music to realize a vision theatrically inapprehensible. In the opera itself theatrical illusion is finally abandoned, for Bunyan emerges, in front of the curtain, to sing the epilogue: which is noble and heroic, but no longer visionary. Pilgrim is again a seventeenth- and twentieth-century mortal man who dreams dreams; and offers to us, the audience, his book, which we must accept 'with head and heart together'.

It is typical of Vaughan Williams that he leaves his operatic morality open to be taken in several ways. Fundamentally, it describes a psychological pilgrimage such as we all may, perhaps must, embark on; we may also take it, if so inclined, as a Christian journey to an after-life.

Either way, it is also a parable about the potential creation of a society – a New Jerusalem born of the rebirths of individual men and women. One of the reasons why *The Pilgrim's Progress* is central to Vaughan Williams's creative life must be because it radiates outwards in these different directions. Its religious, social and political implications colour most of the works of Vaughan Williams's later maturity, whether they carry a literary text or function by way of symphonic argument. A key work in this context is the oratorio *Sancta Civitas*, composed between 1923 and 1925, just after the *Shepherd of the Delectable Mountains* cantata, which ended up in the 'operatic morality'.

The relation between *Sancta Civitas* and Vaughan Williams's Bunyan-inspired works is intimate though its text is drawn not from Bunyan himself but from one of his prime sources, the Authorized Version of the Book of Revelation, which in Greek is Apocalypse. The book was written or compiled around AD 96 by St John of Patmos, a man distinct from the author of the Johannine Gospel. No part of the Bible has exerted a deeper hold over the human imagination than this book, which brought apocalypse into the centre of Christian eschatology. The reason for this is precisely because Revelation is not one book but several. Its images are – as we would say, in Jungian terms – archetypal: pagan myths of sun and moon worship; fertility cults; the zodiacal signs and the prognostications of astrology; the magic of numbers centred around 3 (divine perfection), 4 (creation), and their magical addition 7 and multiple 12; the wondrous old symbols of the man on a white horse and the death-dealing, life-creating dragon – all these and many more offsprings of the collective unconscious are to be found in this revelatory book. They speak direct to us, over so many hundreds of years; even though the original source or text was rewritten, perhaps many times, by Hebraic prophets who bent it to their purposes, and was refashioned yet again by Gentile Christian apologists whose message was not only different from, but opposed to, the pagan world-view.

The apocalyptic theme we now associate with the book was a Jewish invention, though apocalypses of sundry kinds date back at least to the Chaldeans and Egyptians. The Judaic prophecies of Enoch, Daniel and Esdras all start from a recognition of crisis within the world as it is; pronounce judgment on a sinning people reputed to have caused that crisis; and annunciate a stage wherein, the elect having been vindicated, society may be reborn. The difference from pagan prototypes lies in the application of an ethical yardstick whereby degrees of sinfulness and severity of punishment may be adjudicated. Political overtones are usually involved in this, for the Lord's People are oppressed and persecuted by pagan aliens through whose influence the elect themselves may be corrupted. Though there was a factual basis to this oppression, 'Babylon' (the original oppressor of Israel) became a generic symbol for any 'top dog', whether of race or class, who seemed to be having a merrier time than one did oneself. Patriarchs wept as they waited for a deliverer and a day of judgment – a concept taken over by Gentile Christianity when, in Europe's Middle Ages, ecclesiastical exegetists combed the Old and New Testaments for numerological and astrological evidence of the precise date of an imminent Second Coming. Dies illa must be dies irae, for although the doctrine of the Fall hinted at redemption, hope was frail in face of immediate terror.

Matters were complicated when, during the Renaissance, Christianity reformed its Church. Luther and Calvin, though dubious about the doctrinal respectability of the Book of Revelation, were haunted by its age-old mythic imagery, and cannily angled traditional interpretations to support their sectarian creeds. Antichrist, the seven-headed Beast of Revelation, was metamorphosed into the old (Roman) Church itself, now held to have usurped the true faith of the Fathers, handing it over to the Whore of Babylon and her prideful prelates. Puritan horror of the flesh, whatever its obscure psychological origins, added fuel to hate-filled zealotry, which became little short of maniacal. But there was a positive side to the process which, unsurprisingly, is most profoundly described not by a divine, but by a poet. Spenser's *Faerie Queene*, especially its first Book, recounts an apocalyptic quest of the Red Cross Knight for the true, whole Church (personified by unified Una). The dragons, monsters and magicians with whom he often bemusedly contends – as will Bunyan's Pilgrim a century later – have specific identities, intelligible to contemporary readers in terms of international theology and national history. Significantly, however, the poet, as distinct from the prelate, speaks in symbols rather than in allegory. Although Elizabeth I is aligned with Christ the Redeemer, the equation is not narrowly political. Indeed she is affiliated not so much to Christ himself as to his Virgin Queen-Mother, thereby partially reinstating the Great Goddess whom patriarchal Puritan eschatology abominated. And Spenser abandons hope of an immediate epiphany. Had he finished his epic, the Arthurian Matter of Britain, which entailed the establishment of the New Jerusalem, would have been relegated to a future conceivable only outside time.

In the seventeenth century apocalypse again seemed socially and politically urgent, for dualism was spelt out in civil war wherein Armageddon was presumptively re-enacted. Nor did the advance of the scientific spirit substantially stem the flood of millennial prophecy; indeed, mathematical computation was employed to bolster the prognostications of even the craziest zealots; connections between millennianism, social amelioration and later ideas of humanitarian progress were already being forged. Newton himself, the supreme scientist, was a cautious millennialist, not opposed in principle to a Second Coming though reluctant to assign a date. On the whole, millennial prophecy strengthened rather than weakened during these years when the modern world was in labour. Whereas Spenser had believed the apocalyptic purpose to be feasible only outside time, men of Milton's generation, obsessed with the traumatic year 1666 (the number of the apocalyptic Beast preceded by 1 to indicate its imminence), looked for a millennium soon realizable both in spiritual and material (political) terms. Cromwell was regarded as a middle-class millennial Messiah and we have noted that Bunyan, a member of the labouring class, considered his spiritual vision to be a passport to pragmatic fulfilment in political terms.

Nor was the situation radically different after the Restoration. Milton finished *Paradise Lost* in 1667, the year after the presumed defeat of the Revelatory Beast. But God worked in his usual mysterious way, for the triumph of the elect in the war was reversed with the Restoration of the monarchy. Even so, Charles II was hailed as another Messiah, wearing a different hat, or more elaborate peruke, than Puritan Cromwell, let alone tinker Bunyan. Yet his apocalypticism was no less potent; and evidence of a more materialistic and scientific age lies in the fact that the catastrophes attendant on a Second Coming are now accorded a quasi-factual basis – for instance in Defoe's fictional-documentary *Journal of the Plague Year*. By the end of the century we find Swift guying millennial zealots, in his *Tale of a Tub*, in total dismissiveness. Dryden himself, the poet laureate, had treated millennialists satirically and, in his *Annus Mirabilis: the Year of Wonders 1666*, had given a down-to-earth account of the aftermath of the Year of the Beast. The New London, post-plague, post-fire, is 'a Citty of more precious Mold, Rich as the Zone which gives the Indies name, with Silver pav'd, and all Divine with Gold'. Gold and Silver may preserve symbolic divinity but are clearly also metal – hard cash. The New Jerusalem *is* this modern, mercantile, properous community.

But the religious motif in apocalypticism was not totally submerged in the flood of secularization. Even in the seventeenth century Puritan dissenters had escaped from the old country across the Atlantic to the New World: a world wherein the true faith might burgeon, purged at last of the 'loathsome dregs and filth of popery'. In their *New* England men like Cotton Mathers and later Jonathan Edwards could resuscitate the original Word of God, confidently awaiting the Second Coming in the new Eden they had prepared for it; they could even speculate that the native Amerindians might be the lost tribes of Israel, and that biblical prophecy would be fulfilled when they, as missionaries, had completed their conversion to Christianity. To this degree the date of the new Advent was in their hands: which made them an Elect among the elect. Nor did the fact that the Indians were *not* substantially converted and prophecy remained unfulfilled stifle millennial enthusiasm. In Bible-belted nineteenth-century America and in Victorian England apocalyptic prophecies were rampant, both negatively (foretelling sin-generated fire and brimstone), and positively (in forms of social betterment like Morris's medieval-styled Earthly Paradise, not to mention the *Communist Manifesto* itself, in so far as the ultimate explosion of the class war is an Armageddon preparatory for the new Heaven and Earth of a Marxist state). Even a mind as formidable and a social conscience as well developed as George Eliot's toyed with apocalyptic motifs, and not merely in *Daniel Deronda* and *Romola*, novels explicitly concerned with the Jewish problem and with the cycles of world history. To such concepts Eliot found the symbolism of the Book of Revelation seriously applicable, though her sharp intelligence, and perhaps her lapsed evangelicanism, safeguarded her from crudity. Social reformers like Robert Owen were thought of as pragmatists fulfilling a God-directed human destiny.

None the less, as the hold of the Church and its theological dogma weakened, it was inevitable that apocalypse should be viewed in increasingly subjective terms. Poets rather than divines became, in Shelley's words, 'the unacknowledged legislators of the world', as in a sense they always had been. It was in the first years of the seventeenth century that the greatest of all poets, Shakespeare, created the most sublime of apocalyptic utterances; for *King Lear*, first produced in 1603, is a play about a king who divides his kingdom, with consequences as cataclysmic as those in the Book of Revelation itself. The scene on the heath is a war in heaven comparable with those in Revelations and in *Paradise Lost*, but there is no redeemer for 'unaccommodated man', in time or out of it. Cordelia, whose name makes her the heart and eternal beloved, is barbarically destroyed along with the forces of evil. There is no evidence of a divine plan, and at most a slight hope that man, through the cycles of history, may learn from experience. On the evidence of our own century, he may not seem to have learned much. Still, we precariously survive, and pay tribute to Shakespeare's insight, the apparently superhuman nature of which is the most profound manifestation of his humanity. Even Milton, in his late work, tempered his Puritan millennial zeal, yearning for 'a Paradise within thee, Happier far'.

So for Shakespeare certainly, and probably for Milton, the 'new heaven and earth' spoken of in Revelations is not a *thing* proffered to erring but redeemable man but is rather man's own potential to *create*, from the maelstrom of error, a new self. In this context Shakespeare's successor is Blake, though he spoke as a self-styled prophet in biblical tradition, or as a bard who 'Present, Past and Future sees', hymning the cosmic cycles of history at the onslaught of the Industrial Revolution. When he said that all he knew was in the Bible, Blake added the rider that he understood the Bible 'in a spiritual sense': for 'all deities reside in the Human Breast ... I know of no other Gospel than the liberty of both Body and Mind to exercise the Divine Arts of the Imagination. What is the Joy of Heaven but Improvement in the things of the spirit? What are the pains of Hell but Ignorance, Bodily Lust, Idleness and devastation of the things of the Spirit? To labour in knowlege is to build up Jerusalem.' Certainly it was in this Blakean spirit that Vaughan Williams viewed the apocalyptic theme, though we have seen that he was not impervious to the crude ameliorization of a William Morris. It may have been the latter strain that prompted him to call *Sancta Civitas* an oratorio, though it has little in common with the Victorian prototype. Ethical and political implications were overt in its vision of the City's disaffection; wars and rumours of war, apocalyptic disasters were rife in the world at large; the first performance, Michael Kennedy tells us, took place in the turmoil of the General Strike. Even so, the social and political aspects are a physical backcloth; at heart the piece is metaphysical, demonstrating how – as Vaughan Williams had put it in 1920, when asked to define an aesthetic creed – 'the object of all art is to obtain a partial revelation of what is beyond human sense and human faculties'. Not for nothing did he preface his score with words (in Greek) from Plato's *Phaedo* – words which bear directly on the composer's Christian agnosticism:

> A man of sense will not insist that things are exactly as I have described them. But I think he will believe that something of the kind is true of the soul and her habitations, seeing that she is shown to be immortal, and that it is worthwhile to stake everything on this belief. The venture is a fair one, *and he must charm his doubts with spells like these.* (Author's italics.)

The opening of the oratorio is so 'metaphysically' mysterious as to be, like faith, elusive. The large orchestra is hushed in a quietude ambiguous rather than serene, and though the key signature has one sharp, the music is far from the beautitude of G major. Nor is the tonality E minor, Bach's key of crucifixion, for the cavernous bass starts on, and recurrently returns to, a low C, which rises slowly up the scale to F natural. An ostinato chord on three flutes hovers pentatonically between E, A and B and D, E and A; so it would seem that the implicit but never defined modality is phrygian E:

The rising fourth scale then starts from F natural, which aspires to B flat, supporting a piercing motif on solo oboe – a rising fourth A to D, drooping through C sharp and B natural; tonality remains obscure. When the baritone solo enters to declaim the Revelatory words he takes up the oboe phrase, in a rhythm that follows speech. He is a Blakean prophet who invokes dark forces as the flutes' pentatonic chord now wavers on strings, while the chorus sing distant alleluyas derived from it, first chordally, then 'horizontally' in canon, incorporating the oboe motif. The choruses are double – a semi-chorus and a full chorus, used antiphonally; and as this choral section subsides, a third choral group, described as a 'Distant Choir', is heard remotely. This third choir should, the composer directs, be literally distant, and if possible invisible. It should consist of boys' voices; and is not only a third choir, but also a 'third dimension', over the horizon. Being supernatural, the voices are changeless, sufficient unto themselves; their key is always fundamentally A flat major, and they are usually introduced by a distant trumpet, enunciating a godly rising fifth. A flat, enharmonically identical with G sharp, is the upper mediant to E; the implicit false relations sound, in this context, 'out of this world' – as mediant relations often do in the late music of Beethoven.

On this their first appearance their chant wafts over a pedal on cellos and basses – not on A flat, but on the C the work had started from. The voices' chant is homophonically triadic, in swaying triple rhythm, though chromatic alteration, producing a whole-tone augmented fifth, occasionally disturbs the euphony:

The effect is 'planetary', like the Holstian moments referred to in the *Magnificat*. The rising scale in the orchestral basses, now beginning on A flat, is curtailed to a third, against which strings undulate between triads of C and B flat. Modality is still ambivalent, between C, A flat and E: tones which together form a whole-tone augmented fifth, on which the music climaxes. The bass pedal rises to E, and a song of praise ensues, the theme based on Vaughan Williams's familiar upward-thrusting pentatonic scale. The key is apparently C major – another upper mediant; semichorus has the tune, *fortissimo*, to which the full chorus appends alleluyas, softly, in parallel $\frac{6}{3}$ chords. When the bass pedal changes to C the Distant Choir takes up the alleluyas bitonally, on E major triads, *fortissimo*, while full chorus oscillates between E major triads and augmented fifths on D; if paradise is in the offing, it is elusive. Meanwhile the baritone solo calls on God Omnipotent in a declamation shifting between aeolian and lydian E. The triple choruses meet for the ultimate invocation, swaying between parallel triads of E, G and F sharp, proceeding to C sharp, which changes enharmonically to D flat. In this key (it is really C sharp major as lower mediant to E), choirs and orchestra bound in a triple-rhythmed fugato on Vaughan Williams's habitual pentatonic fanfare (tonic, fifth, sixth). The invitation to certitude and 'gladness' is only briefly sustained, for the 'marriage' of the Lamb and his Church is uneasily celebrated – as the notation changes back from flats to sharps – in a scale declining from high G sharp, harmonized in diatonic concords. The key signature is that of E major, though the bass is still rooted on C natural. Division is inherent even in marriage – especially between spirit and a man-made Church. This becomes clear as the first section – it might almost be called a movement – simmers down in retrospective references to the basic motifs. The ambiguous, C-founded bass now wriggles in serpentine triplets, tied across the beats; the baritone's solo hymning marriage is in pentatonic E with lydian overtones; the Distant Choir and their trumpet are still in A flat, their false-related triads disturbingly extended.

The first part of the apocalyptic vision has thus invoked God Omnipotent in his glory, but in its bi- and tri-tonality and its interior divisiveness has also revealed that God has feet of clay! Division is the essence of the next 'movement', which describes St John's vision of the White Horse and Horseman, starting with another abrupt mediant transition to what might be mixolydian G, though it is recurrently undermined by false-related triads (especially triads of B flat minor). The Rider, named Faithful and True, is clearly related in Vaughan Williams's mind to Bunyan's Pilgrim; his triple-rhythmed march, like Bunyan's hymn, is energetically corporeal. The primitive organum-triads are Holstian; rhythms cross the metrical beat; scoring is harsh. The jazzy nature of the cross-accents brings the aggressive music into the context of Britain in the post-war twenties, though there is nothing topical and local about the climax in the vision of the Angel, yelled by full chorus in homophonic major triads, in the dorian mode on a very sharp B. The orchestra, however, moans chromatically declining triads over timpani rolls and ostinatos on G and C natural. Again, doubleness is technically bitonality, and leads into the central, climactic section in which doubleness is the essence, for it describes the war between Heaven and Earth, of which the issue is the destruction of the sinful city of Babylon.

An introductory fugato, in an unstable (Holstian) quintuple pulse, seems to be in the phrygian mode on A, the B flats pressing hard on the tonic – though the orchestral pedal is on E flat, a tritone apart from A. The war music is an astonishing inspiration, not so much bi- as tri-tonal: the latter in more than one sense, since the three keys are spiked with chromatically altered intervals, especially tritones. The full chorus howls in chains of falsely related triads, starting from and returning to B major, though the orchestral timpani are still on C and G. When the orchestra lurches into the wailing triads, starting from G minor, the bass alternates between A flat and E flat, in a 'fallen' version of the distant trumpet. The words 'Great Babylon is fallen' are set to a weird howl, dropping from G minor to B minor, then through triads of F sharp minor, G major, F minor, all in first inversion; the fall occurs melodically through a tritone, sounding the more plangent because the bass is bitonally E flat. This wild outcry becomes a refrain that will recur, always on the semi-chorus; here, it evolves into a grave fugato of which the theme is basically pentatonic on G, though the orchestral bass still teeters between A flat and E flat. The repetitions of the refrain are never radically altered, for this despair seems to be no less 'eternal' than the supernatural music of the Distant Choir. Some progressive momentum is hinted at during triple-rhythmed fugato on a rising pentatonic scale, now beginning on E flat; but movement is stilled as the cries of desolation are interrupted by the Distant Choir and its trumpet, still with its original motif, in its original key of A flat, over its original pedal C. The Distant Choir tranquilly congratulates Heaven on its vengeance over sinful man, the sweet serenity of sonority and rhythm being, in context, spine-chilling. Once again, God's 'mysterious way' baffles mere mortals, including (one suspects) Vaughan Williams.

The Angel's hurling of the avenging millstone is recounted in the baritone soloist's narration, in a dorian B minor with the sevenths occasionally sharpened. The orchestra's wailing chromatic triads turn into a recapitulation of the ululations around G, but over an A flat–E flat ostinato in the bass. The 'voice of the bridegroom and bride' (meaning God and his Church) is stilled, petering out in fragmentary pentatonics; the semi-chorus's haunting tritonal refrain ('Babylon is fallen') resounds for the last time, still at the same pitch, over a bitonal pedal. What happens then is one of the most wondrous moments in Vaughan Williams's work. The bass A flat changes enharmonically to G sharp: which serves as a first inversion bass to a solo violin that almost imperceptibly wells from low register through pentatonic convolutions in a paradisal E. This expresses the 'new Heaven and new Earth' of St John's vision, and not even the lark ascending or Elihu's Dance of Youth and Beauty (in *Job*) is a more magical instance of innocence reborn. Only the fact that the bass pedal is in first inversion, not root position, gives the slow ascent a certain vulnerability – which interestingly echoes that of the Distant Choir's alleluyas, to which the pedal note is always in first inversion. It is fascinating to note that the juxtaposition of the G minor 'fall' with E major 'paradise' recapitulates by inversion the famous fall motif in the arioso of *Orfeo*'s Messenger, at precisely the same pitches.

According to Michael Kennedy, this E major passage was adapted from an early, unpublished Whitman setting, so it is New World music not only in the mystical sense of the Book of Revelation, but also in a psychologically topical and local sense. Certainly Whitman's 'free verse' borrowed some of its cadences from the apocalyptic books of the Old Testament, thereby effecting a link between American Whitman and English Blake. For the actual vision of the holy city the key signature is that of a luminous E major, though the sevenths are often flattened and the fourths sometimes sharpened. Imperceptibly, the pedal bass burgeons into a pentatonic melody mirroring the solo violin which now, having reached the heights, becomes a lark ascending. The lydian fourths gently urge the music towards G sharp minor, the pentatonic arabesques being picked out not by violin, but by a more plangent oboe. Lower strings and harp vacillate in $^6_4$ chords unrelated to the oboe's meandering melody, the bitonal texture here resembling that of *Flos Campi*, composed in the same year. So it would seem that the ultimate vision of the New World is a consequence of *di*vision – which, as our discussion in the following chapters of *Job* and the middle symphonies will reveal, is psychologically on the mark.

As the $^6_4$ chords chromatically undulate, the music is multi-tonal, verging on atonality. But vision seems to be healed in the section about the city's self-illumination and its open-gated state. Pulse stabilizes to a slow $^3_4$, modality becomes aeolian on F, with a key signature of four flats that relates it distantly to the Distant Choir. 'Glory and honour' flow in exuberant cross-rhythms; hunger is banished in parallel triads in a lydian A major, also vigorous in cross-accents. But this is only a transitory interruption of the serene incantation around E, and the pentatonic solo violin, now unmistakably an ascending lark, returns when the people of the New City see God – who presumably is not new, except in the sense that in rebirth he needs us, as we need him: a theme shortly to be explored in *Job*. The chorus wavers around its pentatonic ostinato chord, while both the solo violin and the orchestral basses chant in unsullied pentatonic lyricism, the bass at last freed from its function as a static 'earth'. But the free song subsides again into alternating major and minor thirds, dropping from the heights on solo violin, accompanied by alternations of the second inversion E major triad with the augmented fifth on D. From thence the bass falls to its original C: above which the Distant Choir and trumpet again chant their false-related triads undulating around A flat, unchanged because God is changeless.

In the doxology the three choirs sing antiphonally, offering tribute to God who, we hope, has restored us. Although the pulse firms to a dignified march, all the choirs sway in false-related triads, tonality still veering between the mediants E, C and A flat. The ultimate triumph begins in A flat, powerfully scored for brass in organum-style triads, but moves enharmonically back to E, with the C natural re-established as bass. The Distant Choir sings its incantation a final time, now at last without false relation, with A flat major inviolable. Very softly, the opening of the oratorio is recapitulated, 'as it was in the beginning', and a tenor (not baritone) soloist declaims, on E, 'Behold, I come quickly, I am the bright and morning star'. This is perhaps the most marvellous moment in a piece full of marvels. The tenor's elevation to the high A, followed by G sharp and E, may owe its poignancy to its reminiscence of the semichorus's haunting refrain 'Babylon is fallen', during the War in Heaven episode. The morning star promises light to the City: though not yet, for the full chorus's whispered Amens fade into the original embryonic bass rising from C to F natural, supporting the pentatonic ostinato chord, D, E, A. We the people are left waiting, as deep in the bass, the phrygian F hums to silence.

Vaughan Williams said that *Sancta Civitas* was his favourite among his choral works, and the reason is not far to seek. For the piece confronts head-on the issues of private and public responsibility in the modern world, offers no answers, ends on a question mark, and tempers hope with strength. In this, Vaughan Williams's approach to religious and social experience as a necessary duality has much in common with that of William Blake, the third major literary figure to haunt his imagination through many years. Blake, a visual artist as well as poet, lived at the onset of the Industrial Revolution, as did Samuel Palmer, who was profoundly influenced by him, and whose relationship to Vaughan Williams we have discussed. The composer, an admirer of and successor to Palmer and Blake, lived at a time when the dire as well as beneficial effects of industrialization, foreseen by Blake as bard and prophet, seemed inescapable. Vaughan Williams did not advocate escape; he rather showed how, in a world changing with bewildering rapidity, hope may reanimate tradition, while tradition succours hope.

VIII

THE NEW JERUSALEM

VAUGHAN WILLIAMS, BLAKE AND THE BOOK OF JOB: *JOB, A MASQUE FOR DANCING*

Awake, Albion, awake! reclaim thy Reasoning Spectre ...

Terror struck in the Vale, I stood at the immortal sound.
My bones trembled, I fell outstretch'd upon the path
A moment, & my Soul return'd into its mortal state,
To Resurrection and Judgment in the Vegetable Body,
And my sweet Shadow of Delight stood trembling by my side.

Immediately the Lark mounted with a Loud Trill from Felpham's Vale,
And the Wild Thyme from Wimbledon's green impurpled Hills.

WILLIAM BLAKE, Milton

We have seen how, when British music belatedly experienced a renaissance at the turn into the twentieth century, it was pre-eminently associated with a 'double man', Ralph Vaughan Williams, who in spirit came from pre-industrial rural England while being a Londoner, and who was at once a man of religious sensibility and of agnostic social conscience. Nor is it surprising that first among the literary mentors who inspired him should have been Walt Whitman, a poet of the New World who triggered Old English Vaughan Williams in his quest for a reborn self and society. The second of his literary mentors was undeniably English: John Bunyan, preacher, polemicist, author, mystic, tinker and common man, whose prose rode, even more directly than Whitman's free verse, on the rhythms of the Authorized Version; and who lived in the middle of the seventeenth century, racked by division between the old faith and the new, between country and town, absolutism and parliamentary democracy. In Bunyan's case division drove him to a point that we would call lunacy, since his horror of sin and guilt provoked symptoms, both physiological and psychological, that nowadays would have rendered him certifiable. Moreover we find the concept of an Elect – whereby at a conservative estimate only one man in a thousand and one woman in ten thousand (!) will be spared eternal fire and brimstone – at once grotesque and abhorrent. Even so, the positive aspects of Bunyan, so vitally manifest in his prose, have preserved their potency across the centuries; the Bunyan whom Vaughan Williams loved, to a degree even identified with, was the man of God aware of the numinous, and compassionately concerned with the plight of the underdog. Without such awareness and such compassion any New World would have been, for Vaughan Williams, an empty shell.

But although Bunyan is in these ways spiritually so close to Vaughan Williams, a case might be argued that the most psychologically and philosophically crucial of Vaughan Williams's extra-musical mentors was Blake, who was nearer to him in time. The Civil War that Bunyan was moulded by may have been one of the origins of the cleavage between matter and spirit that went to make industrial society; but it was Blake who was alive while the metamorphosis happened, and who wrote of it and visualized it with prophetic insight. There is a further link between Vaughan Williams and Blake in that the poet, painter and visionary had found in the mythology, as well as the imagery and rhythms, of the Authorized Version the main source of his re-creative mythology. In particular the Book of Job offered a vision his own could mirror. Vaughan Williams in turn discovered in Blake's illustrations to Job a marriage of heaven and hell attuned to his own musical pilgrimage. In this context there is no more important 'key work' in Vaughan Williams's career than his large-scale orchestral piece inspired by Blake's illustrations. Although *Job: a Masque for Dancing* is now usually heard in concert conditions, it was conceived theatrically, as a ballet that owed much to seventeenth-century notions of choreographed ritual. What this ritual was about, in its original environment, was intimately related to the divisions in Britain at the time.

Vaughan Williams's masque was composed in 1930 – the idea was suggested to Vaughan Williams by the Blake scholar Geoffrey Keynes – and first produced, in the superb choreography of Ninette de Valois, in 1931, so that it is chronologically a prelude to the Fourth and Fifth Symphonies, the Piano Concerto and *Dona Nobis Pacem*, a group of works that may count as the crown to the composer's achievement. Because *Job* is so critical a work, we must look closely into its extra-musical origins, both in the Book of Job itself, and in Blake's metamorphosis of it.

Among the books of the Bible, Job has always been regarded at once with reverence and bewilderment. In its seventeenth-century translation it is among the supreme achievements of English literature, as poetically potent as it is theologically mysterious. More than any biblical book it tackles the problem of evil head on; deeply disturbing, it is *crucial* to a religion founded on a Cross. After Freud and Jung we are inevitably more self-conscious about it than were our predecessors, though being aware need not distort. In his book *Answer to Job* Jung has written acutely of the matter, seeing Christ as an image of the self in that through him God comes to consciousness. Job's Old Testament God was a God of power, unconscious and therefore amoral, 'beyond good and evil'. When Moses asked God to reveal his name he replied 'I am that I am', and henceforth was known as Yahweh – He who, or that which, is. This evades any concept of ideas, even of being itself. As the philosopher Collingwood puts it, 'pure being would have a subject matter entirely devoid of peculiarities; a subject matter, therefore, containing nothing to differentiate it from anything else, or from nothing at all'. But when Yahweh torments Job merely in order to demonstrate his almightiness, something occurs that has never happened before in the history of the human race: 'the unheard of fact that without knowing it or wanting it a mortal man is raised by his moral behaviour above the stars in heaven'. Job points out that although Yahweh may be 'king of all proud beasts', the beasts are neither blessed nor cursed with consciousness: which leaves Yahweh as no more than a phenomenon, *not a man*. Yahweh is changed through the failure of his attempt to destroy Job. If at the time of creation he revealed himself through Nature, now he wants to be more specific: God becomes man, in a world-shaking transformation of his own nature.

The birth of Christ was attended by the usual phenomena coincident with the birth of a god or hero. His appearance is preceded by an annunciation; he is lowly but miraculously born, of a virgin; he is persecuted, hidden, and flees on a journey through water, forest and cave; struggles with a dragonish or serpentine adversary; is slain on a hill; is reborn after three days, at a time marking the beginning of a new astrological era. When Christ becomes a dying God his divine origin is attested by his association with a dove, the attribute of a love goddess. But he is demythologized in uttering his despairing cry from the Cross, 'My God, my God, why hast thou forsaken me?' In that moment his human nature becomes divine, while God experiences what it means to be a mortal man and to 'drink to the dregs what he has made his servant Job suffer'. If we call everything that God does good, then evil is good too and both become meaningless. But suffering, whether it be Christ's passion or the suffering of the world, remains the same as before. Stupidity, sin, sickness, old age and death continue to form the 'dark foil to the joyful splendour of life'. In this sense Jesus is the *complexio oppositorum* in the human psyche. He is the perfect man who is crucified, crucifixion being 'that acute state of unredeemedness that comes to an end only with the words *Consummatum Est*. Only the complete person can know how unbearable man is to himself, and in psychological terms Christ saved the world because, if the individual does not become conscious of his inner opposite, there is no alternative but for that conflict to be acted out in violence. All opposites are of God; allowing God to take possession of him, Christ becomes a vessel filled with divine conflict'.

So it would seem to be a two-way process. God wants to become man in growing to consciousness; man wants to become God in surrendering Freudian *id* and entering into the true self. Far from its being God's purpose to exempt man from evil and conflict, God's 'oppositeness' is the heart of, and is symbolized by, his Cross. The conflict in his own nature is so violent that the incarnation can be brought only by an expiatory self-sacrifice to God's dark side. There can be no bliss for God alone in his godliness; he has to be born in the human psyche. Jesus is the 'awakener' because in him the opposites, operative in his Passion, become conscious.

Much of the above is paraphrased from Jung's brilliant monograph; it is in some such terms that we nowadays interpret the Book of Job. But more than a hundred and fifty years ago a great British poet and visual artist had arrived at much the same point not by way of a pseudo-science, but through the crucible of his art: for Blake's private mythology transmuted Christianity in terms apposite to the world he lived in, which was the egg from which we emerged. In his mythology – and here we are deeply indebted to the lucid expositions of Northrop Frye – Blake equated the cyclical movements of history with a recurrent cycle within the human mind. Both cycles exist in four stages, forming a quaternity. The first is the revolutionary birth of Orc, the Son, out of Los's energy, Los being broadly the creative principle. He is a Fall too, as is every artefact once it has been made; his name spells Sol backwards, and includes loss within its meanings. The second stage is the transference of this instinctual power from Orc to Urizen, who is pictured as old, armed with ratio, measure and compasses, the 'mind-forged manacles of Reason', which word is contained within his name. During this stage Orc is chained and pinioned, more or less equated with Prometheus on his rock, Christ on his tree, and Adonis as Dying God. In the third stage religion is consolidated as something existing 'out there' in Kant's 'starry heavens', associated with intellectual computation and pre-ordained moral laws. This is symbolized in Urizen's exploring his 'Dens, manufacturing the Nets of Religion'. The word 'manufacture' implies not merely hand-made (the literal meaning), but also the intervention of machinery: the 'dark Satanic mills' that were already forging the industrial world.

To this Blake in part attributes the fourth stage, wherein chaos is upon us, symbolized in the crucifixion of Orc and the hanging of the serpent on the dead tree. The Son and the Serpent ought to be complementary – as they were in much medieval Christian iconography. They are so no longer; and Blake sees his own age – which was that of Beethoven and the beginning of our own – as confronting catastrophe as the fourth stage engulfs it. Locke and Newton he identifies with Urizen, whom he renames Satan, a fallen angel. 'Single Vision and Newton's sleep' substitutes abstraction for reality, mathematical absolutes for human fallibilities: which is comforting only to those who have themselves become early-nineteenth-century Frankenstein's monsters or twentieth-century bionic men. Not surprisingly this stage is characterized by 'scientific technology and complex machinery', by mechanistic wars springing from egoistic tryranny and the cult of Empire, and by unimaginative anti-art – in which Blake includes most representational painting, such as that of Reynolds.

The only way out of the circle is by admission of the *conjunctio oppositorum*, which Blake called the Marriage of Heaven and Hell. He thus spells out what is implicit in the Book of Job: God, becoming conscious, creates Christ; and 'Jesus Christ IS the Human Imagination', through which or whom heavenly and hellish elements may be united. Blake called this *conjunctio* Jerusalem, the city of God that Albion, or (British) mankind, had failed to find only because he had looked in the wrong place. Jerusalem is primarily a state of mind, which in an unfallen world would be Eden, or 'England's green and pleasant land'.

How closely all this is reflected in Vaughan Williams's music, even before he composed *Job* and the sequent symphonies, is evident in the previous chapters of this book. None the less a decisive re-cognition occurred when Vaughan Williams lighted on Blake's illustrations to Job, and the masque stands as the central pillar in his life's work, drawing together threads, providing impetus for new developments. The complex musical structure of the work is directly based on Blake's engravings, which the composer selected with astute if perhaps unconscious sensitivity to their relationships to Blake's 'fourfold vision'.

Despite the piece's theatrical conception, it is scored for a very large orchestra, including a substantial battery of percussion and an organ, as well as instruments, such as saxophones, that were then considered exotics in a symphony orchestra. Although Vaughan Williams, as was his wont, sanctioned omissions and recastings, the ambitious nature of the project suggests that he was aware of its importance in relation to his work as a whole. He begins with Blake's first illustration, depicting calm before storm. Job is sitting with his wife and children in an age of pastoral innocence – an English Eden. Sheep feed peacefully and are fat; the tree in the centre is Job's strongly rooted, prosperous life. On the left a Gothic church spire rises in front of the setting sun, while on the right glimmers a crescent moon. Since in Blake's symbolism the left or sinister side is associated with materiality, the right or dexterous side with spirituality, this would seem to indicate that the sun of Job's life is declining, and the

Church with it, and that his spiritual life is no more than embryonic. Instruments of music are hung up, soundless, on the tree; Job is *reading* to his progeny, from the Letter of the Law.

In Vaughan Williams's music the pastoral age is initially audible in stepwise flowing lines in the dorian mode on G, scored for flutes and strings, partially doubled by harps. The harmony is concordantly triadic, and since the melodies flow across the bar-lines they efface temporality, or seem to. But elements of darkness soon intrude, for all is not what it seems. The dorian G is disrupted by a pentatonic triplet on E, almost identical with the oboe theme at the beginning of *Flos Campi*; and the bitonality is spelt out in the harmony's alternations between G and E minors. Multiple woodwind take up the triplet figure, oscillating between minor and major third. Remotely, the falling triplet, often revolving on a tritone, may be traced back to the 'Fall' motif in the *Fantasia on a Theme of Thomas Tallis*; here its disturbance is momentary, and the music flows back into the scales on harp and strings.

Within this quietude, Job's sons and daughters pastorally dance. The women's music is indeed that of an Arcadian age, for it is purely pentatonic on G, scored for flutes in overlapping dialogue. Even so, Eden is undermined, for the harmonies – or ostinato chords – mysteriously shift between the falsely related mediants of G and E minor; and the men dance to a tune in the dorian mode on B, each crotchet beat of their $\frac{3}{4}$ tempo equalling a dotted crotchet of the women's $\frac{9}{8}$. When the two dances are combined, duality – the cross of sex – is overt. While the dances continue Job 'blesses his children' in a descending chromatic theme on high violins, expanded from the chromatic and tritonal perturbations that had crept into his originally tranquil modality:

Later this theme will reveal how blessing may be a curse and curse a blessing. The episode ends with the wide-flung blessing-curse theme supported by brass and harps in triads in parallel motion – the initial pastoral undulations in augmentation.

Blake's second and fifth illustrations are the spur to the next section, in which angels are clustered to the side of the stage. Among them is Satan, a fallen God; as Blake put it in 1826, 'Men are born with an Angel and a Devil. . . . Every Man has a Devil in himself and the conflict between his Self and God is perpetually carrying on.' Satan's entry is to shattered rhythms, stabbing in major sevenths and minor ninths:

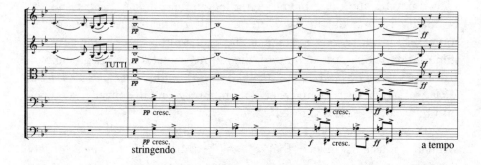

But a chromatic thrust on brass – remarkably similar to a passage in the finale of the Pastoral Symphony – immediately juxtaposes Satan with a vision of God on his throne, his theme grandly unfurling in rising fourths and fifths, moving from (material) left to (spiritual) right. We have commented on these 'instinctually' God-like fourths in many contexts from the Second and Third Symphonies onwards. Here they seem to obliterate Satan's imperfect fourths and fifths, though that there is something odd about this God is indicated by the fact that the major triads at the top of each wave are immediately cancelled by a minor triad. The final chord of this A major vision of God on his throne even incorporates a dissonantly tritonal E flat! This must be why the Sarabande of the Sons of God, though nobly based on rising fourths, has to make several attempts to get on its way. It is relevant to note that its key, A major, was traditionally one of youth and adolescence. God is not yet 'grown up'; in Blake's picture God is up there in the sky, but is in Job's image. 'What is above is Within', as Blake put it; at this stage God as Job images him equals the self. Even in its full statement the sarabande, though harmonized almost exclusively in diatonic concords, presents them in incessant false relation.

Given this falsity, it is inevitable that Satan should step forth – at God's command – to a horrid perversion of the godly rising fourths. God orders

Satan to torment Job in another version of the curse-blessing motif which is linearly as well as metaphorically a Fall. It is less chromatic, though the bass, descending by mediants from C to A to F, ends with a triad in false relation with the melody's aeolian E. The scene ends, massively scored, with a resumption of the sarabande of homage, back in A major but still riddled with false relations. The ceremonial music of a seventeenth-century masque acquires ambiguous grandeur, ending with a resolute, but possibly desperate, unison on the tonic A.

Hope proves illusory, however, in the most extended musical section thus far: which is given to Satan, who prances in a Dance of Triumph. The jagged rhythms and plunging sevenths and ninths to which he had made his entry are transmuted into his theme, aggressive in its wedge-shaped chromatics. God's fourths and fifths are parodied on brass, string tremolandos sizzle like the flames of hell, rythms are inanely repetitive, tonality is unstable or, since the figures are often whole-tone, non-existent. The obsessive self-involvement of the dance is appropriate to Blake's aphorism: 'The Devil is in us, as far as we are Nature.'

Is this thy soft Family-Love,
Thy cruel Patriarchal pride,
Planting thy Family alone,
Destroying all the World beside.

According to Blake, 'the Selfish Virtues of the Natural Heart ... was the Religion of the Pharisees who murdered Jesus'. Job is to learn, through Satan, that 'he who makes his law a curse, By his own law shall surely die'. His dedication to family and property binds him in Urizen's mind-forged manacles, the ravages of which are increasingly evident in industrial society. Blake's wonderful Song of Experience, 'London', which Vaughan Williams was to set in the last year of his life, relates the fate of chimney sweep, soldier and youthful harlot to a Job's patriarchal domination.

Job's error lies in his being trapped in Newton's Single Vision which, cut off from the imagination, corresponds to the 'Analysis of Man into Families and Individuals'. During the ferocious yet idiot march that occurs in the middle section of Satan's dance – scored for heavy brass, blaring out the dotted-rhythmed augmented second – Satan assumes God's mantle, or God is identified with Satan. The devilish disruptiveness of the theme turns into a parody of the plainsong Gloria but ends, more significantly, with a parody of the theme of blessing which is also curse, with Satan's sevenths and ninths incorporated within it. Satan, 'with a big gesture', sits on God's throne:

Both the savagery and the absurdity of this Satanic dance will have repercussions in the later symphonies. Here, for the third scene, we move from supernatural regions back to the real world, only to find that it is curiously unreal. The sons of Job are dancing a minuet with their elegant wives, the minuet being the most genteel of classical baroque dances, favoured by courtly society. When in the prologue the sons had danced with their sisters their pentatonic music had been genuinely Edenic; now, older but not wiser, their music suggests a self-consciously sophisticated, preciously archaic, Arcadianism. The stage direction tells us that the minuet should be 'formal, statuesque and slightly voluptuous': which accurately describes the music, scored for solo woodwind accompanied by harp and cello, with a solo viola serpentinely entwined in an inner part. The voluptuous yet unreal effect springs partly from this scoring, partly from the strangely indeterminate modality, which is melodically dorian on C, though with frequent sharp sevenths and flat seconds:

This tonal no-man's-land sounds oriental, or at least antique, the weirder because the triple-rhythmed harp arpeggios waver bitonally around a triad of E minor. The elegant young things dance in a trance of self-conceit and self-deceit, in their luxurious mansion, as depicted in Blake's illustration. Undulating woodwind enhance the exoticism of the music over pedals on C sharp, until the violin melody crystallizes into a gracefully dancing permutation of the blessing-curse. Far from graceful is its consequence, for the curse suddenly bursts on them in a furious orchestral babel. The sons and their wives fall dead, struck by Satan's thunderbolt – sometimes called an act of God – as depicted in Blake's illustration. This chromatically wailing version of the curse is intensified by duple cross-rhythms against the triple pulse. The scene dissolves in chromatics on the insidious viola, doubled by cor anglais, over a spectral version of the arpeggiated bass. In this scene the viola is an extremely voluptuous instrument but not, as in *Flos Campi*, benignly so.

Blake's sixth engraving is the key to the next scene, Job's Dream. The music at first murmurs in a pentatonic E major, the familiar falling third rising through fourth and fifth. Dreaming in E, Job may be hoping to forget his tribulations in a painless heaven, for the string quavers flow levelly, with never an accidental. Gradually each of the string voices becomes melodic; but that this is only a dream is evident when Satan transmutes dream into uneasy nightmare. Chromatic thrusts speed up the tempo, generating alternating major and minor thirds, the former often notated as diminished fourths. Similar motifs will dominate all the middle symphonies; in *Job* their meaning is spelt out. The destruction of the family is not an end but a prelude to the destruction of the self – which happens as Satan's serpentine chromatics (E, F, E flat, F, E), supported by a marching pizzicato bass, climax in the most violent version thus far of the blessing-curse, strings agilely leaping, brass rampant. This becomes a Ballet of Famine, Pestilence and Battle, whose tramping thirds in march rhythm, oompah basses and aggressive repeated notes will be echoed in the middle symphonies, especially in their scherzi. Whatever their biblical overtones, they belong to our world; the scoring has a virtuosity that might be called Elgarian, though Vaughan Williams's cross-rhythms and whole-tone scales, cackling in parallel thirds, have a more scabrous edge. The vision disappears in another version of the blessing-curse, dissipating on alternating minor thirds G to E, as Job utters the words 'It may be that my children have sinned'. The possibility that the responsibility for famine, pestilence and war, as well as for the death of his children, might be his still does not occur to him.

In the next scene, inspired by Blake's fourth illustration, Job is awakened from his troubled sleep by Three Messengers, who tell him that his material wealth is destroyed. Their woodwind arabesques are chromatic and whole-tone, and therefore mysterious; they may be just neighbours, or they may be messengers from 'beyond'. They introduce a funeral cortège for the dead sons and their wives, the aeolian woodwind melodies being derived from the chromatic version of the blessing-curse, over an unchanging pedal on D, for timpani and basses. The violin melody that intrudes begins with a nobly rising fourth, but embraces voluptuous exoticism in a triplet diminished third. Although death has given the music greater dignity, there is an unreality in the wavering false relations; the cortège, like the minuet, is a show, a playing at death in the same spirit as the minuet played at life. The mysterious arabesques of the Messengers round off the courtège without revealing whether they are malign or benign. They carry us back to Job, who seems to be sleeping peacefully to the pentatonic music of his dream, basically in E major. Only not quite: for the pedal note is not E but C sharp, and the Messengers' false-related triads weave into the tranquilly floating strings.

And at this point the Three Messengers, who may or may not have been from God, are metamorphosed into Three Comforters, who are certainly from Satan. Indeed, they are introduced by Satan's jagged seventh and ninths, in their original disposition; and the 'comfort' they offer is the Messengers' alternating major and minor thirds, now rendered nauseous in being scored for oily E flat saxophone and clarinets, wailing over an oompah bass of unrelated triads:

The psychological insight of this passage is as subtle as that of the minuet. Gradually, the Comforters' chant speeds up from its *andante doloroso*, growing progressively nastier as the rocking thirds reveal their identity with the 'marching bass' in the Ballet of Famine and Pestilence. 'Corporeal friends', said Blake, 'are spiritual enemies'; 'Thy friendship oft has made my heart to ake: Do be my Enemy – for Friendship's sake.' The Comforters are projections of Job's spiritual pride and self-deceit. They get more and more furious until the music breaks off in an abrupt screech, after which the false relations in a retrospect of their original fawning sycophancy sound false indeed! This is the moment of truth: for Job at last 'stands and curses God: "Let the day perish wherein I was born."' The music is the most ferocious and fully scored version of the blessing-curse, with lacerating clashes between the harmonic major thirds and the undulating minor thirds in the bass. This obsessive ostinato will recur throughout the middle symphonies; here it drives the music into a parody of the Dance of the Sons of God in scene 1. The comforters have undermined Job's fortitude by inducing *self*-pity. As Blake says, 'Pity divides the Soul and Man unmans; I have never made friends but by spiritual gifts, by severe contentions of Friendship and the burning Fire of thought.' The ultimate climax of the masque occurs as full orchestra takes up the rising-third-falling-chromatics motif in thunderous organum, reinforced at its utmost fury by 'full organ with solo reeds coupled'. This is a noise of authentic (false-related) terror, whether in concert hall or theatre; as Blake put it, 'In Heaven love begets love; but Fear is the parent of Earthly Love, and he who will not bend to Love must be subdued by Fear'. Heaven is now 'lit up', and the 'beings' in it, lifting their veils, reveal themselves as Satan enthroned, surrounded by the hosts of hell. 'All Love is lost! Terror succeeds and Hatred instead of Love and stern demands of Right and Duty, instead of Liberty.'

As the horrific vision fades God's motif of rising fourth, fifth and octave rings on muted brass, through the shuddering of tremolando strings; an admision that, in Blake's words,

... however loving

And merciful the Individuality; however high
Our palaces and cities, and however fruitful are our fields,
In Selfhood we are nothing. ...

Job, considering himself faultless, is accused of iniquitous fault and falsehood both as regards himself and his God. God's presumed injustice is man's individualized right, or rather self-righteousness. So Blake and Vaughan Williams have borne us from the Single Vision of Newtonian analysis and of the patriarchal family and 'Individualized Man' through the Twofold Vision which recognizes corporeal and spiritual dimensions, while still splitting the soul into conflict. In the next stage Threefold

Vision reveals how Satan and God, if opposites, are necessary comple-
ments. Imagination, represented by Elihu, transforms reason into glory.

Vaughan Williams's impetus for the marvellous seventh scene is Blake's
fourteenth illustration, depicting Elihu's Dance of Youth and Beauty. He
comes to speak *as a human being* ('I also am formed out of the Clay') who
is also God's representative – a human-angelic messenger who wants to
'withdraw Man from his [corporeal] purpose and hide Pride from Man'.
We are not surprised that his music should be entrusted to a solo violin, at
first consistently pentatonic, opening with God's gesture of rising fourth,
fifth and octave (A, D, E, A). That the pentatonicism is rooted on D rather
than paradisal E, as was Job's unreal dream, relates Elihu's youth and
beauty to Nature's lark, who ascended skywards from the (D-founded)
earth. It is to the point that D major (rather than E) seems to be Vaughan
Williams's ultimate tonal 'positive' – as we have observed in several
instances such as the wondrous coda to *Flos Campi*, while the most sublime
D major epilogue, that to the Fifth Symphony, is still to come. We cannot
know how far Vaughan Williams was aware of the correspondence
between his musical symbolism and Blake's mythology, but it would seem
that he shared Blake's trust in the *human* Imagination, which is all we can
know of God. This becomes the more deeply evident when Elihu's violin
cantillation, at first unaccompanied, is supported by sustained triads on
strings, shifting between B minor and D major, C major and E flat major.
The wider the violin-lark spreads his wings, the more he absorbs elements
of contradiction, even pain, as happens in similar passages in *Flos Campi*
and *Sancta Civitas*. The violin cantilena itself, flowing through quavers,
triplets and semiquavers, embraces tritones and alternating major-minor
thirds without surrendering its seraphic grace. Briefly, the melody attains
four sharps, though with a C sharp rather than E bass; but as the sustained
string chords shift stepwise, the melody returns to a pentatonic compromise between D major and B minor, to which the strings are in increasingly
painful false relation. Elihu has initiated spiritual regeneration: which is
acted out in a Dance in Heaven.

The Sons of the Morning, whose Pavane is now danced, are the reborn
Sons of God who, early in the masque, had danced a sarabande. It is
pertinent to recall that the sarabande was the most solemn, even sacral, of
Renaissance court dances, while the pavane, which initiated the masque,
was the most potently human, in that to its stately measure the king and
nobility made their ceremonial entry. Blake's fourteenth illustration is the
trigger to Vaughan Williams's duple-rhythmed dance, which begins in
blessed G major, modulates by mediants, and incorporates on high strings
permutations of the blessing-curse theme, now more blessed than cursed,

animating the dancers to greater sprightliness. Kinship with seventeenth-century dance music is apparent both in the rhythmic openness and in the shifting modalities; the final modally inflected cadence is very grand. Into this positive exuberance Satan bursts, as he had done into the sarabande, with his jagged theme. This time, however, the Sons of Morning are able – since regeneration has happened within the psyche – to expel Satan, as depicted in the sixteenth illustration. They do so in a galliard, a faster, triple-rhythmed dance conventionally paired with the pavane. The key has risen a fifth from G to D and the tune swings in an earthy D major lilt that sounds like a mature, grown-up version of the tune the children had danced to at the beginning. It opens with the same rising third, now major not minor, and is consistently diatonic, though the seventh degree of the scale is evaded, so we cannot know whether it would be sharp or flat. Significantly, the danced song sounds like a sturdy Bunyanesque hymn, thereby making another seventeenth-century equation between spirit and flesh. Man's fulfilment, which is also God's, seems to be in his humanity. God's fourths appear in the texture of the galliard, but inverted and therefore in the descent, as the Sons of the Morning drive Satan 'down' where he belongs. Except that, in so far as he is really part of us, up and down, high and low, even good and evil, are meaningless terms. Without need of words, Vaughan Williams's music again mirrors Blake: 'Forgiveness of Sin is only at the Judgment Seat of Jesus the Saviour, where the accuser is cast out': as he must be when the opposites become one.

For although 'It indeed appeared to Reason as if Desire was cast out, ... the Devil's account is, that the Messiah fell, and formed a Heaven of what he stole from the Abyss.' The affinity between Blake's Satan and Milton's in *Paradise Lost* is obvious, and both have qualities in common with Milton's Comus as villain-hero. By way of Satan, Job discovers that his self-righteousness was worship of selfhood and that the Anti-Christ is a purging power leading, through the bitterness of experience, to beatitude: in Blake's startling words, 'Come Lord Jesus take on thee the Satanic Body of Holiness'. This happens in Vaughan Williams's music when the masque concludes with a return to the original dorian G of the opening: in which mode 'Young Men and Women' dance an altar dance. The pastoral rhythm and the melodic shape are derived from the initial dance, though the metre is more formalized, in $\frac{6}{8}$ instead of $\frac{9}{8}$. Strings sustain a double pedal on a godly open fourth, until the earthly altar dance is joined by a Heavenly Dance of the Sons of the Morning, including, one presumes, Job's dead children. The heavenly dance is a restatement, more fully scored, of the benedictory G major pavane, and the combined dances on earth and in heaven generate, as well they might, a wondrous sense of liberation. Mediant modulations through G, E, D flat (C sharp), B flat, and G induce *ecstasis*, strings and flutes assaying the heavens in a thrilling expansion of the tune, rising through major third, fourth and fifth.

But it is typical of Vaughan Williams, as of Blake, that he does not offer a final apotheosis. At the climax of the ecstasy, we hear again the simultaneous sounding of false-related triads in which the sarabande had culminated, now a tone lower, on G instead of A. In the change of pitch God has, as it were, 'grown up' from adolescent A major, precisely as Jung (and Blake) have said that he must in recognizing that our dependence on him is identical with his dependence on us. The bitonal telescoping of triads of G major and E flat major here is identical with the motif that had launched the allegro of the London Symphony on its course, and the introduction to that allegro had, we may recall, sprung from the rising fourth to fifth to octave which in *Job* is a synonym for the breath of life, or God. The end of the masque proper is unison Gs on all the woodwind and brass, balancing the unison As that had concluded the sarabande.

The unison Gs hint that all Nature may dance as *one man* – what Blake called the Universal Family:

> ... and that One Man
> We call Jesus the Christ: and he in us, and we in him,
> Live in perfect harmony in Eden the Land of Life. ...

That is a prophecy of what might be, not of what is: as is clear when we move into the epilogue, taking us back to the opening of the masque. Job is restored, old but humbled; his wife is still with him, but not of course his slain children. In Blake's picture there is now no God made in Job's image, up in the sky; and he receives gifts from those who love him, whereas his original distribution of largesse had been part of his pride. The music is the same as that of the opening scene, in stepwise flowing quavers in dorian G, occasionally pierced by bitonal pentatonic arabesques on E, usually on woodwind or horns. Everyone, in Blake's twenty-first illustration, is *playing* the instruments that had hung mute on the tree. So this is, and is not, an eternal return; in Blake's terms, it is Essence rather than Identity, and we can now say that what is above is within, at the same time as what is within is above. Heaven is a state wherein each retains his or her identity not by virtue of its preciousness to him- or herself but because it is loved by others, while their identities (essences) are preserved from dissolution by our (and others) love for them: 'This is Jerusalem in every Man, A Tent and Tabernacle of Mutual Forgiveness.'

At the end the strings' cantilena turns into the (diatonic) blessing without the (chromatic) curse, for it has no serpentine tail. Yet Blake's cosmology (and it would seem Vaughan Williams's also) does not accept that such blessedness can be more than momentary, since only the doubleness of Satan can make it possible. The end of Vaughan Williams's *Job*, whether consciously or unconsciously, is in tune with this, for the final chord, unexpectedly, is not a modal G minor, or even a G major tierce de Picardie, but B flat major, G minor's relative. The effect, in the context of the whole work, is oddly unresolved; and there may be point in the fact that B flat major, in the seventeenth and eighteenth centuries, was a 'flat' key of the earth, at first pastorally Arcadian, but later – especially in Beethoven – a key of human power and will. However unconsciously Vaughan Williams's aural imagination functioned, it is characteristic that he leaves us on earth, since the Fourfold Vision, in which the opposites no longer exist, *is* a vision, apprehensible only in brief moments outside time.

The process is millennial. Man, by projecting himself into the world of Nature, discovers the infinite in everything and thus begets God. But from this world of Nature is born Jesus who, projecting himself into the individual, begets the true man in him. Then man again creates God, in the whirlwind; and so on, as it was in the beginning, is now and ever shall be, world without end. Vaughan Williams, a staunch traditionalist, mistrusted mythologies which, like Blake's, had to be invented. Even so, it is clear that the mythology latent in his music is extraordinarily close to Blake's; one might even say that Vaughan Williams, as a Christian agnostic, had no choice but to invent a faith. The evidence is audible in the sequence of symphonies that followed in the wake of *Job*. Though they are not theatrical music, they have a psychological programme in the same sense as do the symphonies of Mahler or Shostakovich, perhaps even of Beethoven himself.

IX

THE WAGES OF WAR

THE DOUBLE MAN IN THE PIANO CONCERTO AND
THE FOURTH SYMPHONY

But this is perfect. The other officers have heard the heavy guns and perhaps I shall. They make perfect cider in this valley: still, like them. There are clouds of dust along the reeds, and in the leaves: but the dust here is native and pure, not like the dust of Aldershot, gritted and fouled by motors and thousands of feet. 'Tis a very limbo lake: set between the tireless railways behind and twenty miles in front the fighting. Drink its cyder and paddle in its rushy streams: and see if you care whether you die tomorrow.

CHARLES HAMILTON SORLEY, letter to a friend, 1915

The middle symphonies are, we have said, a sequel to Vaughan Williams's central testament which, in collusion with William Blake, comes closest of any of his works to defining what his music is 'about'. The Piano Concerto in C, which the composer wrote in 1931, immediately after *Job*, effects a link between that work and the Fourth Symphony, begun around the same time, finished in 1934. The Piano Concerto is not often performed and early acquired a reputation as an odd example of the genre. So it is; no one would associate Vaughan Williams with virtuoso pianism in nineteenth-century romantic tradition, nor is that what he offers. He said that his piano-writing in the Concerto was founded on Busoni's piano arrangements of Bach: which is a key not only to his treatment of the piano, but to a part of his music's imaginative heart. Bach had always been important to Vaughan Williams, originally perhaps as a legacy from Parry's reverence for Bach, but eventually because Vaughan Williams recognized in him an artist whose faith was unperturbed by dubiety – a man as single as he himself was double. Bach's faith is expressed in the unbroken span of his melodic lines, the continuity of his motor rhythms, the consistency of his figurations, the pulse that is steady as the beat of a sanguine heart.

Vaughan Williams paid tribute to Bach practically, in his non-authentic but deeply moving performances of the major choral works at Dorking. Occasionally he consciously emulated Bach's techniques in his own music, admitting to it in the title of his *Concerto Accademico* for solo violin and string orchestra, written in the mid-twenties. Later, Vaughan Williams deplored the title, which he had come to think unnecessarily circumscribing, for the piece is not classical baroque pastiche. Even so, in an era wherein neo-classicism was current and indeed fashionable, the title made its point: the first movement's lines are Bach-like in being unbroken in span and consistent in figuration, while fusing classical diatonicism with the modal source-phrases and motivic transformations of folk song. There are even hints of 'white-note' Stravinsky; no more than the Russian does Vaughan Williams stress the dramatic potential of symphonic argument, though the bitonal arabesques towards the end make for a climax. The beautiful slow movement, with its Ravel-like processions of $^6_3$ chords, is more ritualistic than dramatic; while the finale moves from art-music into fiesta, since the continuous 'present' of a folk-fiddle reel merges into the timelessness of Bach. Towards the end, revel hints at frenzy, and the coda is oddly inconclusive, almost a fade-out, since a double man could hardly attain Bach's affirmation or the folk's simplicity. How much he might do in this direction became evident five years later, in the Piano Concerto in C.

The first movement, under the baroque title of Toccata, is not a sonata allegro, though it flirts with both sonata and rondo. It opens exuberantly, Bachian in its motor rhythm and in its consistent, mainly white-note, figuration in $^6_8$. The theme, thunderous in the piano's bass, consists of a rising pentatonic scale from the low C, capped by another pentatonic scale rising from B flat; it is therefore built from interlocking fourths:

But if the Concerto begins thus positively, its pounding rhythms and cross-accents grow somewhat minatory, so that both the deep triadic writing for piano and the soaring string melodies tend to be frustrated. And the toccata's impetus is dammed by a *senza misura* passage for solo piano, wherein the ghostly presence of Busoni himself joins that of Bach. For the glassy texture resembles that which Busoni cultivated in works like the *Sonatina Seconda*, in the wilder reaches of his excursus around Bach's *Art of Fugue* in his *Fantasia Contrappuntistica*, and in his unfinished opera *Dr Faustus*. The necromantic flavour of late Busoni is technically manifest in a bitonality and an obsession with major-minor ambiguity such as we have traced throughout the music of Vaughan Williams; and the parallel must be experiential as well as technical. For if Vaughan Williams was a double man in his insular condition, Busoni was such in his cosmopolitan context. Vaughan Williams knew what home was, however it might have been threatened, both religiously and humanely, by a rapidly changing world. Busoni, a citizen of Europe, might almost be called homeless, being Italian by birth, German by training, global in his itinerant profession as a concert pianist. His doubleness was between Italy and Germany, between tradition and innovation, between a career as a virtuoso and a life as a composer. How far Vaughan Williams recognized this kinship is unclear.

The slow movement, called Romanza, evolves from the piano's solo interlude, as solo flute steals into the keyboard's mysterious arpeggios. There are three closely related themes all beginning with repeated notes: as though a human voice were trying to speak through the bitonal arabesques with which the piano garlands the diatonic melodies. The goal of the modality seems to be a cross between dorian E and G major, such as is often a synonym for beatitude in Vaughan Williams's music, as it is in that of Ravel. Here there is another link with the secret garden of Ravel's *L'Enfant et les Sortilèges*, remembering that the literal meaning of the word paradise is an enclosed park. But Vaughan Williams's bitonality is more dangerous, offering harbingers too of the slow movement of Tippett's Piano Concerto, closely related to his magic opera *The Midsummer Marriage*; and perhaps even of the Magic Wood in Britten's *A Midsummer Night's Dream*, and of the spooky nocturnal garden in *The Turn of the Screw*. In any case, the luxuriant magic of *Flos Campi* has acquired a more elusive savour, creating a sound-world beyond the horizon, marvellous in orchestral and pianistic resource. The winding oboe solo, leading into string polyphony in visionary extension of the repeated note theme, is surely one of Vaughan Williams's strangest and most moving inspirations. Towards the end, the piano's glassy treble line is poised above viscid chords low in the bass, and leads into a thrilling climax based on alternating minor and major thirds: a Fall from the romanza's presumptive paradise identical with that of Vaughan Williams's fallen angels in *Job* and elsewhere. Here the grumpy chords and the scintillating treble are themselves an image of doubleness: which generates, without break, the theme of a Fuga Chromatica:

This, in turn but surprisingly, will be metamorphosed into a Danza alla tedesca.

Does late Beethoven, especially his B flat Quartet opus 130, join Bach and Busoni not as an influence, but as another ghostly presence? We are tempted to such a speculation because at this moment the Piano Concerto's relation to the immediately sequent Fourth Symphony becomes explicit. Up to this point most of the features in the Concerto that are to be developed in the Symphony have been present in *Job* also; the Fuga Chromatica, however, directly anticipates the epilogo fugato to the Fourth. The Concerto's tightly chromatic fugal subject has grown from the romanza's cantilena of descending minor and major thirds; with that romantic vision dissipated, the motif is spiky and screwed-up. Contrapuntal devices of stretto, augmentation, diminution and inversion are used, as they will be in the Symphony, to build dramatic intensity, the piano texture being steely, tough, modern, as compared with the bitonal insecurity and impressionistic haze of the slow movement. This harsh chromatic fugue explodes into a piano cadenza, very Bach-Busoni-like in idiom. Thick-textured, it turns the fugue subject upside-down so that, pushing upwards instead of falling, it metamorphoses the theme into an improbable German waltz. After the constriction of the fugue, the waltz is expansive, though this is far from a triumphant apotheosis. It rather generates hysteria, perhaps related – like Ravel's scary parody of a Viennese waltz in the symphonic poem *La Valse* – to Europe's post- and pre-war ravagement. Indeed it is almost a Mephisto waltz, recalling those of Liszt, again by way of Busoni who as innovative pianist-composer was Liszt's successor. Although an analogy between Vaughan Williams, Mephisto and Faust – or for that matter between Vaughan Williams and Liszt – seems unlikely, we must remember that his Satan, in *Job*, is a fallen angel of Faustian propensities.

In the twenties original, the Piano Concerto ended with the German waltz. But Vaughan Williams decided, surely correctly, that this was not a satisfactory conclusion; and twenty years later, in 1946, appended a coda more adequate to the concerto's emotional complexity. This coda begins in a mysterious, disturbingly tranquil, bitonality, from which it moves into a long piano solo in 'white' C major, slowly processional in rhythm. It might even be mistaken for the 'white-note' piano music Stravinsky was creating during the twenties, as it annihilates time in telescoping tonics, dominants and subdominants. The conventional norms of progression in European music, elided, paradoxically create an ineffable calm: which is another, and different, instance of Vaughan Williams's 'transcendence'. Embracing the whole range of Vaughan Williams's experience thus far, the Concerto glimpses new worlds that might be born of destruction and decay.

The Piano Concerto now sounds like one of its composer's greatest works, and the magnificent recording made in 1984 by Howard Shelley and Vernon Handley has done something to rehabilitate it. Of course, coming at a crucial point in the composer's creative life, it *was* problematical; Vaughan Williams, uneasy in any case about the musicality of the grand piano, had doubts about the piece, some of which he belatedly resolved in the masterly 1946 coda. He also seems to have thought, and was encouraged to think, that there were problems of balance between piano and orchestra, which he attempted to solve in a version for two pianos, still occasionally heard. Shelley's recording, however, has proved that this problem was illusory: the element of contest between soloist and tutti is in this concerto even more significant than it is in most piano concertos of the last two centuries. Projecting conflict outwards into rival forces may be a peculiarly violent form of doubleness – which Vaughan Williams needed to go through before he could objectify strife in a pair of symphonies which are polar opposites yet at the same time complementary.

Vaughan Williams had embarked on sketches for a fourth symphony alongside both *Job* and the Piano Concerto, so the commonly canvassed notion that when the Symphony was first heard in 1934 it contradicted the tenor of all his previous work is without foundation. The Concerto leads directly to the Fourth Symphony, to which it transmits, from *Job*, intimations of the philosophical and psychological interdependence of God and Satan, now incarnate in a purely musical argument. The relation of the Fourth Symphony to *Job* is as intimate as is the relation of the Fifth Symphony to *The Pilgrim's Progress*. Both symphonies are realized with an economy less likely to typify a 'masque for dancing' or an 'operatic morality'.

Formally, the Fourth is a fairly strict classical symphony in the usual four movements; and it is the most tightly constructed of his works because it is emotionally the most disruptive. In the first place, it is traditional in that its key is F minor which, as we have noted, in the baroque age was the tonality of *chants lugubres*, of darkness, death and the infernal regions. In the second place, the Symphony is traditional in being a post-Beethovenian conflict symphony in which the first three movements tell us that we must, as Henry James put it, 'in the destructive element immerse', while the finale affords, if not resolution, at least a potentially Beethovenian apotheosis. The end is not positive; but it indicates how, through rigorous control, even so ferocious a tumult may be withstood. The basic paradox is that the two cells or motto themes from which all the material of the four movements is derived are both, in terms of orthodox classical tonality, disintegrative. The first is a chromatic figure that eats its own tail: F, E, G flat, F – almost but not quite the Bach motif. The other is a succession of open fourths, bounding up from F. Although one constricts, the other liberates, both were destructive forces in European tonality. Advanced chromaticism undermined both sixteenth-century modality (consider Gesualdo) and eighteenth-century tonality based on the cycle of fifths (consider Wagner and Schoenberg); while the fourth (although, with its inversion the fifth, the most acoustically perfect of intervals) has always worked against the clever contrivances of post-Renaissance man's functional harmony. Parallel fourths and fifths were, and still are, forbidden in academic textbooks because they obviate progressive harmony; the notorious piled-up fourths in Schoenberg's early Chamber Symphony were hardly less potent than his extreme chromaticism in subverting tonal orthodoxy. Not much later, the neo-medievalist Holst was revelling in those parallel fourths and fifths that were the bane of academicism. Given God's 'otherness', it may make sense that his acoustically perfect intervals should undermine man's temporary, temporal-harmonic pursuits. In this matter Vaughan Williams was less extreme than Holst, though we have seen that melodic fourths dominate much of his music, reaching an apex in this Fourth Symphony.

The ferocity of the piece inevitably encouraged reponse in programmatic terms, the most common interpretation being that the Symphony is a prophecy of the Second World War. Vaughan Williams denied any such naïve literalism, though the fact that the Symphony was composed alongside *Dona Nobis Pacem*, the text of which explicitly concerns war, suggests that it was a product of the decade's turbulence. It could not have been otherwise, for Vaughan Williams could not regard the battleground of his art as separable from the outside world. No less than the Cantata, the Symphony is an appeal, if not for peace (that comes in the Fifth), then at least for the renunciation of war – in a psychological rather than material sense. Certainly war's horror is incarnate in the first bar, in which the familiar semitonic descent is screeched out in double *forte* by full orchestra, the D flat being harmonized, or rather disharmonized, with its resolution C – the starkest possible form of dissonant appoggiatura. Lower voices imitate the appoggiatura, which is then screwed up by diminution and double diminution. Tonal moorings are sundered by the chromatics, and the rising pitch and the progressively shorter note-durations (intensified by squeaking piccolo) make for mounting frenzy. This is the initial statement of the first (chromatic, tail-eating) cell:

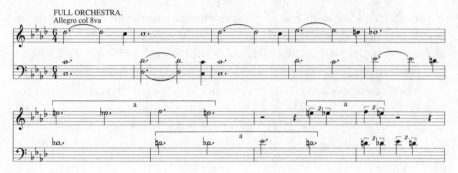

The upward surge results in a painfully syncopated chromatic scale, which explodes in rising fourths on the brass – the second motto. By this time it has registered that the plunging appoggiatura and the rising chromatics are derived from, or related to, Satan's theme in *Job*, while the open fourths are the motif associated with Job's God who, we remember, is also Satan, and vice versa. The fourths when syncopated are close to Satan's Dance of Triumph; at the repeat of the plunging appoggiatura, now on the tonic F minor instead of its dominant, the leaps vastly expand Satan's original theme. Vaughan Williams calls for chromatic timpani to emphasize the devilishness of tritones; and climaxes in snarling repetitions of the chromatic figure that nags around itself with ever-increasing venom, driven by the bounding fourths. It ends in that ultimate fingerprint, major and minor thirds in frenetic alternation.

At this point the key signature of four flat is abandoned and the pulse changes from $\frac{6}{4}$ two beats a bar to $\frac{3}{2}$ with three beats, each of which equals the duple pulse of the opening; so the tempo is proportionally slower, though still remorseless. Brass and woodwind blare repeated note chords in syncopation, while the strings in octave unison initiate a palpable second subject: long, sweeping, irresistible in momentum as, oblivious of bar-lines, it springs as well as sings:

The range of the melody is vast and so rhythmically flexible that, if its effect is positive compared with the nagging first subject, it is still distraught. The tonality is obscure, though it has attributes of lydian B flat, and the string basses and brass chords have a B-flattish flavour. A flats typically interlace with the A naturals; when four flats return to the key signature, the natural is still as frequent as the flat third. The bounding, physical dance-song tries to gravitate towards F major, especially when it is taken over by string basses and bassoons, intrepid throughout its writhings and cavortings. Canonic counterpoints gird the texture, massively scored, imposing order on chaos: until the theme, in what may be the aeolian mode on F *sharp*, is chanted more broadly, with a motif of hammering syncopations on brass. The figure, though based on stabilizing repeated notes, preserves a serpentine wriggle in its tail, and generates serpentine modulations. This may count as a classical codetta theme, fusing some of the features of both first and second subjects. It ends with savage reiterations of descending thirds and tritones: from which the blessing-curse motif from *Job* is not far distant.

The development begins, classically enough, with a return to the first subject's anguished appoggiatura, plunging from E flat through D to A. Speed quickens with a sudden *pianissimo*; bassoons and cellos extend the chromatic wriggle through tremolando lower strings, while the violins transmute God's fourths into rocking undulations that will have weird consequences later on in the Symphony. The quiet dynamics last only a moment before the rising scale motif of the exposition induces a vast crescendo and a return to the lurching chromatic motif, back in $\frac{6}{4}$, close to Satan's Dance of Triumph. The climax of the development is the upward-bounding fourths on brass – one of the mottoes of this symphony, here in a form almost identical to the music to which, in the stage directions to *Job*, Satan 'assumes God's mantle.'

With a return to the original four flats, the recapitulation is upon us. The first motif of appoggiatura and wriggling chromatics is curtailed, but the lyrical, if energetic, second subject proves even more irresistible in momentum. The wide-flung bass line at once sings and dances, dominated by a figure (A, B, C, E flat, D, C) that involves both rising and falling minor third, and a tritone. This part of the recapitualtion is also telescoped, suddenly collapsing into a coda centred around D flat major, passive flat submediant in relation to F minor, though that key has never been clearly defined. The bass line teeters between God's perfect fourth and the Devil's tritone, until the violins float con sordino from the heights in a permutation of Job's curse that is also a blessing. The tonality is inched up from D flat to D natural, perhaps in a fleeting glimpse of the 'wholeness' that D major so often represents in Vaughan Williams's music. But the ambivalent tonality settles on a D *flat* major triad, over a cavernous D flat pedal, above which the strings' major and minor thirds clash in piquant false relation. The effect of this coda, in the context of the movement's turmoil, is both moving and mysterious, since D flat major is experienced not as resolution, but as a glimpse over the horizon, as illusory as a dream. There is a parallel with Schubert's dreamy flat submediants, which are, of course, less violent in the context of classical tonality.

The slow movement is not very slow but rather a forlornly meandering march. It demonstrates the almost fanatically close-knit textures of the Symphony in that its themes, though indigenous to it, are all permutations of motifs from the first movement (including the two mottoes) and from *Job*. The key signature is again four flats, and we begin with an introductory motif of the open fourths, on muted brass. The andante theme itself, however, moves over a padding pizzicato bass beginning in the aeolian mode on F, the main theme being on first violins in what would be lydian F (with sharp third and fourth), were not the sevenths usually flat. This theme, moving by step, shares the constriction of the first cell, for it undulates around a nodal point of A natural, and does not modulate when an answering voice in fugato enters on D flat. The bass shifts as the part-writing is chromaticized until solo oboe extends the tune into chromatically rocking fourths – already hinted at in the development of the first movement. Texture grows increasingly polyphonic as tonality weakens; the 'nagging' figures expand in uneasy lyricism. Climax occurs in alternating minor and major sixths and in the fourths, now chromaticized and reflecting oddly on God's perfect fourths chanted by brass. When the turmoil subsides, solo flute sings something very close to Job's blessing-curse:

This becomes a trigger for fugal evolution, the slow march pulse providing continuity through near-atonal vagaries.

At the return to an F minor signature the padding bass itself becomes a triple *forte* theme, which disolves into permutations of the fugato. With a brief change of key signature to two sharps, solo oboe tries to create from the interlacing polyphonies a level, crotchet-pulsed song in the aeolian mode on B. The attempt dissipates, however, into the chromatically rocking fourths and into a stretched-out version of the blessing-curse. The key signature changes to that of F major as the original theme is sung in free canon on the strings, while the blessing-curse floats down on solo flute. But the canons shift from major to minor, and the movement ends with a cadenza on solo flute which turns into the alternating thirds in slow descent, over minor triads on muted brass. Although the strings, also muted, slide in with a triple-*piano* chord of F major, the flute's cadenza attempts to come to earth through the descent A flat, G, E, with the A flat serving as both diminished fourth to the E and as enharmonically identical with G sharp. The unresolved E natural was an afterthought; in the original version – as is audible in the composer's magnificent 1937 recording – the final note was F.

This strange movement thus ends where it began, in limbo: from which the scherzo leaps like a dog shaking itself after dreamful slumber. The leaping, once more, is in the guise of the 'motto' fourths, and there is nothing godly about these prancings in a syncopated $\frac{6}{8}$. The first (chromatic) cell immediately follows the fourths, on muted but *fortissimo* brass, and is twice repeated in diminution. Woodwind impudently interject the syncopated fourths into the strings' chattering until momentum explodes in a whirlwind of semiquavers, punctured by the fourths on brass. Any suggestion of buccaneering jollity in this is obliterated by the stabbing dislocations of metre in the next section, which returns to the nagging chromatics of the first movement:

Solo trumpet and horn pick out a motif of rising fourth, softly but perkily: which to a degree heals the dislocations, carrying the music into a jig-like dance. But jigging turns into gibbering, punctured by the two cells, in sundry metrical permutations. The scherzo is then repeated da capo but in shortened form, its various segments telescoped with an effect at once vivacious and bizarre.

The trio is a simpler matter, as trios often are, being bucolic, if not exactly beer-garden music like so many trios of the Viennese classics. Its tempo is a straight $\frac{3}{4}$, the modality pentatonic E flat, the theme being based on the rising fourths, now recognizably a tune, not just a gesture. That the tune is introduced by solo tuba defines its character, though extensions of it on flute and oboe have the grace as well as vigour of the old agrarian world. The brass canonically reconvert grace into brash energy and so lead to a da capo of the scherzo, still more toughly curtailed. The rising fourths, canonically generated from the tune, turn into something close to Satan's motto of plunging major seventh and minor ninth; and lead into a coda that proves to be a link to the finale, built over a 'revolving cam' that recalls the famous transition between the third and fourth movements of Beethoven's Fifth. The dislocated nagging of the ostinato is on G sharp and A; the leaping fourths are on bassoon; clarinets and violas lurch in the chromatic cell: until with an immense crescendo the scherzo becomes the finale which, opening *fortissimo* in F major and in a martial duple time, is in sonata form and as much a 'conflict' piece as the first allegro.

Though its fast, forward-thrusting march seems to resolve positively the meandering march of the slow movement, ambiguity is evident even in the opening bars, for the falling third from A to F is harmonized in falsely related triads, and the continuing descent of the tune turns into the pattern of alternating thirds:

The metrical basis, driven by unrelated concords in oompah rhythm, is assertive, even cheerily so; but the music-hall energy grows more exacerbated in the second part of the first subject, since its sustained semibreves are capped by a lydian descent from C to B natural. As the scoring becomes denser, a theme defines itself, the contours of which – F, G flat, D flat, C, G flat F – betray their origins in the Symphony's very first bars. When the first half of the tune recurs, it explodes in cascades of quavers in alternating major and minor thirds, with lydian B naturals counteracting the flatness.

A second subject begins in B flat, the subdominant, not dominant; again lydian fourths are prominent. The tune itself has a brash swagger, its fourths tootling and footling, so that the jollity is suspect. Still, so much energy is life-enhancing, especially when rhythm shifts to a thrusting $\frac{6}{4}$ for a codetta motif on brass. Returning to $\frac{2}{2}$, a wild development section ensues, densely scored. The texture is riddled with alternating thirds in a tornado which not even the tuba's ponderously rising fourths can quell. The second phase of the tune, with its repeated semibreves and semitonic descent, is gradually dampened by timpani beats, while the oompahs grow more chromatically unstable. The motif derived from the first movement's cataclysm now appears a semitone higher (F sharp, G, D, C sharp G), on muted strings; and serves as a transition to a brief but deeply affecting slow interlude, distantly recalling the repeated note theme of the first movement. There, it had been bellicose; now it softly sings in triads rocking in piercing false relation, over an ostinato bass in which the fourths fall instead of rise. Their C, B flat, F, C matrix is in bitonal relationship with the upper strings, which distantly hint at the human fulfilment of D major. Gradually, with a return to the four-flat key signature, the two cells of chromatic wriggle and rising fourths reinvade the texture, sweeping into a sonata recapitulation. This follows classical precedent in that all the material of the exposition reappears with appropriate modifications of tonality and pitch, but it does not culminate in sonata-style resolution.

Instead, we are left with nagging alternations of major and minor thirds divided between high and low sections of the orchestra, leading into an Epilogo Fugato – closely related, as noted, to the fugue in the finale of the Piano Concerto. The seminal sources of the Symphony, enunciated in its first bars, are combined in a double fugue on the two cells: the doubleness of Satan's 'closed' chromatics and God's 'open' fourths, remembering that in Blake's mythology God and Satan mirror one another. No sonata resolution could be adequate to such a savage contradiction, which may be controlled only by the steely discipline of fugal unity, imposed by the will. The forces that prompted this fugal epilogue are thus comparable with those that impelled Beethoven to conclude the Hammerklavier Sonata with a fugue to end all fugues, though this is not to elevate Vaughan Williams to Beethoven's transcendent heights. The difference is that whereas Beethoven's fugue is vast and multifarious, Vaughan Williams's is brief and single-, even simple-minded in its wilfulness. Its juggling with the cells in various metrical permutations – augmentations, diminutions, stretti, cross-rhythms – becomes a somewhat hysterical game in which the duality of closed chromatics and open fourths desperately seeks identity. Fugal unity fails; it cannot engulf, or gobble up, the contradictions. True, we experience an elevation of spirits when the 'jolly' second subject of the allegro finale bounces (in D major, too) above a close stretto of the chromatic motto. But screaming trills and hammering tritones carry us back to the finale's first subject, combined with the chromatic cell in ever more frenetic diminutions, whence we move, by way of cascading major-minor thirds, to a final recapitulation of the *first* movement's satanic opening. Despite the fugue's brave wilfulness, we end where we started, with the semitonic appoggiatura G flat to F. The hammered repeated chords at the end contain both major and minor third, as well as the flat seventh. The very last chord is a bare fifth on F, triple *forte* for all the orchestra except the potentially celestial flutes.

Vaughan Williams's much-quoted remark that though he did not know whether he *liked* the Fourth Symphony, it was what he *meant*, is very much to the point. One can hardly describe a work of such superabundant energy as negative; yet it concentrates on the dark side of his moon and perhaps for that reason cannot count among his greatest pieces. What one can say is that it was necessary, at that moment, for him to write it: to bring into the open the turmoil behind works like *Job* and the Piano Concerto, allowing violence, with almost gleeful abandon, to do its worst. Only then could he say, with Beethoven, from the horror of 'war within and without', dona nobis pacem; and proceed to make the Fifth Symphony, which may fairly claim to be his ultimate masterpiece.

X

PRAYER FOR PEACE, 'WITHIN AND WITHOUT'

THE DOUBLE MAN IN *DONA NOBIS PACEM* AND THE FIFTH SYMPHONY

Blessed is he whose lot it will be to see this Holy City descending, and lighting upon the place that shall be prepared for situation and rest. Then will be a golden world, wickedness shall then be ashamed, especially that which persecutes the Church. Holiness, Goodness, and Truth shall then with great Boldness, Countenance and Reverence walk upon the face of the earth. It will then be always summer, always sunshine, always pleasant, green, fruitful and beautiful to the Sons of God.

JOHN BUNYAN, *The Holy City*

Sketches for a fifth symphony were being made more or less at the same time as the Piano Concerto and the Fourth Symphony, though the new symphony was not to be heard until 1943. Just as the Piano Concerto links *Job* to the Fourth Symphony, so another work links the Fourth to the Fifth. Like the Concerto, this cantata, *Dona Nobis Pacem*, is not only transitional, but also one of its composer's most powerful creations. Composed between 1934 and 1936, it belongs to the English choral tradition, while being at the same time more concerned with new worlds than with old: for Vaughan Williams, working during the troubled thirties, intended it to be an appeal for 'inner and outer peace' – as Beethoven said of the Agnus Dei of his *Missa Solemnis*. More overtly than *Sancta Civitas*, composed a decade earlier, *Dona Nobis Pacem* stresses the social and even political ramifications of the New Jerusalem, as well as the spiritual vision which may make rebirth possible. Significantly enough, in bringing his vision into the heart of modern life, Vaughan Williams returned, in his sixties, to the poet of his youth and of the New World – Walt Whitman. In the last movement, however, he battens on his heritage from England's seventeenth century, for he calls on words from the Old and New Testament in the Authorized Version. No startling disparity of literary style results, since the cadences of Whitman's free verse are themselves in part moulded by those of the English Bible.

The work opens, in universal terms, with Latin words from the Eucharistical Agnus Dei: an appeal to the Lamb of God, who takes away the sins of the world, to give us peace, in our desperately divided condition. Orchestral strings sustain a D beneath which $^6_4$ chords undulate chromatically. Soprano solo enters with the liturgical phrase, wavering up and down through a minor third from D; the F naturals of her top note acutely clash with the F sharps in the orchestral triad:

On the word 'dona' the soprano's dissonant appoggiaturas intensify the anguish; and although the music quietens as the chorus enters canonically with the rising and falling third, the calm is deceptive. For suddenly they take up the sighing appoggiaturas, loudly. As they sway from D flat major to C minor triads over a pedal G, the soloist wails aloft on A flat, with the effect of a dominant ninth. On 'pacem' texture clears to C major, though often with A instead of C as bass; and flows through chains of (now diatonic) suspensions. The soloist is left alone to round off the phrase with a decline from G to F sharp, not F natural. Her last 'dona nobis pacem' is aeolian on E, which then droops a further semitone to E flat.

During this declension orchestral timpani and basses have softly crept in, bitonally on A flat and E flat. The doubleness of their bitonality with the fundamental G signals war, which is soon empowered by brass fanfares on A and E naturals, in further bitonal relationship with the drums. The poem, from Whitman's *Drum-Taps*, is one of his finest, combining his 'democratic' cataloguing with stanzaic control; and it is pertinent to recall that although in youth Vaughan Williams was fascinated by Whitman as a New World explorer, the poet was also, like Vaughan Williams himself and seventeenth-century Bunyan, a bard of conflict and division. The New World too had been racked by war: a war of separation from the old country, and, still more painfully, a civil war of division of self against self, North against South. In this war Whitman was directly involved as poet-journalist and as preacher-tractarian. The *Drum-Taps* poem prompts the composer to bellicose immediacy; the chorus homophonically exhorts drums to beat and bugles to blow in rhythms furiously propelled by the words. Thematically, the lines stem from the alternating seconds (E to E flat) at the end of the soprano's solo. Syncopations enact 'ruthless force', in stark textures tending to unisons or an organum of parallel fifths and fourths. Modulations or tonal shifts are, borne on the whirlwind, volatile, though they recurrently gravitate back, as though by magnetic force, to the axis of E and E flat. At the words 'mind not the timid, mind not the weeper' the motif of rising minor third and declining chromatics gives sinew to the texture; for the 'mother's entreaties' the motif is very close to Job's blessing-curse. This does not promote development; the movement ends with war's stabbing rhythms and raucous organum chords, dispersing in the fanfare and the oscillating semitone.

Without break this leads into the next movement, 'Reconciliation', one of the most wondrous inspirations of both poet and composer. The burden of the text is that, for all the carnage, 'Death and night incessantly, softly, wash again and ever again this soiled world'. The free yet at the same time meticulous 'laving' rhythm works in the same way as Vaughan Williams's flexible melodies, of which the tonal root is still E. The E flat-A flat bitonality has vanished; the key signature is one sharp, though the music veers between phrygian E minor and E major. Strings sing a gently undulating melody over a syncopated ostinato with phrygian F natural; the tailpiece of rising fourth and falling pentatonics is another fingerprint, dispensing balm. The baritone solo, above which soars a solo violin, flowers out of this lovely cadential figure, flowing from the rhythm of the words, affirming humanity through the heart-beat of the syncopated accompaniment. He ends the stanza, on the words 'this soiled world', with the refrain phrase (E, G, F sharp E) diatonically harmonized, moving to an E major consummation:

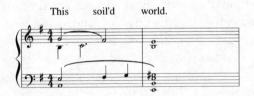

This music is expanded by the chorus, sopranos singing the baritone's melody, on which the other voices comment homophonically. Dissonant tensions accruing from the falling bass do not affect the benignity of the cadential resolutions. With the baritone soloist's return, dualism intrudes in bitonality between triads of E major and C minor – prompted by a vision of 'my enemy ... a man divine as myself ... white-faced and still in the coffin': a prophecy of Wilfred Owen's famous poem of World War I, 'Strange Meeting'. The unaccompanied choral passage about Death and Night as agents of purgation breaks the heart; and sunders the musical texture, too, since the solo soprano returns with the liturgical 'Dona nobis' phrase, the dissonance latent in her falling appoggiaturas being hardly less poignant, though she is now unaccompanied. She fades to silence between G sharp and F natural, with E as implicit bass: the same motif, at the same pitch, as had been associated with Satan's destruction of the self-regarding serenity of Job's sons, minueting with their wives. Here the purgation is the more moving because it is on behalf of humanity, not of an elect social group.

But of its nature war opposes reconciliation; and war is omnipresent in the next movement, a setting of Whitman's 'Dirge for two veterans'. The poem, also from *Drum-Taps*, describes the burial of a father and son, together slaughtered in the war, and Vaughan Williams's music enacts Whitman's prescription: 'a strong dead march enwraps me'. This is simpler than the previous movements, perhaps because the situation is objectified in physical action. The funereal pulse never relaxes; the drum taps on E and A imply no bitonal disturbance; the modality is dorian or aeolian A. The chorus's vision of the full moon over the double grave is unaccompanied, though the quiet drumming returns as the modality shifts to aeolian D. Over the steady pulse, the harmony acquires discreet chromatics: the 'immense and silent moon' unsurprisingly prompts an almost Delian luxuriance, with sequential modulations by way of seventh and ninth chords. The 'full-keyed bugle', however, calls us back to diatonic order, with a climax for the 'great drums' in a resonant C major, while side-drums side-step to triads of G minor and A major. A more linear texture pervades the verses about the son and father doubly dead, and a dotted-rhythmed melody climaxes with the timpani once more off-key on A flat and E flat. The Delius-like sequences recur to soothe war's divisiveness, introducing another invocation to the moon, whose light may transfigure the shapes of death and transmute bugles and drums into celestial airs. This is what happens in the unaccompanied setting of the words 'My heart gives you love': music with the sublime simplicity of the 'this soiled earth' phrase in the third movement. The funeral procession trudges, orchestrally, into the distance, still unperturbed in pulse, between aeolian and dorian A in modality.

Some of the music for the Dirge was revised from an early Whitman setting Vaughan Williams had made in 1908, and the piece as a whole sounds of earlier vintage than the previous movements. Its simplicity is right in context, however, and steers the rest of the work to more overt social and political commitment. In an interlude the dirge's As and Es are taken over by a baritone soloist who intones words at first neither from Whitman nor from the Bible, but from a speech of John Bright to the House of Commons, delivered in 1855: which brings us back from the New World to home, with its rumours of imperial war. The intonation echoes the soprano's solo in the first movement in that it slides from its obsessive Es to E flat, and so to C and a recapitulation of the introduction's wailing appoggiaturas in a 'filled-in' ninth chord over the dominant pedal of C. With the words 'We looked for peace, but no peace came' Vaughan Williams returns home in a deeper sense, for the text is from Jeremiah, whose Lamentations Tallis had so poingnantly set four centuries previously. In this universal threnody the distant Crimean War merges into the First World War and into the birth-pangs of the approaching Second.

At first the music is canonic, with a theme based on a fifth, as though seeking certitude out of desperation. Doubleness works both negatively and positively: for while a phrygian second (D flat) suggests constriction and bondage, D flat itself becomes a key centre as the baritone calls on the 'strong man who will give peace'. His arioso begins pentatonically, but shifts from triads of D flat to D natural and then B natural, which is perhaps really C flat. From there, with a mediant transition, Vaughan Williams reaches E flat major, and stays there for a long time as the strength of simplicity reveals the simplicity of strength. For ultimately, it is a matter of belief, of 'making' a faith – which happens as stepwise undulations on cellos and basses grow into a diatonic theme, extended in fugato by all the strings. The chorus enters to tell us that 'nation shall not lift up sword against nation, and none shall make them afraid'. A tonic E flat pedal is fundamental to this vision of concord; for several pages no accidental sullies the diatonicism, though the vocal parts are humanely responsive to the rhythms of the words, often creating passing dissonances and crossing the metrical beat. This interior animation propels the music at long last into another mediant modulation, to C major. The orchestra dances in pentatonic patterns; an ostinato of repeated minims bandied between the parts is powerfully affirmative, in effect a cantus firmus without the theological dimension of a plainsong theme. Textures remain consistent through further modulations from aeolian D to B flat and to a potent G major celebrating the 'new heaven and earth'. Falling scales emulate chiming bells; cross-metres inject energy, carrying us back to diatonic E flat major for the doxology. This homage to God's glory and hope for men of good will is sustained by a tonic pedal, hanging on, as it were, for dear life: so the music's momentum is not compromised by the acute passing dissonances or by stepwise shifts to the tonality. The tune and rhythm have the flavour of a Bunyan hymn, such as the final dance of the Sons of the Morning in *Job*. The key is not, however, Vaughan Williams's humanely consummatory D major, but E flat major, a semitone higher.

The ultimate climax comes with another mediant transition, from E flat back to C major – once a social key of Enlightenment – and a grand, unequivocally diatonic peroration. Over the affirmation of good will towards men the solo soprano floats her declining appoggiaturas on 'Dona nobis pacem', stilling the chorus to a triple *piano* C major triad, the bass's low C humming like the turning earth. The solo soprano whispers 'pacem' on her low E, but at last does not fall to E flat, remaining consonant as she fades into silence. Although latish Vaughan Williams characteristically does not end in triumph, the tranquillity of this conclusion is positive in effect: at least in comparison with the mere cessation of *Sancta Civitas*. He foresees a potential resolution of vision into social reality, though it remains potential, and perhaps always must. He will not tackle this theme again; the resolutions his symphonies seek are within the psyche rather than in the external world.

We saw that the Fourth Symphony, however fierce, is not merely a war symphony. It does not deal in entirely negative emotions, for its energy is itself a positive; it is sometimes (especially in the scherzo) outrageously funny, and often (in the scherzo and finale) obstreperously vulgar. The Fifth Symphony – which was first performed in the War years, though it was under way by 1937 – is similarly not merely a peace symphony: indeed, its peace passes understanding precisely because it is so deeply entwined with the strife more overt in *Job*, the Piano Concerto, *Dona Nobis Pacem* and the Fourth Symphony. The Fifth's pastoralism, like that of the symphony designated 'Pastoral', is no vegetative quietude but a state of mind attained through a passionate pilgrimage. Offering the musical quintessence of the 'operatic morality' *The Pilgrim's Progress*, on which Vaughan Williams had laboured so long, it encapsulates all the elements that had gone to make him: the clumping of Eliot's 'loam feet', the mystical transcendence of the lark, the inner conflict of Blake's opposites, the anguish consequent on those conflicts, their sublimation in a quest. Technically, it is his most accomplished work.

The Fifth was called by the composer 'Symphony in D', and with reason. Yet the key signature of the first movement has only one sharp, being in the mixolydian mode on D, with no sharp sevenths. Yet that is too simple, for the first note we hear is the flat C as pedal in the bass; and although two horns undulate in dotted rhythm through a D major chord, the violins' answering melody is at first pentatonic with an A–C basis. We begin, that is, in doubleness and ambiguity, however gently in comparison with the violently dichotomous opening of No. 4. This is borne out by Vaughan Williams's designation of the movement as Preludio – which suggests an emergent state. And although the movement will display some of the characteristics of a sonata, it is not overtly a dramatic conflict, like the first movements of Symphonies 2 and 4. In this opening, the music does indeed open like a flower. The undulating D-centred horns recall the instinctually breathing Nature-music of the Pastoral; the violin's theme, with its rise through a fourth extended to a fifth, is that incipiently pentatonic fingerprint so natural that it may be taken as a synonym for the breath of life. The bass earths us deeply to its flat seventh which has no need to resolve, either up or down. Yet by the ninth bar a latent duality is already active. Nature's wavering horns change from major to minor, not in dramatic contrast but in an embracement of other aspects of experience that may prove liberating – and does so when the violins change gear (if so inappropriately mechanistic a metaphor be permitted), shifting to D rather than C or A. Their lyrical melody floats pentatonically down from a high D, flowing in lark-like, metrically free cantilena, and fluctuating, without stress, between major and minor third. The bass still undulates, stepwise, around its pedal C; horns breathe their undulation more distantly, first major, then minor. While strings fuse their fourth-founded motif on G, C and D with their floating pentatonic descent, the woodwind transform the horns' dotted-rhythmed undulation into continuous song. Since the thirds are minor, the harmonic texture is 'white-note', softly sensuous in passing dissonance.

Through this opening paragraph the music has evolved by way of polyphonic interweaving, not harmonic progression, though that is latent, and becomes patent with another change of gear, for the bass's pedal becomes itself a tonic when the key signature changes to three flats. Violas sustain C as a pedal, while the stepwise moving bass acquires lyrical identity and the violins soar pentatonically. The tonality has become aeolian or dorian on C, as horns sing the motif of fourth rising to fifth as though it were a cantus firmus (a song of affirmation); flutes double the violins stratospherically. When the modality shifts to the upper mediant E the dotted-rhythmed undulations continue on horns and woodwind, but the violins evolve a new melody almost in E major, though sharp sevenths are not conspicuous. The bass, now pizzicato, is melodically as well as harmonically supportive; texture is richer since the flowing lines embrace scrunchy suspensions and passing notes. This is intensified when the sixth is flattened, and the music vacillates between E major and minor; though dynamics are still soft, the texture is ripe, with divided strings as well as interlacing woodwind. One can hardly describe this E-based section as an orthodox second subject since it has evolved inevitably from the flowing lines, in a manner almost comparable with the symphonic Sibelius (to whom Vaughan Williams dedicated his symphony, 'without permission'). Yet this music, hymnic in contour and march-like in gait, does change the mood as well as tonality, and initiates what may count as development as well as evolution. The symbolism of this event in time is not the less potent for being simple, even naïve: for it is literally a Fall – a sudden descent by a chromatic semitone, which we have met before in the approach to the coda of the Tallis Fantasia, in Satan's music from *Job*, *The Pilgrim's Progress*, and recurrently in the works discussed in the last two chapters. It is as though the exquisitely scored lyricism of the Symphony thus far proves to be not an illusion, but only a partial truth: as was already implicit in that its innocence contained seeds of division. The pentatonic descents, floating down from E, softly lurch to E flat, intensified with a *marcato* fall from F natural to E to E flat:

At this point the key signature changes to three flats. The strings' figuration, still pentatonic around C, murmurs like the voice of Nature, recalling one of Sibelius's whirring moto perpetuos that evoke winds and waters, though Vaughan Williams's English Nature is relatively benign. Even so, the tempo is now *allegro*, and into the hushed scurrying of strings woodwind and horns interject the fateful descending semitone. We know from *Job* that this semitone may be satanic; obliterating song, it leaves for the moment only Nature's non-human humming. The semitone expands to a tone, and is further extended to a minor third, canonically imitated by woodwind. Canon may possibly order Nature's indeterminacy; with modulations shifting by mediants through C and E flat minors to G flat minor (notated as F sharp), the destructive chromatics, gradually dechromaticized, gather energy to work for good rather than evil. Having descended another third to pentatonic D minor, the strings' tremolandos shimmer in Sibelian Nature-noises: which woodwind and brass control because their Fall motif has been metamorphosed into a hymnic march, still beginning with a pentatonic descent (D, C, A on trumpets), but now canonically ordered:

Yet as dynamics subside we are carried back rather than forward in that developent is superseded by a recapitulation that is unmistakably such, though the bass line, still rotating around a C pedal, now has more melodic identity. But if this is a classical-style recapitulation, it is also still development – as were, of course, many of Beethoven's recapitulations, at least from the Eroica Symphony onwards. The 'God' motif of fourth and fifth – A, D, E, D – is more obtrusive, inverting the canonic brass descents at the climax of the development, and leading to its own climax with a fully scored version of the quasi-second subject. The melody's hymnic character is nobly affirmative, and even the passing dissonances and the ambiguous tonality, teetering between B or E flat major and G major and minor, induce exultation rather than anguish. The hymn swells into a pilgrim's march (basically in E flat major) which, after a triple *forte*, resolves into the violins' pentatonic melisma, now on G. Into this the woodwinds' and horns' satanic semitone – a nagging worm of corruption – unexpectedly yet inevitably intrudes. So the hymnic climax is not a final triumph, only a momentary victory; the pilgrims live, and die, and live to fight again. The movement ends as ambiguously as it had begun, horns undulating through their dotted-rhythmed D major, string basses earthed on their pedal C. The nature of their descent is, however, slightly but significantly different for, with a key signature of two flats instead of one sharp, they fall to C by way of E flat.

The first movement is a true symphonic argument, though it does not function by way of tonal and thematic conflict in the same sense as does an allegro of middle-period Beethoven. Its dualism is rather between pentatonic innocence and chromatic experience; its development is anti-developmental in that it threatens disintegration; and its recapitulation is a lyrical rebirth which is not consummatory: the cycle of birth, growth and decay is perennial. The scherzo, moving *presto* in crotchets, also has close affinities with *Job* and the Fourth Symphony, for it opens with the strings, triple *piano* and con sordini, flickering through the rising fourths that seem to pertain arbitrarily to God and to Satan. In *The Pilgrim's Progress* they have a comparably double function, spectrally appearing in Pilgrim's fight with the hobgoblins. If this is fight-music, it is a struggle recollected in tranquillity, for the dynamics are mostly soft, and the fleet-footed movement is sprite-like as well as sprightly. The modality is pentatonic on E or A, and the texture is more a matter of pattern than of melody, though flute and bassoon insinuate a little dance-song, moving up and down through a third from E. Figurations are gossamer-like, sustained by a horn ostinato on bare fifths moving from D to E and back. The thematic fourths interlace in woodwind canons; dissonant acciaccaturas on E flat-E natural turn into the alternating major and minor thirds familiar from all the works since *Job*, leaving us in no doubt that the airy-fairy dance has a devilish undertow. Threat intensifies as the basses lollop in false-related fifths and the thirds become an almost rollicking tune hopefully beginning in D major. The diaphanous flurry of the strings is pierced by the woodwinds' alternating thirds, and by the rising fourths in cross-rhythm on brass. Dynamics are the more minatory for being still soft.

In the trio, beginning in aeolian C sharp (really D flat, reached by a mediant shift from B flat minor), the fourths are moulded into a tune that might by a Bunyanesque hymn; a tune close to it is associated, in Vaughan Williams's 'operatic morality', with Mr Good-Deeds. When the tonality becomes E major-minor, the tune is fully stated on trombones, harmonized in parallel triads, with a duple metre within the triple pulse that suggests a modest girding of the loins. Yet this positive pilgrim-hymn does not carry the day: the fourth-founded scherzo returns da capo and from afar, and this time the tune, perky on piccolo, is routed by the hobgoblins' duple-rhythmed alternating thirds, and by the falsely related acciacatura chords on brass. Duality becomes overt between the duple-metred gibbering and the rising fourths' approach to lyricism. Both metrically and tonally the sprites are disintegrative, though momentarily strings mutate the fourth into a song of infinite longing, oscillating between C and A:

Song vanishes in a wisp of smoke, the muted strings quivering in the fourths, dissolving in a pentatonic descent. The pitches are identical with those of the affirmative canon at the climax of the first movement's development, now heard in a glass darkly, in wraith-like retrospection.

This scherzo is not a closed structure, as the classical scherzo-and-trio commonly was. In containing dualism, it is implicitly dramatic, even progressive; and the strings' visionary moment of yearning just before the final dissolution is a harbinger of the fulfilled vision (which is also drama) of the slow movement. Vaughan Williams labelled it Romanza, a term he often used for his deepest utterances, as we have noticed in reference to *The Lark Ascending*, Jane Scroop's lament for her sparrow, and the slow movement of the Piano Concerto. Here it is a romance because it tells a tale, as is evident in the fact that, as we have seen, some of the music occurs in the opera *The Pilgrim's Progress*. It is not clear whether the passage was first part of the opera, occurring at the point when Pilgrim sets out on his quest, and was later incorporated into the Symphony; but Vaughan Williams never disguised the borrowing since he prefaced the original score of the romanza with Bunyan's words: 'Upon that place there stood a cross and a little below a sepulchre. Then he said: "he hath given us rest by his sorrow and life by his death".' The composer omitted this text from the published score, no doubt feeling that the music stood on its own and would be unnecessarily circumscribed by a seventeenth-century text. In any case the meaning of any parallel passage must be changed by the symphonic context.

The romanza opens with diatonic concords on divided strings, each in false relation, ceremonially moving through C major, A major, G minor, A major, G minor, back to C major. The sublimity of the sound recalls, over more than thirty years, the opening of the crucial *Fantasia on a Theme of Thomas Tallis*. Through this mystical impersonality, solo cor anglais intones a theme basically in aeolian A, beginning with humanly speaking repeated notes, then undulating up and down through a third, the sixth being sharp in the ascent, flat in the descent:

The cor anglais's intonation is preludial; strings initiate the movement proper, with an almost imperceptible increase of pace. Violas and cellos are divided, and all the string voices, germinating from the habitual rising fourths, sing lyrically, the aeolian texture unspotted with a single accidental. Dissonant suspensions occur because each line is songfully independent, but there is no hint, in this spacious paragraph, of division or disruption. A slight unease is, however, generated when the strings, in parallel triads, take up the cor anglais's rising and falling third, and when solo woodwind interject pentatonic arabesques, springing from the leaping fourths. We may hear these arabesques as birds, Nature's perhaps angelic messengers, while the gestures of the undulating string triads suggest human stress and distress. The woodwind birds are transmuted into a version of the Tallis-like concords of the opening: spirit and flesh coalesce as the strings transform the cor anglais's speaking intonation into song. The aeolian texture is again devoid of accidentals, the music's lyrical flow being enhanced, rather than broken, by the suspensions and dissonant passing notes.

But when song dies back into the stepwise undulating thirds, division becomes overt. At first it seems to be simply between mankind and Nature, for the pentatonic melismata on oboe and cor anglais float ecstatically, while clarinet and bassoons writhe, muddily in low register, through the thirds. Woodwind become a bird–chorus, chanting both the fourths and the undulating thirds. But Hardys 'pain of consciousness' is audible when, with a quickening of tempo, the strings embark on a chromaticized version of the minor third motif, stressing the semitonic sigh and recalling the satanic semitones of the first movement. The woodwind too exacerbate their fourth-founded melismata chromatically, so that blithe birds become distressed humans, the figure being close to that to which Pilgrim cried for salvation at the foot of the Cross. The climax to this passage is unexpectedly ferocious. The chromatic wail becomes unmistakably a Fall, while the woodwind arabesques turn into the alternating major and minor thirds, hardly less violent than in *Job*, and at the same pitch (A, A flat, F, E), accompanied bitonally by a string triad of F sharp minor. This is the beginning of what amounts to a symphonic development by opposition. The horns have the cor anglais's initial intonation, echoed by trumpets through tremolando strings; the chromatic wails howl on brass. And although both woodwind and strings join in the fourth-founded arabesques, as if man and Nature were seeking harmony, this only rouses the strings to vehement outcry, ending in alternating thirds the more anguished as their high F natural clashes with a canonic entry on E.

The psychological 'programme' of the Symphony proves to be Blakean in telling us once more that without contraries there is no progression. Division promotes a still further increase in momentum, until strings, woodwind and brass, healing division, together unfold a more spacious version of their aeolian melody. Again the texture is void of accidentals, though the dissonant passing notes are riper and richer. This is the Symphony's ultimate climax, which subsides in the humanly expressive rising and falling third on first violins doubled by oboe. Out of this soars a solo violin, carolling the rising fourths and pentatonic arabesques, and recalling both the ascending lark and Elihu dancing in youth and beauty. We end with a reference back to the Tallis-like concords, through which muted horn sings the cor anglais intonation shorn of its initial repeated notes – perhaps because, being fulfilled, it no longer needs to 'speak'. The dissolving cadences on strings resolve aeolian A minor into radiant A major, a key of youth and beauty, though the chromatically dissonant passing notes tenderly impart (in the Greek sense) pathos.

The developmentally symphonic nature of this work is confirmed by the finale, a passacaglia. In the seventeenth century – an era we have seen to be of deep significance for Vaughan Williams – passacaglia or chaconne was the fundamental musical synonym for unity, for it was a triple-rhythmed dance on an ostinato which remained constant throughout. Originally, the dance seems to have been associated with marriage, which is about unity within duality, both in a sexual and sacramental sense; a chaconne or passacaglia (the distinction between them is obscure) was habitually performed as an exit dance at the weddings of kings and other very important persons. That a passacaglia should end what has proved to be a symphony about division and conflict, notwithstanding its prevailing lyricism, makes its potent point; nor is it fortuitous that the key signature for this movement should be unambiguously that of D major. For the first time the sevenths are not flat but sharp: leading notes that promise cadential finality.

The passacaglia theme, appearing traditionally in the bass, is another permutation of the pentatonic third, fourth and fifth; the main melody, sung by first violins and flutes, begins with a rising D major scale, answered by a falling scale related to the hymn-like aeolian song in the romanza (see the music example on p.184). The passacaglia theme and the hymnic air, combined, make unity out of duality, the more so since nothing disturbs the D major certitude. There is an analogy with other sturdily triple-rhythmed hymns such as the Galliard of the Sons of the Morning in *Job*, the hymn of pilgrimage in the Bunyan opera, the hymn at the end of *Flos Campi*, and the opening and closing chorus of the 1928

Benedicite, an exuberantly earthy D major setting of that great canticle of Christian praise triggered off, we are told, by Vaughan Williams's reading of Prescott's descriptions of pagan ceremonial in his *The Conquest of Mexico*! In the Fifth Symphony Vaughan Williams does not flirt with such exoticism, though the first variation on the passacaglia bass is vigorously corporeal and even jazzily syncopated. The next variation further fosters worldly glory, beginning with the main theme in canon on brass, triumphantly asserting oneness. Moreover, although the music at last modulates, moving *down* the cycle of fifths from D to G to C, modulation (which means movement) *augments* energy. Strings have the main theme, woodwind dance in variants of the passacaglia ostinato, carrying us back to D major and to tempo primo, with both themes in fugato on full brass, bolstered by tremolando strings. This blaze of D major would seem to signify a worldly apotheosis, as the passacaglia theme on bass trombone, reinforced by tonic and dominant timpani, supports the rising scale tune in canonic stretti.

But this is not an end, since worldly glory is not the goal of this symphony. The apparently final D major triad on trombones abruptly changes to minor, and is joined by shivering string tremolandos. The time signature alters from $\frac{3}{4}$ to $\frac{4}{4}$, in which metre a variant of the ostinato is sung by clarinet and flute. What ensues is a kind of development section – or at least a recognition of other modes of experience – occurring within the ultimate unity of a passacaglia! Modulations grow restless, especially in comparison with the tonal lucidity of the first part of the movement; and it soon becomes evident that restlessness is promoted by retrospection. The metrically altered version of the passacaglia theme reveals a relationship to both the romanza's aria and the first movement's as it were second subject; and these covert relationships become overt in direct quotation from earlier sections of the Symphony. The chromatic wail, returning on horns, increasingly dominates the texture through increasingly wayward modulations. Rising scales in triplets increase momentum until climax arrives in an octave unison statement of the passacaglia theme by all the strings and woodwind, the key perhaps being C major, underpinned by alternating $\frac{6}{4}$ chords of F major and minor on brass. A pedal C quietly emerges on timpani as the figuration simmers down, introducing a recapitulation of the germinating themes of the preludio, with the original pedal C supporting dotted-rhythmed, false-related triads of D major and minor. The key signature, unlike that of the passacaglia but like that of the Symphony's opening, has one sharp; the tonality, if fundamentally D, again makes ambivalent reference to G and C.

The end, however, is not ambivalent, for the sharp sevenths return to the signature as Vaughan Williams appends an epilogue, though he does not so title it. For the rest of the work D major is pristine, through level crotchets moving linearly by step. The music is derived from – for much of the time identical with – that to which Pilgrim passed over the River of Death in the incidental music Vaughan Williams wrote for the broadcast dramatization of Bunyan's book, and incorporated into his operatic morality. The declining scales beginning on the second beat sing alleluyas such as are manifest in the second half of the passacaglia theme itself.

Psychologically as well as musically, it is interesting that, in the epilogue to the Fifth Symphony, we hear these alleluyas as a derivative of the declining semitone that, in the first movement, had been associated with a Fall. The theology, philosophy or psychology is again close to Blake, and implies a Jungian rebirth, whether or not one thinks that the sharp-seventhed alleluyas herald another life. 'When the Day that he must go hence was come, many accompanied him to the River side, into which, as he went, he said "Death, where is thy Sting?" And as he went down deeper, he said "Grave, where is thy Victory?" So he passed over, and the Trumpets sounded for him on the other side' (*The Pilgrim's Progress*). Slowly, almost imperceptibly, entry upon entry, the strings, earthed on a deep tonic pedal, fan out until the vision is fulfilled. Despite the beautiful prologue to Part II of *Gerontius* which to a degree resembles Vaughan Williams, Elgar stops short at the river-bank, as Vaughan Williams does not. Whereas Delius and Holst, in their search for metaphysical ecstasy, in their very different ways disintegrate cadential resolution, Vaughan Williams, who had never been partial to it, rediscovers it; and paradoxically finds in it a gateway to Paradise.

It has often been remarked that the second half of the Fifth Symphony's passacaglia theme, and still more its transformation in the epilogue, reminds us of the alleluyas in Vaughan Williams's great hymn *Sine Nomine* ('For all the Saints'). We sing the hymn, in church, in the world out there, 'hoping it might be so', as Hardy put it: perhaps almost believing it might be, so inspiring is the sweep of the tune. Yet we know that the New Jerusalem does not, cannot, exist in social reality: whereas in the Symphony the validity of art for a moment makes the vision true. It is difficult to know precisely what that tells us about Vaughan Williams's faith, but one may hazard that the Fifth Symphony is Vaughan Williams's greatest work because it is a quest that *attains* its goal. In the context of his life's work, however, it is a station on the way. If he does not again achieve its perfection, that may be because once was enough. He had miles to go before he slept.

XI

THE AFTERMATH OF WAR

THE DOUBLE MAN IN THE SIXTH SYMPHONY AND THE SEVENTH SYMPHONY, WITH AN INTERLUDE ON *RIDERS TO THE SEA*

Old men ought to be explorers
Here and there does not matter
We must be still and still moving
Into another intensity
For a further union, a deeper communion
Through the dark cold and the empty desolation.

T.S. ELIOT, 'East Coker'

Solitude is dangerous to reason, without being favourable to virtue. Remember that the solitary mortal is certainly luxurious, probably superstitious, and possibly mad.

SAMUEL JOHNSON

Vaughan Williams's Fifth Symphony seemed, at the time it appeared, to be not only a masterpiece but also a consummation. If it was puzzling that the previous symphony had been the violent Fourth, one realized that the Fifth did not evade but rather transcended that conflict; and it soon became evident that the Fifth was also an end in a sense other than consummatory. A climax to Vaughan Williams's religious sensibility, it was also a farewell to Eden, at least in a traditionally religious context.

Immediately after the Fifth Vaughan Williams wrote a small work which is an appendix to it and both consciously and unconsciously borrows from it. This is the Concerto for Oboe and Strings, written in 1944 for Leon Goossens. The oboe was by heritage a pastoral instrument favoured by the god Pan, who haunted the Samuel Palmer-like dells and glades that were the scene of Vaughan Williams's English Edens, wherein lived the shepherds of the Delectable Mountains. In the first movement of this concerto – described as being in A minor though it is more accurately in or around the aeolian mode – the oboe's pentatonic arabesques are halfway between Pan-music and the twitters of birds; the string melodies, in their sighing declensions in triple pulse, recall the Fifth Symphony vividly if without direct quotation. Though the piece is too slight to be called an elegy, it sounds like a valediction to the Forgotten Garden, especially since the 'human' folk dance that steals into it is curiously wispy. A quiet questioning suffuses the final pages, and although there is no introspective slow movement, the minuet and musette that serve in lieu of one are wistful in their tenuity. The third and last movement, called scherzo, was consciously based on material discarded from the scherzo of the Fifth, beginning as a will-o'-the-wisp dance, and growing increasingly angular within its folkiness. Towards the end, sighing strings immobiloze the folk dance. Something ceases, a loss is experienced. In the coda the solo oboe, piping monodically, is a primitive shepherd stranded.

That the Oboe Concerto was in the nature of a goodbye to much of, if not all, that, is supported by our knowledge that the Sixth Symphony, first performed in 1948 in the composer's mid-seventies, had been started as early as 1944, the year of the Concerto, and possibly earlier if one counts the 1943 music for the film *The Flemish Farm* as a contributory source. The Sixth Symphony was a bombshell that made an extraordinary impact: so much so that it was performed nearly a hundred times during its first year of life, a record exceeded only be Elgar's First Symphony. Like any real music, it has not lost its force, being, in Ezra Pound's phrase, 'news that STAYS news'. What this news was and is has led to much bootless speculation by commentators. Vaughan Williams always insisted that the Symphony was not 'about' the war and its aftermath, the hazardously hopeful or hopeless future. In a literal sense he was right, though it is certainly about his spiritual and psychological state and is a social testament in so far as he had become, rather more than do most composers, our representative.

The Symphony is described as being in E minor, though it is not so clearly or for long. Even so, the ascription has its symbolic relevance if we think of the key as the negative minor of paradisal E major. E minor was Bach's key of Crucifixion; Vaughan Williams's Sixth is crucial in relation to his creative evolution. In the furious turmoil of the first few bars Eden is indeed obliterated; and the first note contradicts the one sharp of the key signature by being F natural! The whirlwind, powerfully scored, sweeps us into permutations of the satanic alternating thirds first spelt out as such in *Job*. Over a pedal E, the motif stabs up from F to G to A flat, then lurches between A flat, G and E. Again there is an implicit doubleness between F minor and E minor-major (with the A flat substituting for G sharp) (see the music example on the facing page. The torrent surges down, then see-saws up, reinforced by barking brass in syncopated triads. When a singing theme emerges from the babel, it does not release tension, since the strings bound in syncopations across the beat, their leaps springing from the oscillating thirds. The brass still barks, lower strings and woodwind still

sizzle in the semiquaver figuration, if less ferociously. The key signature becomes three flats – a variously modalized C; one sharp returns in a flurry of woodwind, who freely invert the semiquaver figure; and the first section – it is hardly a first subject – disperses in declining chromatics in the bass and alternations between C and E on tuba. It is by now clear that this movement is not an orthodox sonata structure. The key signature is two flats and the modality seems at first to be phrygian D minor, the metre an animated $\frac{12}{8}$ over a lumpish oompah bass, emphasized by side-drum. In contrast to the furious first subject group the mood is low and jaunty, even comic and grotesque, though hardly positive, since the rocking minor thirds, false-related triads, and hiccuping syncopations are still pervasive. The main tune bounds between minor triads and 'rootless' augmented fifths and tritones, gradually revealing affinities with the soaring string melody of the turbulent first section: its rhythms, despite the hint of music-hall, are far from cosy since accents are dislocated. Even so, the compulsive beat and the increasingly massive scoring give the music forward momentum; and where this points to is revealed when the ambivalent D and G minors are transmuted into a swinging $\frac{6}{4}$ tune in a mode on B which cannot decide whether it is aeolian or dorian, for the sixth is sometimes flat, sometimes sharp. The oompah accompaniment survives, but is now subservient to the lyricism; and although this section fulfils something of the function of a codetta theme in a sonata exposition, that would not be an adequate description since, far from being a tail-piece, this melody has been the goal of the movement thus far. Thesis and antithesis between the first section's negations and this ostensibly fulfilled song are the heart of the movement's psychological warfare. On this its first appearance this folk-like, self-revolving, would-be self-subsistent tune does not long survive. With a shift back to a key signature of one flat it is engulfed in sundry metamorphoses of the earlier hurly-burly, and although brass makes an attempt to reinstate it a third lower, this unleashes not merely the oompah accompanied themes in full pelt, but also the initial whirlwind and brass barks, still more savage in cross-rhythms.

Yet if the (*Job*-like) powers of darkness seem to have triumphed, their victory, too, is short-lived. The alternation of war and peace is perennial, and out of the savage development which is simultaneously a recapitulation tranquility is born in a return to the folk-song-like theme, actually marked *tranquillo*. The key has changed from a modal B minor to an E major whose paradisal associations are justified, for the song is chanted by unisonal strings on the G and D strings, a tone higher than its original pitch, and accompanied by triadic harps. The falsely related but concordant harmonies and the modal alterations in the lines liberate the melody which, no longer revolving on itself, springs onwards and ultimately upwards, in increasingly flexible rhythms:

This marvellous tune creates a true symphonic climax by melodic means distinct from conventional symphonic techniques; and demonstrates how close are Vaughan Williams's methods of thematic transformation to those of the 'folk' themselves. Folk songs, as Cecil Sharp long ago demonstrated, tend to be accretions from several well-springs; the pentatonic and other modal formulae that, given acoustical facts, people naturally sing become a storehouse of melodic and rhythmic patterns that may be instinctively combined in sundry permutations to make tunes. These formulae are aural equivalents of the clichés – 'As I went out one May morning', and so on – used by folk poets to get them going. The parallel with Vaughan Williams's methods is revealed in a work like the accurately titled *Five Variants on Dives and Lazarus*, a retrospective piece written in 1939, at the onslaught of the Second World War. The difference between a folk song and Vaughan Williams's variant of it is that his patterns are not self-enclosed: as is still more patent and potent in the expanding modalized E major melody that concludes, apparently consummates, this movement. Only the consummation is not, after all, final for with the bass settled on a pedal E, the melody unexpectedly dissolves into the opening's semitonic wail between major and minor third – the notation being now unambiguously that, with no punning A flats for G sharps.

Nothing but the E pedal survives as, without break, the allegro merges into the second movement which, if relatively slow, is far from being relaxed. On the contrary, the liberation fleetingly attained in the E major song is denied, for the tonality of the moderato is basically B flat minor, a devilish tritone away from the first movement's E; and the theme, if it may be called such, is anchored to an ostinato B flat, around which it writhes in nagging chromatics. Spiritual exultation, in the E major song, is superseded by a funeral march and a remorseless ta-ta-ta metre, soon reinforced by brass and side-drum:

Strings attempt a more lyrical melody, first in unison, then in organum fifths and fourths, but this proves to be a descent, almost a Fall, not unrelated to Job's curse. This movement, like the first, is a tug-of-war between contradictory forces, only here the lyricism cannot positively define its identity, but is increasingly threatened by the ostinato rhythm's bellicosity. Eventually the string melody is itself invaded by tritones; rhythmic flow is damned by brass and timpani vacillating in false-related triads between the Symphony's fanatical minor thirds; until the strings float in almost metreless chromatic monody, turning into organum in parallel triads, first on woodwind, then on divided strings. We have heard harbingers of such 'limbo' music in works like the Fourth Symphony and *Sancta Civitas*; here, it is prophetic of the Symphony's extraordinary epilogue, though we cannot know this at the moment of hearing. The weird effect is due to the music's very ambiguity: we cannot be sure whether it is a potential escape from the prison of the nagging B flats and

C flats, or whether its lost rootlessness may not be their cause. Does the ostinato pattern hang on for grim life, or is it a dark angel of death?

At the moment, the return of the B flat ostinato on soft but *pesante* trumpets, backed by muffled side-drum and then timpani, leads incrementally to frenzy: the ostinato rhythm and the wavering chromatic organum prove to be electrical charges that ignite in ferociously rocking, false-related triads see-sawing between G flat major and G minor. On this catastrophic contrariety the movement expires, the ostinato still tethered to its by now terrifyingly oppressive B flat. Solo cor anglais floats in a metreless, stepwise-moving undulation, anticipating the epilogue. Its tentative melody is drowned by the ostinato, still teetering between B flat and C flat. The latter (dissonant) tone fades to silence, as the scherzo crashes in like a juggernaut. In it the interval of the tritone, previously a diabolic undercurrent, becomes an obsession no less relentless than that of the second movement's ostinato.

The scherzo's pulse is fast duple and the thematic content, canonically presented by brass and strings, is consistently, indeed infuriatingly, tritonal. Whirling semiquaver scales and syncopated oompah rhythms cannot obliterate the canonic tritones on brass, and the more the metrical durations vary – from two crotchets to four quavers to six triplet quavers a bar – the more hellishly constricted the music seems, since its unvarying pulse is a prison. Contrapuntal augmentation on brass reinforces the tritonal obsession; and although a trio-like tune first presented on tenor saxophone hints that a relatively cheery, music-hall dance might break the tritonal circle, it gives up in an extended solo passage, accompanied by side-drum beats, flickering semiquaver scales and low pizzicato strings. Abandoning the not very meaningful one flat key signature, the music turns into spectrally tremolando tritones on strings, with solo bassoon grotesquely cavorting through tritones in triplets. From this point the tritones take over contrapuntally in a multiplicity of metrical durations. The effect is similar to that of the parodistic counterpoint in the Rondo Burleske of Mahler's Ninth Symphony, and the scoring is comparably raucous. The counterpoint, too, is of Mahlerian sophistication, the tritonal theme being ingeniously combined with its inversion. Ingenuity causes not delight but something not far from terror when the moronic music-hall tune of the trio returns as an aggressively stomping march. Parallels with Nazi militarism and tyranny were made but were unnecessary, even misleading. The death of the heart may occur in many contexts, especially in our brutishly mechanized world.

After the march's fury, the scherozo vanishes in a puff of tritonally mephisthophelean smoke. The epilogue is unique among symphonic finales in that the last thing it seeks is finality. Consistently soft in dynamics, it floats levelly without change of pace or pulse, strings and brass muted. The theme – if it can be called such, since it defies definition – encapsulates the seminal motives of the Symphony – and indeed of the music of Vaughan Williams's middle years. The undulation between major and minor third (the former sometimes notated as a diminished fourth) is pervasive, as is the tritone; and these negations are carried to an ultimate since any hint of direction, let alone progression, is effaced in the lines' wispy drifting, in several different note-durations; the augmented version of this basic motif seems to make time stop and to disembody pitch sequence:

The return of the moderato's chromatic organum on remote horns makes desolation yet more desolate; joined by muted trumpets, the horns emit a faint expiration in parallel sevenths, echoed by multiply divided strings, over the initially cavernous pedal E. A remote echo of the blessing-curse theme strays into the cellos and basses, and softly creeps through the upper strings. The lines never get far, however, from their major-minor undulation, which is picked out by harp harmonics through a haze of tremolando strings. Again, the simultaneous drifting of the motivic pattern in several different note-durations creates an illusion of immobility, as the theme winds slowly up from the bass clarinet's bottom register to dissolve in parallel fifths on strings. Solo oboe transmutes this into the 'Fall' motif, whispered monodically. It subsides into pizzicato cellos and basses, while the upper strings fade *a niente,* wavering between first inversion of an E flat major triad and second inversion of an E minor triad. A state of limbo is implicit in this too, for what sounds like an E flat major triad is punningly notated as G natural, A sharp and D sharp, the sharpened tones being appoggiaturas to the second inversion E minor chord on which they resolve. Never was resolution less resolving, nor a tonic triad more indeterminate as conclusion to a symphony.

It is not surprising that this movement, which made a deeply disturbing impression on audiences at the time of the first performances, should have been submitted to a variety of interpretations. The most commonly canvassed was that it was some kind of lunar landscape or post-atomic devastation: literally an aftermath to the rest of the Symphony, which was supposed to be concerned with the late war. Vaughan Williams as usual deplored such literalism, which must limit the work's metaphorical references. He said that if the last movement meant anything other than its sounds, it was literally an epilogue in telling us that, in Prospero's words,

> We are such stuff
> As dreams are made on, and our little life
> Is rounded with a sleep.

This may embrace the more crudely literal accounts, if considered both in Shakespeare's context and in that of Vaughan Williams himself. For Shakespeare's Prospero was prosperous post-Renaissance man who, having tried to play God, came to recognize that this was folly, and to abjure his magic book and break his wand, casting it back into the ooze of the unconscious, whence it came. This is a death of humanism in which, as we have seen, Vaughan Williams shared; the epilogue is perhaps the ultimate auralization of agnosticism, telling us that that Unknown Region which the hopeful young Vaughan Williams had set out to explore, is not a metaphysical 'other world', but is unknown, and always will be, simply because it is unknowable. The epilogue discovers that in the unknown region there must be nowhere: a fact offering occasion for neither hope nor regret. The difficult faith of the Fifth Symphony is relinquished; man is alone, in the dark cold and empty desolation. Acceptance brings to this strange music a serene insecurity: a courageous testament of our frightful century, the power of which has not weakened with the passage of years.

Late in life (1951) Vaughan Williams set a fragment of Prospero's 'farewell' speech for unaccompanied choir – along with Ariel's song to Ferdinand, 'Full fathom five'. The latter is indeed magic music, using the ding-dongs of the sea's bells to evoke an other-worldly sonority. The wonderful poem is about the power of the unconscious sea to mutate eyes into pearls, materiality into 'something rich and strange'. Returning to the unconscious may be a gateway to rebirth, though the evolution is remote from that envisaged in Vaughan Williams's early appeals to the sea not only as Great Mother, but also as the nurse of social progress. In the Ariel song metamorphosis is expressed in disembodied triads floating in false relation, similar to those in the Sixth Symphony's epilogue. The same techniques appear in the setting of Prospero's 'cloud-capped towers' speech, for the 'insubstantial pageant' dissolves in almost vaporized triads; release from tonal direction or harmonic root is at once fearful and wonderful. The sea *is* the Unknown Region: into which, in his next symphony, Vaughan Williams will plunge to sink or swim. Interestingly, the Seventh Symphony had an extra-musical dimension in the film about Scott of the Antarctic for which Vaughan Williams was commissioned to write music. Clearly this occasional task assumed a significance he had not consciously bargained for. The epilogue to the Sixth is, we have said, strictly speaking agnostic; on the ultimate mysteries Vaughan Williams can have nothing to say, since whatever he may feel, he does not know. So the pilgrim Bunyan, who did know or thought he knew, is replaced by a dourer pilgrim from the context not of the seventeenth century, but of modern life. Whereas Bunyan's pilgrimage was spiritual, Scott's was in a sense physical, as he entered an ultimate Waste Land. Even so, for Vaughan Williams, Scott becomes a modern mythic hero, symbolizing man's capacity for endurance in a land laid waste not necessarily by atomic explosion, but by a decay of traditional sanctions, whether associated with Church or State. The words Scott wrote in his final journal read as an apposite comment on the epilogue to Vaughan Williams's Sixth Symphony, as well as on Scott's own life:

> I do not regret this journey; we took risks, we knew we took them, things have come out against us, therefore we have no cause for complaint.

This is a death of man, succeeding Nietzsche's death of God.

Vaughan Williams had approached the elemental sea as symbol of the ultimate (unknowable) mystery of life and death once before – in a one-act opera that is an almost verbatim setting of J.M. Synge's *Riders to the Sea*. This was composed, though not produced, in 1925, the year of Vaughan Williams's most 'mystical' (and favourite) choral work, *Sancta Civitas*. Offering a startling anticipation of the epilogue to the Sixth Symphony and of the Seventh (Antarctic) Symphony, it merits comment for the further reason that it is a masterpiece – its composer's most perfectly realized theatrical work. Synge, an Irish poet and dramatist with a *fin de siècle* background, lived for the early years of this century among fishermen on the remote Aran Islands, shared their archaic life as fully as a sophisticated modern man could hope to, and wrote in the poetic rhythms and imagery of the language they spoke – which had affinities with both biblical English and Whitman's free verse. No life could have been more elemental, for they were Lear's 'unaccommodated' men and women waging war against the elements, especially the eternal and all-encompassing sea. Maurya, the tragic heroine – Greek in evoking both pity and terror – has had grandfather, father, husband and five sons claimed by the ravenous ocean: which during the play exacts the tribute of the youngest son and sole survivor. At the time he composed the opera Vaughan Williams cannot have known how appropriate the play's uncompromising austerity would be to his later years, when the ambivalent faith of *Job* and the Fifth Symphony was more elusive. Vaughan Williams stripped his technique to the bare minimum of Synge's islanders, creating vocal lines that are a sublimation of poetic speech – as for that matter were Monteverdi's at the highly sophisticated birth of opera; and as were Moussorgsky's in dealing with elemental Russian nature, and Debussy's in his elegantly artful *Pelléas et Mélisande* which also set, more or less verbatim, a play dealing with people lost, if not in inchoate Nature, in the dark forest of the subconscious mind.

Vaughan Williams's opera – 'play in music' would be a more accurate description – is through-composed, and since the characters lead such rudimentary lives and speak a language itself almost song, one might even regard it, naturalistically, as a slice of life; certainly the conventional stylizations of opera intrude less than in any other piece of music theatre. The prelude for the small orchestra evokes the raging storm economically but with uncanny realism: not because it employs a sea-machine, but by way of typical Vaughan Williams fingerprints. A wail, undulating up and down through a third, is bitonally supported by tremolando triads in organum; the familiar chromatic semitone (E to E flat) whines in an inner part; an upward pentatonic gesture (E, G, A, B) unfurls above. The top line is transmuted into one of Vaughan Williams's motto-themes – a pentatonic rise through B, D, and E to F, which then curls up to A flat and subsides down the scale, while the tremolando bass shivers like the sea, subsiding on a bare fifth on C. A meandering incantation on cor anglais declines into sighing $\frac{6}{3}$ chords that may be the wind, but are also overburdened human hearts. Nora and Cathleen, daughters of the woman who has lost so many menfolk, are talking of the storm's havoc, wondering whether the last son Michael may be destroyed in it – some clothes, stranded on the beach, may, they fear, be his. Their song-speech is unmeasured in rhythm, in chromaticized pentatonicism close to the inflexions in which people relatively in a state of nature naturally talk. Their lines are riddled with those oscillations between major and minor third, or between diminished fourth and minor third, which we have traced throughout Vaughan Williams's mature work, reaching maximum intensity in the Sixth Symphony. The orchestral accompaniment is sparse; solo woodwind, especially oboe, simultaneously recall human speech and the cries of sea-birds. At the reference to the young priest who will be needed to bury Michael, if dead he be, the orchestra wavers between parallel major and minor thirds, anticipating passages in the second and last movements of the Sixth Symphony. If the manner sounds faintly liturgical, the Church is dehumanized, God being synonymous with the unknowing sea.

With the entrance of the old woman Maurya, whom her daughters hope to shield from desperate knowledge as long as possible, a new but related motif emerges, again as potent in effect as it is exiguous in means:

This undulation up and down through a third (we meet it in several life-affirming contexts in earlier and later works) becomes a marvellous musical image for fortitude against a remorseless destiny. The pattern is repeated, like a refrain, while the orchestral texture is seldom free of the agitatedly alternating major-minor thirds. The passage wherein Maurya sings of the making of Michael's coffin generates intense harmonic anguish from only two parts, since the rising and falling third and its vacillating bass are in fluctuating false relation. Maurya's vocal line creates apparently artless song from sublimated speech, in a manner that contrasts with the art-full verbal inflexions in the early *On Wenlock Edge*.

In the empirical, through-composed idiom there are no seams, and the music reaches its first climax at the daughters' recognition that the sea-disgorged clothes are indeed Michael's. For the first time, movement becomes metrical, in a swaying $\frac{6}{4}$ as compulsive as the sea itself. Thematically, the lines stem from Maurya's fateful rising and falling third, the texture being bitonal in that the vocal line is frequently in the relation of unresolved appoggiatura to the organum fifths in the orchestra. Intensity is incremental as phrases, even whole clauses, are repeated a tone higher, much as speaking voices rise in pitch when excited; but the music droops into song-speech when the girls gird themselves to tell their mother of her last son's fate. When Maurya enters her theme of undulating third is harmonized at the tenth, so that major triads are persistently in false relation; there is pain in the false relations, but strength in the resonance of the tenths, even though – or perhaps the more so because – there are only two luminously spaced parts. When Maurya sings of her vision of Michael drowned, the motivic major and minor thirds climax in lyrical lament. The triadic harmony then shifts from E flat to E minor; $^6_4$ triads waver between F major and E flat minor, an effect close to the fade-out of the Sixth Symphony.

Maurya's 'vision' is arioso that might almost be called aria, for there is now a regular if asymmetrical pulse, initially in $^7_4$, later in $^5_4$ – a legacy from the asymmetrical ostinatos favoured by Holst. The texture is still exiguous, the $^6_3$ chords in parallel motion hardly counting as harmony, any more than they do in medieval organum with which Vaughan Williams's music has here some affinity. After the recognition of the last death the opera is all Maurya's; she sings a threnody not merely for her own dead, but for everyone's. The lament begins with an expansion of her scalewise-rising third to a fifth, harmonized mostly by diatonic concords in mediant relationship. Beginning on C, the theme is repeated and extended on E, the triads fluctuating between E major and the falsely related G major. Into her song the daughters and other women chorically interlace keenings, rotating around the rising pentatonic cry and the major-minor wail; bitonal storm-music in the background intermittently becomes foreground. It is worth noting that the storm-music, throughout the opera, is always at the same pitch (pentatonic G against A flat-E flat fifths): which may underline the obliviousness of Nature.

When the dead body is brought ashore this is both imitated and symbolized by levelly rising stepwise quavers, slurred in pairs. They survive throughout Maurya's magnificent final lament, which opens with her rising third from F to A, harmonized in false relation between F and D major. When the threnody is elevated a tone to E major-minor, she achieves something like acceptance, as well as stoic resignation. Four sharps appear as key signature, and her beautiful expansion of the third-based phrase on 'But it's a great rest I'll have now' is in heavenly E major, though with the tang of a sharp lydian fourth. The stepwise-rising motif in parallel triads gains strength; is interrupted for her blessings on the dead, accompanied by the 'liturgical' triads, with a key signature of four flats instead of sharps; but returns to lydian E major for her heroic blessing on 'my soul and on the soul of everyone is left living in the world':

The drama ends with choral keenings, flowing from the alternating major and minor thirds. Lydian E and the 'footsteps' motif in paired quavers return for the ultimate testament of acceptance: 'No man at all can be living for ever, and we must be satisfied'. This is not far from the Sixth Symphony's, epilogic recognition that 'We are such stuff As dreams are made on,' and the opera's music is a remarkably direct premonition of the Symphony, written fifty years later. The final vocal keening is on the tones F, E, C sharp; C sharp, C natural, A; A, A flat, F, E – ending with the exact pitches of the augmented motto in the Symphony's epilogue. In the opera, however, acceptance brings a kind of peace – perhaps because its environment, if elemental, is real, as compared with the spiritual limbo into which the Symphony evaporates.

Riders to the Sea was scored for a normal small orchestra with the addition of a sea-machine – which might be considered a contradiction in terms since it represents elemental Nature, as opposed to anything man-made, let alone mechanistic. The Seventh Symphony, over half a century later, is scored for a very large orchestra with, in addition to the normal symphonic apparatus, a celesta, harps, piano, organ, wordless voices, and an immense battery of exotic percussion, including a wind-machine. The purpose of the abnormal instruments is much the same as that of the sea-machine in *Riders*, though the lavish scoring in part springs from the music's origin in an ambitious film score. In this sense the exotic instruments indeed belong to another world, though Vaughan Williams imbues cinematic illusion with uncompromising truth; and could do so because the theme of Scott's Antarctic exploration coincided with his own spiritual pilgrimage, after the waste land of the Sixth Symphony's epilogue. We may think of that as a ruined landscape – bleaker than though related to that of the Pastoral Symphony; and also as Prospero's dream-stuff, for the two meanings coexist. Then Symphony No. 7, taking its cue from the frozen wastes of the Antarctic, asks where, if anywhere, we may go from here. Again there is a parallel with the Third (Pastoral) Symphony. Both works call on a wordless soprano solo in the last movement, her identity being at once human and non-human. In the Seventh the voices combine with the exotic instruments prompted by the visual images of the film to evoke magic.

Criticism has been levelled against the *Sinfonia Antartica* – the composer's use of the Italian title was perhaps intended to differentiate it from his 'straight' symphonies – on the grounds that it is hybrid; the film score, though brilliantly inventive as such, was of its nature too gimmick-ridden to be turned into a concert symphony. There is a measure of truth in this, but not enough to militate against the work's impressive originality. We have seen that it was not merely a matter of transforming an elaborate film score into a self-subsistent symphonic work; it was rather a consequence of the composer's realization that his Scott music was also his own story, in sequel to the crucial Sixth Symphony. And the first movement, called Prelude like the first movement of the Fifth and for similar reasons, immediately establishes parallels with the Sixth, for it is not in sonata form though it involves sonata-like oppositions. The first theme, in a slow-swaying triple pulse, is a marvellous aural image for the strifeful aspiration referred to in the epigraph from Shelley's *Prometheus Unbound* that precedes the score. It consists of a scale pressing up from E flat to C, with the B sharpened. Having descended to G, it rises in a wider arch from G to G; in the first rise the third is major, in the second, minor. The phrase is harmonized in diatonic concords, related either by minor second or major third: an instability that gives the music a sense of wonder, but also of fear:

We may find a close parallel in a superficially improbable place: the music which the American Virgil Thomson wrote for another film score, that to Flaherty's *Louisiana Story*. The music to which the oil-derrick floats down the Mississippi in ceremonious solemnity is built from diatonic concords similarly unrelated, harmonizing slowly flowing scales. Thus is evoked the mingled wonder and fear in the small boy's watching eye and listening ear. He, a denizen of that Acadian and Arcadian Southern environment, accepts wide-eyed and open-eared the clash between (moribund) rural innocence and (exploitative) industrial progress. Given the different context, the theme is basic Vaughan Williams; and Scott's exploration would not have been possible but for a similar precarious equilibrium between innocence and experience.

The opening theme, with its whole-tone instability, has no defined key and is always in flux, as is Thomson's Mississippi. Gradually, as the arches of the scales are extended, it gravitates to a phrygian G: at which point there is a sudden cessation and silence. This opening paragraph has been thickly scored; now, as Nature's supernatural instruments appear, texture thins. Xylophone, piano and harp quiver in impressionistic whole-tone timelessness; woodwind and strings stretch the undulating scale into a tritone-ridden cantillation; brass sustain soft dissonances, suggesting creaking ice. The opening paragraph would seem to present man in the wilderness; this second paragraph is Nature herself, not so much inimical to as oblivious of him. So the duality of sonata is manifest in a peculiarly direct form, and one hardly conducive to resolution. At this point soprano solo and wordless chorus distantly sound, without recognizably human identity; altos sigh in a declining semitone at that basic pitch of F to E, while soprano solo transmutes the string cantillation into slowly drooping alternations of major and minor third. This is almost identical with the keening at the end of *Riders to the Sea*; then it was human voices becoming elemental lament, here it is a voice of Nature which we may hear anthropomorphically. It prompts the 'human' rising scale to return cavernously on cellos, basses, bass clarinet and double bassoon, starting this time from E natural; but vanishes when the magic instruments (glockenspiel and vibraphone as well as celesta, harp and piano) shimmer again in their self-revolving patterns. If this began as illustrative Nature-music, its similarity to the mystical moments in Vaughan Williams's middle-period music is unmistakable, as is its kinship with the non-Western aspects of Holst.

The rest of the movement consists of gradually intensifying metamorphoses of the human/non-human opposition. With a change, *più mosso*, to $\frac{2}{2}$, the level crotchet pulse undulates chromatically, while brass expands in aspiring arabesques, rotating around the diminished fourth and minor third. The Nature-noises are always static since Nature has no reasons or purposes, but the brass hint in dissonantly rocking triplets at a pilgrim-like fanfare. Again the music breaks off in silence, as human effort falters; another limbo-like passage for woodwind in alternating thirds and fourths wanders through semitonic tremolandi on high violins. Tritones predominate in a slow-thumping march: through which solo soprano floats a long cantilena of alternating major and minor thirds, again almost identical with passages in the soprano solo of the Pastoral Symphony, as well as with the keenings in *Riders to the Sea*. Here she is perhaps a human rather than supernatural voice; for after the music has expired in viola tremolandos between the basic F and E, the first theme returns in more lyrically spacious form, in consort with what are explicitly called fanfares on distant trumpets. Their pentatonic figuration recalls the heroism of an earlier pilgrim, John Bunyan's Christian; the hope may be that his spiritual fortitude may be operative, even in the frozen wastes. Significantly, the key signature acquires four sharps, and the rising scale theme at least starts from E, though the sixth and seventh of the scale are usually flat. At this stage apotheosis for the pilgrim-in-limbo seems remotely feasible. The brass fanfares fuse with the singing strings and woodwind, persisting through the whirrings of Nature's magic instruments as tonality shifts from E to G. The first theme now incorporates the fanfares; despite further fluctuations between mediants, the final cadence shifts from second inversion A flat major to G major in root position. The fully scored conclusion is a G major triad; traditionally G major was a key of blessedness.

The prelude hymns man's aspiration in an arduous present. The scherzo – concerned, according to the epigraph from Psalm 104, with the ships and leviathans that cavort on and in the ocean – abandons strenuous endeavour and lives up to the jokiness of its genre, whether it is depicting the galumphing of sea-beasts and the yellings of sea-birds, or whether it allows man the respite of retrospection. The G-minorish pentatonic pastoral tunes that germinate, in $\frac{9}{8}$, on woodwind seem merrily oblivious of the strings' softly whirring winds and waters; spurred on by solo trumpet, the violins themselves lilt in an Arcadian dance, changing the G minor pentatonics to G major with some bitonal ambiguities. The magic instruments join in the dance, now in a frisky $\frac{6}{8}$. On a radiant morning at sea, Nature and man may for the moment love one another. Nature-music itself seems humane: at least the passage which, in the film, accompanies parading penguins conveys the creatures' comicality in a boogie-rhythmed music in Vaughan Williams's music-hall vein. Penguins can look like vaudeville clowns and, given a sunny day, may even render the Antarctic amiable. Not entirely so, however: for the penguin-music is based on rootless whole-tone non-progressions, and is swallowed by fragmented oscillations of thirds and tritones – which become a small whirlwind, transmuting penguins from anthropomorphic figures of fun back into denizens of the wilderness. Quavering woodwind birds and a disembodied version of the humanly pastoral dance disperse in ocillating dissonances on woodwind: music not so far from the 'limbo' passages in the second and last movements of the Sixth Symphony.

The third movement is that in which the human element intrudes least – as its title, 'Landscape', indicates. Out of wind and water noises four muted horns chant the basic motif of the Sixth Symphony's epilogue, E, F, A flat, F, E. Brass sing a kind of cantus firmus on the major-minor thirds but this, going nowhere, acquires no melodic identity. Gradually the pulse stills, as though frozen. Descending thirds on brass usher in a very slow $\frac{3}{2}$ section, the theme being an almost immobile procession of minims, mostly tritonal. These tritones are not so much devilish as neutral. One may construe neutrality as devilish in relation to time-dominated human feeling, but that is not Nature's intention, since she has none. The inexorable march of the minims is interrupted by sighing parallel triads on horns and woodwind, accompanied by the magic whirrings. In saying that they sigh we are of course speaking anthropomorphically, as though they were ourselves, conscious of our solitariness. When the tritonal march resumes it fades into a flute solo, piercing a dissonant chord sustained on divided strings, its contours again being those of the basic motif of the Sixth Symphony's epilogue. Slowly, permutations of this meandering theme reveal affinities with the chromatic wriggle that initiates the second movement of the Sixth. In a tonality that may be a chromaticized A, the melody almost acquires lyricism, though it is too lost, revolving around itself, to count as a humanly expressive song. Still, it is not nothing, even in face of a climactic statement of the tritonal procession, now *fortissimo*, scored for full orchestra, joined by organ moving in massive unrelated concords. The effect is scary, and the use of the 'mighty machine' in association with the inexorability of ice-floes was an inspired stroke. The most elaborately mechanized of instruments – at least before the invention of electrophonics – expresses Nature's non-humanity.

The final triadic concords clash excruciatingly with syncopated inverted pedals on B natural, sustained by strings, which make a brief attempt to re-establish the chromatically meandering theme. It disperses on muted trumpet, in sighing woodwinds, shimmering cymbals and glittering harp glissandos. This non-human landscape prompts human retaliation, however forlorn. For the intermezzo is just that: a retrospect of a human past, perhaps in childhood and youth. The oboe tune, in a swaying triple rhythm and with an unambiguous key signature of D major, so often Vaughan Williams's key of human fulfilment, begins with a rising major third, arching up to embrace the flat third in the upper octave, recalling a lost agrarian world. The tune is very close to several Bunyanesque hymn tunes we have noted in *Job*, the *Benedicite*, *Flos Campi* and the Fifth Symphony, not to mention *The Pilgrim's Progress* itself; and it is relevant to note that in the film this passage was associated with the explorer Wilson's day-dreaming about his distant wife. In an Antarctic context the tune, and D major, cannot be long sustained. Nature-noises undermine its simplicity; with a change from triple to duple pulse it becomes metrically syncopated and garners chromatics, which turn into the declining thirds. Even so, the tune learns by experience, for a solo violin, stealing out of the lyrical polyphony, becomes a slightly distraught lark! One would not expect him to live long in such an environment, nor does he. The music freezes into a slow march, reiterating a dissonant chord rooted on F, not E; the woodwind theme fuses the rising third of the 'folk song' with the self-revolving chromatics. In a brief coda, the quasi-folk tune sings, still in D, but from an immense distance, frostily. The final *pianissimo* harp chords are not D major, but B minor.

So the prelude has concerned man's courageous aspiration from within limbo, not necessarily in terms of Antarctic desolation. The scherzo has momentarily presented man and Nature in equipoise, *homo ludens* being fleetingly smiled on by an illusorily benign Nature. 'Landscape' deals with Nature's imperviousness, with minimal intrusion from man; while in the intermezzo man is for the time being allowed the luxury of memory. The epilogue gathers together the threads, which is what Vaughan Williams's epilogues are for. Through trilling and tremolando Nature-noises three trumpets chant a pentatonic fanfare – a heroic gesture recalling that of the first movement. The rhythm, however, is more jagged, as well it might be, that much further along the frozen way; and the original rising scale, blazed on brass as it seeks stronger affirmation, acquires too a motif of quavers slurred in pairs, similar to those at the end of *Riders to the Sea* – another unconscious memory recurring after a gap of half a century. Brass take up this quaver motif; violins metamorphose the chromatic oscillation into a lyricism that embraces the paired quavers also. The original pitches (E, F, G, A flat) recur at a climactic point, and the arches of the melody sound sea-sick. The see-saw is steadied by hammered crotchet triplets, thickly scored. Wordless voices creep in, undulating between that basic E and F natural, and are linked, in a rare allegro, with the aspiring fanfare on brass. Tremolando strings cascade down through the alternating thirds, leading to a recapitulation of the Symphony's opening, harmonized in the same unrelated concords. Aspiration, it seems has weathered – spiritually as well as physically – the pain that flesh is heir to: as it had, judging from Scott's last words in his journal, in the case of this particular pilgrim through the unknown region. If the end is nirvana, or nothingness, this is a victory not for evil, but for Nature's neutrality. The distant soprano solo fades into a cantilena of falling thirds. She may be both the human spirit disembodied and the voice of Nature herself; but the sighing $^6_3$ chords of the women's chorus would seem to be inanimate winds rather than crying humans. They fade into the noise of the wind-machine, which is irremediably other than human. Even so, the pedal G on which the sighs are earthed is a tonic, of sorts; the triumphal G major triad with which the prelude had concluded is not totally forgotten. Man lives to fight another day: or at least if Scott did not, Vaughan Williams did, way into his eighties. The music of his last years does not deny the death of the heart, though it tells us that miracles may still happen. However we may rate the *Sinfonia Antartica* in relation to his supreme masterpieces – its position is perhaps comparable with that of the Fourth Symphony – we can have no doubt that it was a necessary stage in his pilgrimage. Without it, the final phase would have been impossible.

XII

SECOND CHILDHOOD

VAUGHAN WILLIAMS, THE CHRISTMAS STORY AND
THE LIGHT OF GOD: *FANTASIA ON THE OLD 104th;*
HODIE; THE SONS OF LIGHT

Thou meetest with things dying, I with things new born.
SHAKESPEARE, The Old Shepherd, in *The Winter's Tale*

We were young, we were merry, we were very, very wise.
MARY COLERIDGE

With all your science can you tell me how it is, and whence it is, that light comes into the soul?

HENRY THOREAU

Vaughan Williams's Sixth and Seventh Symphonies, composed during the fifties when he was in his seventies, ended in something that might be mistaken for nihilism, though it is not quite that. Clearly, however, a kind of rebirth was imperative if he was to go on; and that is what happened during his eighties and the century's sixth decade. As a preliminary, Vaughan Williams clears the decks in the last year of the fifties by composing two works, one of which is entirely valedictory while the other combines elegy with prophecy. Neither is a major work, though the second of them is of peculiar fascination.

The valedictory piece is explicitly called *An Oxford Elegy*, and is retrospective not merely in setting parts of Matthew Arnold's threnodies 'The Scholar-Gipsy' and 'Thyrsis', but also in being a throwback to the earliest years of Vaughan Williams's creativity. As long ago as 1901 he had considered using these poems as the basis for a theatrical work, and we can see that Victorian Arnold's laments, in 'The Scholar-Gipsy', about 'this strange disease of modern life, With its sick hurry, its divided aims', and his dismay in 'Dover Beach', over the 'ignorant armies' that 'clash by night', would have struck chords in the young composer. The later elegies must have appealed to Vaughan Williams the more since Arnold's nostalgia is there deeply sensuous in evoking an English Eden for ever lost. Significantly, Arnold's poems fuse a mythical past – that of the legendary Scholar-Gipsy who, some two hundred years back, mysteriously vanished from Oxford – and a painful personal event, the early death of his Oxford friend, the poet Arthur Hugh Clough. It may be that the Second World War recalled to Vaughan Williams the loss, in the First World War, of friends and colleagues of his own, such as George Butterworth; certainly he might have seen himself as a Pan-like scholar-gipsy who in youth had tramped miles through Palmer's English countryside in the wake of another scholar-gipsy, George Borrow, to whose *Lavengro* he was addicted. The idea of making an opera out of Arnold's meditative poems was surely doomed from the start; yet when Vaughan Williams, in old age, compromised on spoken narration with choral and orchestral commentary it works, making an elegy not so much in a social context as in general reference to Spenserian mutability.

Musically, the piece is unusual in Vaughan Williams's work in being unashamedly nostalgic, harking back to the English Eden of *The Shepherd of the Delectable Mountains* and still more to the sensory luxuriance of the more recent *Serenade to Music*. The use of (often wordless) chorus recalls the magic choralism of *Flos Campi*, less dangerously, because retrospectively; and the speaker, too, distances the experience, for moments of transcendence are recollected in tranquility rather than being, as in *The Lark Ascending*, immediately manifest. The speaker is, as it were, Vaughan Williams, or you or I, whose memories evoke the past in ripe orchestral sonorities and in choral music that catches Blake's 'dream as it flies.' Throughout, the work, though patently nostalgic, concerns a quest which, in the section about the 'high mountain tops where is the throne of Truth', relates to the progress of the Pilgrim who had dominated Vaughan Williams's creative life. For a brief moment, setting the words about the 'causeway chill', the choric voices almost suggest that the pilgrimage may end in the wailing winds of the *Sinfornia Antartica*. But when the epilogue tell us that 'the light we sought is shining still', this valedictory work presages the music of the composer's last decade.

The *Oxford Elegy* concerns the 'things dying' referred to by Shakespeare's Old Shepherd. In the other transitional work of 1949 – the *Fantasia on the Old 104th*, for piano solo, chorus and orchestra – things dying meet with 'things new born'; even for the scoring of the work there is no precedent, except in Beethoven's *Choral Fantasia*. Whereas *An Oxford Elegy* taps Vaughan Williams's rural well-springs, the *Fantasia on the Old 104th* does as much for his heritage in English Anglican tradition which, we have noted, still precariously survived. In basing the piece on what Hardy called 'Ravenscroft's terse old tune', Vaughan Williams pays homage to that tradition, not so much as religious experience, but rather as a continuing manifestation of English communal life. At the same time, in juxtaposing that communal conservatism with solo piano music, often in the form of free cadenza, Vaughan Williams offers perhaps the most extreme instance of doubleness in his work. The choral-orchestral music, closely related to the seventeenth-century tune, maintains communal life in sturdy diatonicism and modality; the solo piano writing, on the other hand, is wildly improvisatory and is – even more than the solo pianism in the Piano Concerto – rooted in false relation and bitonality. The parallel with Busoni, discussed in relation to Vaughan Williams's Piano Concerto, is here even more pertinent.

Duality is evident in the unusual form of the work – a cross between rondo and variations, in which the hymn serves as an evolving (varied) rondo tune, while the piano provides disparate episodes, usually in the form of solo cadenzas. After the orchestra has announced the first phrase of Ravenscroft's melody in aeolian D minor, the piano immediately fragments the tune into clangorous sevenths and whirling arabesques, usually based on ambiguous thirds. This first cadenza ends by re-establishing the hymn in massively harmonized concords in a mode that seems to be a cross between lydian D flat and aeolian F; the point of the 'flatness' will not be fully apprehensible until the end of the work, when the hymn triumphs in D major. The chorus, supported by strings, enters with the hymn slightly decorated. Climactically, chorus, piano and tutti 'shine most clear' in a melismatic act of praise. This 'light of God' is again dimmed by the piano's second cadenza, much longer than the first, more glassily bitonal in texture, flowing through many modalities, with cross rhythms, false-related triads, and a remarkably Busoni-like passage of $\frac{6}{4}$ chords, peppered with off-key arabesques:

Stealthily, the chorus reintroduces the hymn in octave unisons, and the next variation, back in aeolian D minor, is affirmatively fugal. Yet again this is disrupted, initially in aeolian-lydian F, by a still longer piano cadenza, in which Busonian major-minor figuration attains a spectral translucency, near atonal rather than bitonal. Rhythm also is fragmented; in total effect this cadenza is as mysterious as the most hermetic passages of Busoni's *Fantasia Contrappuntistica*. This is not a matter of conscious influence, but of consanguinity of mind. Just as Busoni remakes Bach's contrapuntal faith in the glimmering light of his uncertain aspiration, so Vaughan Williams as double man remoulds an Anglican metrical psalm: which seems to survive, however bewilderingly double the piano's textures may be, since hymn and piano coalesce, at the end of the cadenza, in a simple if remote statement of the tune in stellar register, in the aeolian mode on F. Triumph is indisputable when another statement of the hymn succeeds in mixolydian D, which is often straight D major, with two brave sharps in the key signature. Chorus and orchestra reverberate, bell-like, in the key which for Vaughan Williams so often seems to mean home, haleness and wholeness, if not holiness; and the piano has lost its 'double' quality, for it clatters in toccata-like repeated notes and triadic figuration, gloriously gilding, but in no way subverting, the hymn. This would seem to be a victory for the 'terse old' Anglican tune (and for the church organ, which exuberantly joins in the final peroration) over the vagaries of the piano's solitary heart. It is oddly moving that some of Vaughan Williams's most weirdly individualistic music – that of the piano cadenzas – should hark back to the dichotomies of the Tallis Fantasia of thirty years earlier; and that the potency of the seventeenth-century Anglican hymn should finally blaze through as it was, is now, and hopefully ever shall be, in this church (rather than concert hall), in this performance. Perhaps this positive statement was no less necessary for the fruition of Vaughan Williams's final phase than was the uncompromising fortitude of the Sixth and Seventh Symphonies.

However this may be, Vaughan Williams's 'second childhood' finds wondrous expression in his Christmas cantata *Hodie*, a large-scale work for large forces, first performed in 1954, when he was eighty-two. Vaughan Williams characteristically said that he hated Christmas but liked the idea of it. Now, in old age, he sees the Christmas story as that of the Boy who was born: thereby echoing the title of the first major work of Britten's adolescent genius and demonstrating, no less than the young man's piece, how deeply the Christmas myth may be relevant to our bruised and battered century. Even so, it is significant that Vaughan Williams should treat the story archetypically (in the Jungian sense), setting it in a traditionally Christian social context. England's past, as well as the individual psyche, is here renascent, the convention being that of a pristine English oratorio, merged into an Anglicized version of the Bachian Passion or sacred history – a convention which, by then, was a part of English life. Simply harmonized carols take the place of Lutheran chorales, representing us the people; unisonal treble soloists become boy evangelists, narrating the story in recitative suggested by the liturgy of the English Reformed, instead of the German Lutheran, Church. The music for the boy evangelists is close to that of the Woodcutter's Boy in the Delectable Mountains scene of *The Pilgrim's Progress*; and we have noted the sense in which he was a rebirth. Despite the early date (1922) of the original Delectable Mountains cantata, the Woodcutter's Boy was almost certainly added for the final version of the opera, produced in 1951, just before *Hodie:* in which piece the words of the narratives are from the Gospels, while choral numbers are from the Vespers for Christmas Day and from early Milton, solo songs from George Herbert and William Drumond, and carols from Miles Coverdale and Hardy. Two poems were specially written by Ursula Vaughan Williams; all the texts, sixteenth-, seventeenth-, nineteenth- and twentieth-century, are in tune with the composer's life-long preoccupations.

The prologue, for four-part chorus and orchestra, is in a sense liturgical, since the words are from the Vesper Service for Christmas Day. But Vaughan Williams treats this celebration of a Saviour's birth, carolled by us along with choirs of angels and archangels, with a pristine immediacy that is of the earth, earthy. The metre is a vivacious $\frac{6}{8}$ often crossed with $\frac{3}{4}$; the texture is at first unisonal or in parallel fourths, which is as non-harmonic as one can get. Modality, however, is ambiguous, for though the key signature has three flats, the scale seems to be E flat, F, G, A flat, B flat, C flat, D flat. One might at a pinch call it mixolydian (with flat sixth); certainly its flavour is oddly archaic, quasi-medieval and faintly oriental. The choir's cries of 'Nowell' in organum fourths clang like bells; the bass line often rotates in a primitive ostinato in dotted rhythm. The choir's tune, when they have one, is also ostinato-like, rocking through a minor third B flat to G, then careening up and down through B flat, C flat, D flat and E flat. By such means the music creates an eternal present as vernal as medieval cantillation. In the context of the modern world it sounds like a child's rune; there is some affinity with the children's music of Carl Orff.

As one might expect, compositional procedures are sectional rather than devlopmental. When, for the Glorias, the key signature changes to one sharp, the rhythm also becomes more seductive; Vaughan Williams marks it *allegro alla tedesca*, recalling the strange ländler in the Piano Concerto. Here the G major tonality is consistently lydian, with sharp fourth, though the choral Glorias make many triadic side-steps, and the $\frac{3}{4}$ waltz rhythm is often broken into $\frac{6}{8}$. The climactic Glorias are canonic bells in cross rhythms, which expand into alleluyas in $\frac{3}{2}$, the seventh of the G major scale now being flattened. This music is rather grand, if still pristine. But with a shift down a tone to lydian F the manner abruptly becomes impudently dance-like in $\frac{2}{4}$, and the choral harmony, though all the parts move by step, is undermined by whole-tone progressions. This is a Puckish gloss on the presumed innocence of childhood: which leads into a brief, almost laconic coda returning first to the $\frac{3}{2}$ alleluyas, then to a shortened da capo of the original section at the original pitch.

The first of the Narrations, telling the tale of Christ's miraculous birth and the visitation of the angelic messenger, is taken from the Gospel of St. Matthew. Here as throughout it is sung by choirboy trebles, not solo but in unison: a device which ensures impersonality and neutrality. The words themselves, as well as their setting, suggest that this is an old tale that happened in the once-upon-a-time, yet is vital to us all: as is appropriate to Vaughan Williams's view of the matter, which takes the tale as psychologically true but in the strict sense mythical rather than historical. But 'history' is inherent in the manner of presentation, for the accompaniment is for a small Anglican church organ such as was and is in use throughout the parish churches of England. It begins with a pentatonic melisma, but then supports the vocal declamation with simple concords freely related – an extension of the technique of harmonic underlining as practised in the sixteenth-century liturgy of the Reformed Church. Basically, the pentatonic declamation echoes that of the spoken words, with a minimum of expressivity, let alone drama. The boys merely tell the tale; only occasionally does an unexpected (but still concordant) triad point a detail of the text, as when the 'angel of the Lord appeared unto him in a dream'. The parallel is perhaps with the sacred histories of Bach's predecessor Heinrich Schütz (which Vaughan Williams knew and loved), rather than with Tudor liturgical music itself.

Certainly the angelic music itself is Schützian, for the heavenly visitor is characterized in music for tenor solo far more impassioned than the treble narrative. Indeed, his song turns out to be another permutation of the blessing-curse motif that plays so crucial a part in *Job* and the later symphonies. His descending cry is harmonized with false-related concords of light C major and dark E flat minor – a dichotomy that will haunt the rest of the cantata:

The Angel veers between such dramatically impassioned outbursts and syllabic narration similar to that of the boys, though his fluctuating concords (between F sharp major and F minor) are far more falsely mysterious, recalling the desolation of *Riders to the Sea* and related passages in the Sixth and Seventh Symphonies. And out of mystery springs triumph, in the vision of Emmanuel ('God be with us'), wherein C major trumpet fanfares rout the darkness of E and A flat minors.

The Angel's visitation makes briefly possible a state of blessedness. What Vaughan Williams accurately calls a Song sets part of the young Milton's hymn 'On the Morning of Christs Nativity': seventeenth-century poetry which typically fuses sophisticated post-Renaissance artifice with a dewy morning atmosphere. This Vaughan Williams's music exquisitely catches as it flows in an equable pastoral $\frac{6}{8}$, delicately scored for woodwind and strings. The key is benedictory G major with hints of aeolian E. The soprano solo's line moves either by step or pentatonically, lyrically but scrupulously following the elaborate metrics of the verse. In the last section about the Prince of Light the soloist is echoed by women of the chorus in head voice. Note how beautifully the vocal rhythm responds to the calm expansion of Milton's final lines:

> ... the mild ocean,
> Who now hath quite forgot to rave,
> While birds of calm sit brooding on the charmed wave.

The next narration tells of the visit to Bethlehem for the gathering of taxes. The music, recalling a distant past, is initially unchanged, though the minute chromatic alterations are, given the events recounted, more acute: consider the sudden A flat within the radiant F major, and the shift therefrom to lydian F sharp for the Child's birth. At this point follows the first chorale, which is also a carol: a four-part homophonic setting of words adapted by Miles Coverdale, one of the makers of the Tudor Bible, from Luther himself. The flowing, triple-rhythmed tune is in the aeolian mode on D; the harmony is purely diatonic, with not a single accidental throughout the three stanzas. Though the music is Vaughan Williams's own, the carol serves exactly the same function as a 'traditional' chorale in a Bach Passion, relating the sacred story to us the people. Such simplicity, without fear or evasion, must count in our fallen world as a creation of genius. Especially touching is the effect of the Kyries at the end, when vestigial canons emerge from the homophonic texture to cadence plagally, in hemiola rhythm.

The Angelic Messenger reappears in the next narration, to which the organ prelude is itself more urgent, embracing cross-relations between triads of F and D majors. The Angel, bringing good tidings, chants the same blessing-curse theme sung at his first appearance, with the same harmonies alternating between light C major and dark E flat minor. But his melismata are more ecstatically extended, while the orchestra's triadic oscillations are even more precariously balanced between F sharp and F, now both minor. Whereas the treble evangelists are always accompanied by church organ, the Angel is orchestrally supported: a device borrowed from Bach's obbligato (rather than continuo) accompaniment to the words of Christ. The vision of the Birth prompts a recapitulation of the first movement's jubilation, embracing the *allegro alla tedesca*, the lydian Glorias (at first in the original G, then in lydian C), and the duple-rhythmed dance, now in lydian A major, a key hinting at both healing and hope. A recurrence of the chorically tolling bells, again canonic in G major, is not unlike a tonally 'ironed-out' version of the blessing-curse. The final Glorias in the German waltz add E flat to the lydian C sharps, creating whole-tone ambiguities: as befits a reborn child like octogenarian Vaughan Williams. When the trebles round off the narration accompanied only by organ, however, the music regains pentatonic innocence, the mode veering between G major and minor, with touches of aeolian E.

The seventh movement is another song which is also a carol; and is a little miracle, the emotional core of the work. There is point in this since Thomas Hardy's poem, recounting an old folk legend that on Christmas Eve the cattle in their 'strawy pen' are wont to kneel in homage to the newborn Son of God, encapsulates Vaughan Williams's approach to the Christ Mass. The tale is recounted as a memory of childhood:

> In the lonely barton by yonder coomb
> Our childhood used to know,
> I should go with him in the gloom,
> Hoping it might be so.

The key slightly modifies the narration's G major to dorian E, as the music opens with a diaphanous canon between flute and cor anglais, soon joined by oboe and bassoon. Baritone solo tells the story and paints the scene with much of the simplicity of the treble's narration, this being a tale within a tale, far away and long ago, yet also within living memory. Mystery accrues from modal alteration until a momentary modulation to diatonic A major – that key of youth and hope – prepares us for the 'fair fancy' that just possibly we today might glimpse the kneeling beasts. The final stanza returns to a modified version of the falling canons in dorian E, though a wondrous shift to what is almost Edenic E major prefaces the words 'Hoping it might be so'. The movement fades in its vestigial canon:

The next narration, which is brief, is pentatonic on F over a gently stalking pizzicato bass. It serves as prelude to a recapitulation of the *alla tedesca* Glorias, still in lydian G, though their whole-tone ambivalence is reinforced by a magic celesta. This visionary gleam is not at first present in the ninth movement, a song for baritone solo, headed Pastoral, similar to but less pristine than the soprano's setting of early Milton. This time the text is by George Herbert; we recall that Vaughan Williams had set Herbert early in his career in the Five Mystical Songs. Then he was too close to Edwardian convention fully to reveal Herbert's heart and soul. This beautiful song, however, penetrates to Herbert's essence, reflecting the poem's discreet sensuality, domestic wit and ultimate transcendence when the candle is metamorphosed into a sun which, although 'frost-nipt', is a 'willing shiner'. Vaughan Williams responds adequately, which is saying a lot, to Herbert's fusion of the metaphors of singing and shining:

the sun's 'beams shall cheer my breast, and both so twine That even his beams sing, and my music shine'. Here, as in the soprano's Milton setting, the pulse flows levelly in $\frac{9}{8}$ rather than $\frac{6}{8}$. The texture is freely polyphonic, always about to take off through volatile modulations. Even so, the 'home' of fulfilled and fulfilling D major is never lost sight of, and the baritone solo, responsive to the minutest verbal inflexion, steers the final 'singing and shining' into a radiant D major, with a long sustained tonic D on the word 'shine' which has no need of a crescendo. The final D major chord sounds as though we have never heard one before: as in a sense we have not, since true creation is always a birth.

Only a very brief narration separates this song from the hardly less exquisite Lullaby, for soprano solo and the women of the chorus, in antiphony. The narration is in G flat – really F sharp as upper mediant to the Pastoral's D. But the lullaby – a setting of a sixteenth-century carol set to music as an ayre by John Attey in 1622 – is in E flat. Vaughan Williams's version pays deference to Attey's, and has something of his dew-on-the-grass quality, perhaps accruing from the emergent tonality, which cannot decide whether it is aeolian C or straight E flat major. The middle section, telling of God's descent from on high to our terrestrial world, is more darkly in aeolian F, over a tonic pedal; but diatonic E flat major returns for the last stanza and 'lullas'. Throughout, the level quaver movement is hardly disturbed by accidentals, though the final cadence has an acutely tender secundal dissonance. The final E flat major triad sounds new-born.

Paired with this soprano carol is a hymn for tenor solo, setting another seventeenth-century poet. This song of praise is very different from the lullaby in both mood and manner, for the words offer a more consciously rhetorical version of the young Milton's artifice in his hymn on the Nativity. They key is still E flat, and the movement still in level quavers, but one could not call this music child-like. The mode on E flat resists classification, though it has analogies with that of the opening movement of the cantata. But it makes more of the scale's whole-tone implications, tending towards an exoticism that matches Drummond's ornate rhetoric. The effect, evoking 'bright portals of the sky', 'sparkling stars' and the 'doors of eternity', is appropriately magical, and magic instruments – first heard in *Flos Campi* but reappearing in the Sixth and Seventh Symphonies – are again active, enhancing with their tinklings the music's incipient orientalism. Tonality is in flux, undermined by whole-tone triads and undulations. The quite long movement has a luxuriance very different from the purity of the carols, though it has an innocence of its own, since its whole-tone mysteries induce, especially in the coda, a wide-eyed expectation: as the (re)birth of God well might.

In context the hymn is cannily placed, for it introduces the most extended dramatic, and pictorial, episode in the cantata: the visit of the Wise Men from the East. The trebles' narration begins in unsullied pentatonicism on E, at first monodically, then in organum. At the appearance of the star over the manger tonality momentarily becomes an equally unsullied E major, though the narration fades out in pentatonic E minor. This drops a tone for the March of the Three Kings, which begins darkly in pentatonic organum in D minor, the metre trudging, and with the familiar God-motif of rising fourth lifting to fifth on trombone and viola. The quasi-oriental manner is close to that of the march in *Flos Campi*, though the 'dark strangers' here do not have the minatory undertones of the earlier march. If there is savagery in their simplicity, that is not necessarily a negative quality; the carol-like poem, which was written for the occasion by Ursula Vaughan Williams, is about the interdependence of life and death, and ends with a vision of the 'star of dayspring' whose 'sharp radiance lights the stable and the broken walls'.

At this point Vaughan Williams transmutes the lumpish march into a spacious hymn beginning with a noble fifth, in variously modalized G and D. The winding descent from high D to low D flat may be another permutation of Job's blessing-curse. Major-minor vacillations pervade the homophony also, especially when the three soloists (soprano, tenor and baritone) together hymn the 'bitter gift' of myrrh with weird teeterings similar to those associated with the Angel earlier in the cantata, and manifest too in *Riders to the Sea* and the second and fourth movements of Symphony No. 6. The passage again suggests that, but for darkness, light would be inapprehensible. The movement – by far the most substantial in the piece – ends with the chorus in resonant antiphony, as the dayspring sheds radiance on the hill-top. Finally the G major-minor bitonality settles on a pedal D, above which soloists and chorus weave polyphonies basically in D major, though with many modal alterations. The movement subsides in the original pentatonic ostinato-march, with the fundmental motif of fourth rising to fifth to flat seventh ringing on muted horns.

That is the end of the cantata's dramatic argument – or more accurately of its story-telling. Before the epilogue Vaughan Williams inserts another chorale-carol, the first verse of which is anonymous while the second was added, at Vaughan Williams's request, by his wife. The theme of this poem is consummatory, telling how

> Promise fills the sky with light. ...
> Never since the world began
> Such a light such dark did span.

And for it Vaughan Williams finds a consummate musical image: again a symmetrical tune in four pulse, in D flat, but oscillating between major and minor, as between light and darkness. This fundamental 'false' relation does not destroy the music's serenity, though it deepens its effect; for this reason the carol-chorale, sung unaccompanied, sounds, like the poem, consummatory as well as consummate. The texture's compromise between organum-style parallel fifths and false-related chromatics is precisely apposite to the equilibrium between darkness and light; the triumph of light may be symbolized by the narration's boy trebles joining in the second stanza.

This is the last we hear of them, the tale's timeless narrators; for although the epilogue begins with declamation, starting from the weirdly undulating F sharp and F minor triads previously associated with the Angel, it is sung by the three soloists in sequence, moving upwards from baritone to tenor to soprano. It is as though supernatural power has become natural, because manifest in us through the incarnation. The words begin with the apocalyptic Word of St John the Divine, telling us that 'in him was life and the life was the light of men'. Outbursts of the Emmanuel motif of the first movement make the ultimate climax, the magic instruments clattering in whole-tone mysteries while the chorus resonates on C major triads. The blessing-curse motif, after recurrent declensions on woodwind, ends in a phrygian descent to G: which ushers in the final chorus, the words again being from Milton's youthful hymn 'On the Morning of Christs Nativity'. Youthfulness is appropriate to a piece about birth, and is manifest in this galliard-hymn, comparable with the Sons of the Morning music in *Job*. The opening choric phrase is pentatonic; for many pages there are no accidentals, though momentum springs from cross-accents between the verbal rhythms and the prancing beat of the dance. There are momentary modulations when, in the hymn's words, the 'well-balanced world' is hung on 'hinges' and the 'weltering waves' are channelled by the Great Creator – as though the buoyantly youthful Milton were anticipating the Newtonian mechanistic universe. But he does so as a jubilant (G major) game, which Vaughan Williams shares in as he swings the music into majestic hemiola rhythms, veering between diatonic G major and aeolian E. Still there are virtually no accidentals, and the grand homophony – in which the soloists are instructed to participate – is undisturbed until the massive final cadence. This is not, however, a dominant-tonic but a III, IV, II, I progression, without the crudity of a 'leading' note. Such music is at once old and new. We are not 'getting anywhere', but are what we are; Vaughan Williams's conservatism itself becomes rebirth.

This is why *Hodie* may be unique in musical history. It owes its perennial youthfulness to its being the creation of an octogenarian; 'second childhood' may be the opposite of senility, and however vulnerable his new-born Boy may be, he can end his Christmas cantata in unblinking but far from absurd optimism. Since the work asks Thoreau's question – 'Can you tell me how it is, and whence it is, that light comes into the soul?' – it would seem relevant to append a note on a minor work, composed a year or two before, which is specifically about the 'Sons of Light'. Its text, again specially written by Ursula Vaughan Williams, explores the theme of darkness and light, as do the verses she contributed to *Hodie*. *The Sons of Light* was commissioned by Bernard Shore, who was then head of Her Majesty's Inspectorate of Schools Music and director of the Schools Music Association. Scored for massed youth-choirs and the London Philharmonic Orchestra (initially conducted by Sir Adrian Boult), it was first performed by a choir of 1,150 young people. The composer made no concession either to youth or to amateurs; that the choral parts include a high proportion of unisonal writing is probably due mainly to the fact that massed unison voices are intrinsically effective. Although the cantata is not a major work like *Hodie*, its exhuberance would be astonishing from any, let alone an octogenarian, composer. The orchestra is large, the scoring, to compete with the massed voices, at once luxuriant and sharp-edged. The energy and potentiality of the young are incarnate in the bounding rhythms, thrusting lines, and dense orchestration, now glowing, now glassy.

The first movement, actually called 'Darkness and Light', telescopes several creation myths. The Greek story of the sun driven across the sky by Apollo becomes a myth of generation, as light and darkness are separated at the birth of time. The moon follows the stars and the poem ends with a procession of the stars: the celestial lights by which man will live 'till Time is done'. Magic instruments appear for the 'swan-feathered plains of arctic snow' and the stellar spaces. The music no longer recalls the Holst of *The Planets* but is essential Vaughan Williams, stemming from the Sixth and Seventh Symphonies. The second movement, 'The Song of the Zodiac', is a set of runic rhymes about the astrological signs. The music shines, as do the signs, and makes magic in being hieratic, metrically tight, repetitive, and therefore anticipatory of the child-like, runic episodes in *Hodie*. The Sign of the Virgin introduces Edenic relaxation into the tight textures, but the magic of Scorpion and Archer is again rigorously formalistic, weaving spells. The Goat has moments of frivolity in a fast waltz *alla tedesca*: which suggests, along with the *tedesca* episodes in the Piano Concerto and in *Hodie*, that this genre of music may have been associated by Vaughan Williams with folly. Fools, like little children, are sometimes very wise – as Mary Coleridge pointed out in one of the epigraphs to this chapter.

The last movement – youth needs no slow movement – extends the Creation myth into Genesis. 'Winged Messengers' give man the gift of speech. Inspired by the morning star, he must name the creatures, thereby giving them conscious identity. Out of the darkness 'Light is scattered jewels that you wear. Light shall be light for ever and the darkness night, man shall awake and speak their names aloud and set a name on fire and wind and cloud. . . . Rejoice, man stands among the 'Sons of Light'. The piece ends – of course in E major – with riotous fanfares and pounding drums, a simple but not simple-minded affirmation which is as energetic, and as purposeful in direction, as youth may hope to be. If we think this coda crude, that is because man is, in the context of eternity, a crude animal. We hear the music with ears still tingling with the magic shimmerings of the end of the first movement, and the crystalline sonorities of the zodiac music. These are indeed sounds that 'never were' on land or sea, though we will hear much of them, transformed and transforming, in Vaughan Williams's two final major works, his Symphony No. 8 and Symphony No. 9.

XIII

A DOUBLE MAN'S LAST HARVEST

INNOCENCE AND EXPERIENCE
IN *TEN BLAKE SONGS*, THE EIGHTH SYMPHONY
AND THE NINTH SYMPHONY

A Stranger here
Strange Things doth meet, strange Glory see.
Strange Treasures lodg'd in this fair World appeare,
Strange and all New to me:
But that they *mine* should be who Nothing was,
That strangest is of all; *yet brought to pass.*

THOMAS TRAHERNE, 'The Salutation'

I give you the end of a golden string,
Only wind it into a ball,
It will lead you in at heaven's gate
Built in Jerusalem's wall.

England, awake! awake! awake!
Jerusalem thy Sister calls!
Why wilt thou sleep the sleep of death
And close her from thy ancient walls?

WILLIAM BLAKE, 'Jerusalem'

Vaughan Williams's Eighth and Ninth Symphonies form a pair of complementary opposites, as do the Second and Third and the Fourth and Fifth (though not the Sixth and Seventh, which are more complementary than opposite). The duality they embrace – that between innocence and experience – had been a seminal force behind all Vaughan Williams's music, from early years; but nowhere is the *conjunctio oppositorum* – in Blake's and Jung's sense – more palpable than in Symphonies Eight and Nine. We may approach them by way of another work of Vaughan Williams's final years, the ten settings for solo voice or for voice and oboe of poems selected specifically from Blake's *Songs of Innocence and Experience*. Though in an obvious sense a small work, this must count as one of Vaughan Williams's supreme masterpieces. In returning to the oneness of monody, the songs might seem to be an apotheosis of innocence; they tell us, however, that oneness that was purely so might be heartless and mindless; whereas twoness, if pure, may have its own truth, which is the innocence of its honesty.

Technically, the profundity of these small songs cannot be separated from their polymodality. None is in a straight diatonic major or minor key; neither is any in a clearly defined mode. Modality is in flux, at the behest of the emotive significance of intervals. This, of course, is how modes always function: for a mode is not an abstraction within which tunes may be fitted, but is a deduction from acoustical phenomena and from the ways in which sounds behave as people use them. Thus the first song, 'Infant joy', is undeniably a song of innocence since the singer is a baby 'but two days old', for whom, as far as he or she knows, 'all is summer, all is sunshine, always'. Yet for human creatures instinctual joy is a beginning, not an end: as may be implicit in Blake's curious final line, 'Sweet joy befall thee!', which sounds a little like a threat. Moreover, Vaughan Williams's setting is not a monody but a duologue between tenor or soprano voice and oboe – traditionally a pastoral instrument at home in English Edens yet also, in its orchestral evolution during the nineteenth century, an instrument at once introspective and expressive. In this first song the oboe's role is Arcadian; it sings – croons to itself, like a baby – a little phrase stemming from that most instinctual interval the fourth, with a pentatonic tailpiece rotating around E flat and D flat. Either note might be the tonic, though the key signature is that of G flat, on which note the voice part ends. One might call the oboe's mode pentatonic with an occasional extra tone, though never with a leading note. The voice part, being human, is more articulate: more lyrically extended and more rhythmically formulated. If we think of its tonic as E flat (there are other possible choices), it is in the dorian mode, the sharp sixths of which often form the interval of a third or sixth with the momentarily stationary oboe line. From this euphony the song's infantile sweetness is distilled – and also perhaps its wistfulness, since the mellifluous consonance passes like a dream. Innocence is inherent in the free rhythm of the oboe's arabesques, which are Nature's voice, coming to us through the agency of Pan or a piping shepherd. The rhythmic flexibility of the vocal part has a different source – its response to the spoken inflexions of the poem, in an attempt to be humanly articulate, as the bird-like baby grows to consciousness.

'Infant joy' is ambiguous in modality, as befits infancy, rather than polymodal. The second song, 'A Poison Tree', is as polymodal as we would expect Experience to be, demonstrating how heavy a burden of 'negative' emotions a single line may carry, let alone a vocal line in dialogue with another instrumental melody. The mysterious poem is about anger, jealousy and deceit, exhibiting that 'terrifying honesty' which T. S. Eliot attributed to Blake.

I was angry with my friend;
I told my wrath, my wrath did end.
I was angry with my foe;
I told it not, my wrath did grow.

These words are preceded by a serpentine oboe melody in what might be the dorian mode on D, though the seventh is sometimes sharpened. The extension of the phrase after the voice has entered, in stepwise movement, thrusts up to the flattened fifth, the devilish tritone, while in the descent to the tonic D the E is flattened into the phrygian mode. So although the contours of both oboe and voice melody spring from the instinctual behaviour of intervals and from the pressure of words, they generate a powerful electrical charge. It is hardly extravagant to say that between them the two melodies create a psychological drama related to that of the composer's mature symphonies. Thus the poem offers images for the monstrous fruit that jealousy nurtures, with murderous consequence; and to match it Vaughan Williams's two lines grow ever more polymodal and more dissonant in relation to one another. Permutations of the obsessive declining thirds entwine into the arabesques, vividly evoking in their serpentine convolutions a Fall from Eden; the duo climaxes as the oboe soars in ecstatic pain while the voice presses up chromatically, to reach E flat:

And in-to my gar-den stole When the night had veil'd the pole:

This ascent is intensified by the expansion of the oboe melody, both modally and in rhythmically ambiguous chromatics; consonances of third or sixth may be no less poignant than dissonances, since they define temporal sequence – growth and decay. The gleeful triumph in destruction manifest in Blake's last stanza is echoed as the lines wind their way back to a tonic D; tritones are devilishly acute both vertically in the harmony, and horizontally in the movement of each line. 'My foe' is 'outstretch'd beneath the tree' in a Fall from G sharp to D, and then from F to D by way of the phrygian E flat. Never has a descending second sounded more oppressive. Here the exiguousness of means gives added force to a trait typical of the symphonic Vaughan Williams.

The third song, 'The Piper', is again Arcadian, for the shepherd, piping 'songs of glee', meets a child who, laughing, asks for a song about a lamb. But shepherd and child are in 'a valley *wild*'; and although the oboe's frisking $\frac{6}{8}$ tune begins in pastoral F major, the third and seventh are almost immediately flattened. The voice echoes this, while the oboe's answer incorporates a tritone. When the child appears on a cloud, the tonic moves up to G, and the mode, beginning with flat third and fourth, sharpens them into the lydian mode of healing. And there seems to be something to heal, since the child weeps at the song. Although his tears may be of joy, the lamb is sacrifical and purgatorial; and that pain is in question is suggested by the child's asking the shepherd to 'drop his pipe' and to resume his Edenic 'songs of happy cheer'. A further tone higher, in a youthfully pentatonic A major, the child asks the piper to write the songs down 'in a book, that all may read'. With a sudden shift to the minor third, the child vanishes and the singer, left alone, 'plucks a hollow reed' and fashions a 'rural pen', with which he 'stains the water clear' as he writes down his 'happy songs'. There may be a suggestion, in that staining, that the act of writing down must be to a degree a betrayal; the making of an artefact is of its nature a Fall, as is any conscious attempt to perpetuate Eden. This is beautifully conveyed in Vaughan Williams's polymodality when the tonic returns to F, the vocal part being wistfully lydian, the oboe in an indeterminate mode that contains both A natural and A flat, E natural and E flat. Irresolutely, the voice ceases not on F but on G. The oboe's coda begins on G, is substantially 'in' F major-minor, but stops rather than ends on B flat.

The fourth song, 'London', is perhaps the greatest and most terrifying of Blake's *Songs of Experience*. It is about the corruption of the City of Destruction as opposed to the New Jerusalem which Blake prophetically envisaged. For him, the 'mind-forg'd manacles' of 'Single Vision and Newton's sleep' have chartered the once-flowing Thames, stained the infant's face with fear, blackened the walls of churches, squandered the blood of the hapless soldier, blighted with plagues the marriage hearse. The fiery intensity of Blake's indictment of the evils of industrial capitalism – which by Vaughan Williams's time had become yet more palpable – imparts rigour to his symmetrical four-lined stanzas; and it may have been awareness of such rigorous necessity that encouraged Vaughan Williams to set this most dualistically experienced of Blake's songs not as a duologue, but as a monody. The solo voice is free to follow the words' rhythms, opening with a phrase that marvellously conveys the poet's 'wandering' through the blackened streets. The mode is initially phrygian D, though the flat second is sharpened at the end of the first line, which peters out in a melisma wavering between B flat and A, to suggest the river's scarce-flowing turgidity. With the reference to 'marks of weakness and of woe' the mode darkens to F minor (traditional key of *chants lugubres*) with tritonally flattened fifth. But the line stretches chromatically upwards to embrace D natural, from which it descends by way of C and B natural. So the line gyrates painfully, in a series of spirals, reaching the high F, which has become a sort of tonic: only to droop down, for the 'mind-forg'd manacles', to phrygian D. The melisma on E flat and D is as doom-laden as the end of 'A Poison Tree':

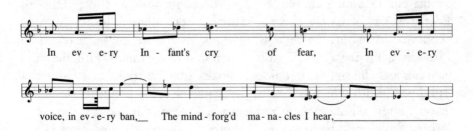

The difference is that whereas the speaker in 'A Poison Tree' himself had created evil, in 'London' he is a victim, and to that degree an experienced innocent. The climax comes with an expansion of the phrase for the chimney sweeper's cry, which soars through a tenth without relinquishing its phrygian second. In context the wail of the chimney sweeper sounds like a universal lament of mankind oppressed: a point technically accomplished when the spiral slowly winds down from the chimney sweeper's high F, returning by way of the hapless soldier and youthful harlot through the tritonal F minor complex, to the phrygian D for the new-born infant and blighted marriage-hearse. The final melisma on this marvellous image of life-become-death exactly echoes that on the mind-forg'd manacles. Whether or not Blake intended a cross-reference between 'hear' and 'hearse', Vaughan Williams reveals it.

From this fiercely dualistic yet monodic Song of Experience Vaughan Williams returns to an innocence comparable with that of the first song. The setting of 'The Lamb', a child's image of Jesus, is seemingly without the undercurrents of irony in the previous innocent songs – unless one counts it as ironic that the Lamb has four dark flats in his key signature! Still, the song is not in F minor, but consistently in the aeolian mode on F, with only one accidental in either the vocal or instrumental line. The rhythm follows the words, gently questioning: 'Little Lamb, who made thee?' – and there may be a hint that such guilelessness is in part a deceit. Vaughan Williams said that he could not abide the poem and was surprised to find himself setting it spontaneously and, he decided, effectively. The reason must be that he saw it, as Blake intended, in the light and dark of the *Songs of Innocence* and *Experience* as a whole. If it is regression to 'infant joy', it is also aware that the Lamb is a sacrificial victim. Placing the song immediately after 'London', which is about unknowing victims, makes a point: as does the single chromatic alteration in the song, which occurs at the moment when the words identify the Lamb with Christ. A cadential substitution of D natural for D flat in the oboe part resolves a suspension into the dorian instead of aeolian mode. The sharp, 'open' sixth registers, even though its effect is momentary: for the aeolian mode is immediately re-established and the song, although a duologue, continues to do its best to translate duality into unity. This is the only song in the cycle in which the two parts sometimes double one another in unison. That sounds as though in some circumstances monody might paradoxically be a Fall – which has some psychological truth in that the 'pain of consciousness' (which Jung relates to the Incarnation) cannot, once experienced, be undone, however desperately man may cry, with Hardy, 'Ere Nescience can be reaffirmed, How long, how long, how long?'

The sixth and seventh songs form another pair of opposites. 'The Shepherd' is a monody of innocence to balance the monody of experience, 'London', and its Arcadian heaven approaches closer than any of the songs to a genuine rural folk melody. The tune swings gently in a pentatonic F major, though it later garners a lydian fourth, which may imply a momentary modulation. The rural paradise has Christian overtones, for the shepherd's song to his sheep becomes a canticle of praise to his and their maker. This shepherd is clearly in the Delectable Mountains; his Christian affiliations mean that he is also aware of pilgrimage as temporal progression. The pentatonic descent at the end augments the note durations in a hemiola $\frac{3}{2}$ metre within the prevailing $\frac{3}{4}$; and the single line defines, in the last bars, a dominant-tonic cadence.

'Ah, Sunflower' is again a duologue, setting one of the subtlest of Blake's *Songs of Experience*. The tenor and oboe are both free in rhythm, even *senza misura*, and although in dialogue they maintain separate identities. The oboe' opening arabesque is pentatonic on D, though the fifth (A) is literally dominant. This is Edenic music without being specifically Christian; as in *Flos Campi* or the Oboe Concerto the piper may be Pan. The likelihood of this is increased by the fact that the poem is sexual, being about oppression and suppression in a psychological rather than (as in 'London') a social context. The sexual constraint within which Youth and Virgin 'pined away with desire' is imaged in the way in which both vocal and instrumental line wind narcissistically around themselves, with A – dominant of what proves to be the tonic D – as pivotal point. The mysterious poem tells how the youth and virgin ('shrouded in snow') arise from their graves and aspire, with the sunflower, to seek the sun, the source of life. The tenor has the same kind of melismata as the oboe without the exotic semiquaver triplets, so he is more trammelled in the coils of his unfulfilled desire. And the form of the poem, like that of 'London', is a spiral that returns to its source: as is mirrored in Vaughan Williams's setting when, on the word 'graves', the oboe's A is flattened in its descent from a high F, while the voice slowly winds down from *its* high F to the D a tenth lower, again approached by a phrygian E flat. This is a Song of Experience which is also a tragedy, for aspiration, indeed life itself, is defeated.

And the next song, 'Cruelty has a human heart', is an apex to the negative aspects of Experience, since it makes a universal statement about the evil expressed in personal terms in 'A Poison Tree'. The song, though it lasts a mere page and is scored for only two instruments, has deep analogies with the middle symphonies, springing thematically from their pervasively sighing chromatic semitones (beginning at the same pitch, F to E natural, as in Symphonies 4, 5 and 6), and from Job's drooping major and minor thirds. This had been the burden of Pilgrim's 'forsaken' cry to his God; but in this Song of Experience it is man himself who has forsaken his true identity. The crying semitones, plagent on oboe, and the chromaticized falling thirds are agonizedly bandied between voice and instrument, revealing how we have made ourselves into 'fiery forge', 'furnace sealed', and 'hungry gorge'. There is no defined modality; what might be diatonic tonality is undermined by enharmony as well as chromaticism, as voice and oboe chase one another's tails in free canon:

The voice ends with a murmur of the undulating thirds at the same pitch – E, E flat, C – they had recurrently sunk to in *Job* and the middle symphonies; the oboe's final moan F to E fades on the E unresolved, as in the slow movement of the Fourth Symphony.

After this duologue – the cycle's dramatic climax – the next song, 'The Divine Image', is both monodic and hymnic. The point of the poem, which is at once innocent and experienced, as is the case with many of Blake's complementary songs, is that if the negative forces of Cruelty and Jealousy have a human heart and face, the positive forces of Mercy, Pity, Peace and Love are human attributes also. In the previous song, for voice and oboe, human potential for evil was rampant; in this song, for voice alone, man's potential divinity is manifest. Symmetrically simple in the dorian mode on F, the tune is as plain as a Wesleyan hymn, with which Blake was familiar. We are told that he sang his songs to his own presumably improvised tunes, which were half-way between folk song and hymn and between religious instinct and institutionalized social conscience. This comes out in the sobriety of the tune, as compared not only with the lacerated line of the previous song, but also with the relative exoticism of 'Ah, Sunflower'. The shifts in the time signature between $\frac{4}{4}$ and $\frac{5}{4}$ do not imply irregularity of even asymmetry; they are Vaughan Williams's way of notating the pauses – for breath or cogitation – that an improvising amateur singer might introduce.

Since the (potentially divine) values of mercy, pity, peace and love are man's discovery, this hymn is not static. In the second verse, identifying man and God through their attributes ('Jesus Christ IS the Human Imagination'), the mode changes from dorian to aeolian; but swings, in the sequent stanza, between the two. In the final stanza resolution occurs in a change of time signature – from $\frac{4}{4}$ to $\frac{3}{4}$ – as well as of key signature – from four flats to one. The ultimate recognition that

> 'All must love the human form
> In heathen, Turk or Jew;
> Where Mercy, Love and Pity dwell
> There God is dwelling too'

is in the healing lydian mode on F, rather than in straight F major. The balm of the 'open' major thirds is as positively consummatory as the flat phrygian seconds, in earlier songs, had been negatively oppressive.

Vaughan Williams does not end his cycle with this song, though it would seem to have healed the breach between innocence and experience. His probably unconscious reason may be that his vision of Albion, like Blake's, was of its nature open-ended, having no final consummation, which is impossible except in death, and perhaps not even then. The final song, 'Eternity', is again a duo which sums up the themes of the cycle,

since it is about bondage and freedom; 'He who binds himself to a joy' –
even that Infant Joy of the first song –

> 'Doth the winged life destroy:
> But he who kisses a joy as it flies
> Lives in eternity's sunrise'.

The mode is again dorian on F in the voice part, though the oboe's
persistent D flats are aeolian, and are constricted in their undulations
around the fifth. The vocal rhythm, flowing from the words, mingles $\frac{3}{2}$ and
$\frac{6}{4}$, while the oboe never abandons its slowly swinging $\frac{3}{2}$. The latter part of
the poem is a reversal of values, for

> 'The look of love alarms
> Because it's filled with fire,
> But the look of soft deceit
> Shall win the lover's hire'.

The mercantile metaphor links this deceit with the corruption of
'London', so Vaughan Williams offers no apotheosis to his cycle. He does,
however, as in the previous song, change the key signature from four flats
to one; the voice is in the lydian mode on F for the 'soft deceit' – reminding
us that the lydian mode, if associated with healing, could also have the
enervating implications of Milton's injunction to 'lap me in soft Lydian
airs'. The oboe, at first tethered to its wailing semitone D flat to C, ends
in weirdly ambiguous modality, through which the *Job*-like descent from
D flat to C to A natural is obtrusive. The instrument's final tone is A
natural, fading to triple *piano*. It does not sound like a major third in F, but
like a tone in limbo, and therefore timeless, like eternity, which is the title
of the poem. In its small way, therefore, Vaughan Williams's cycle ends
where the Sixth Symphony ends; that is Vaughan Williams's terrifying
honesty, to balance Blake's.

The Eighth Symphony was written when its composer was eighty-three
and was, on its first performance in 1956, not dismissed, but condescended
to as a slight, light work in comparison with the middle symphonies. So in
a sense it is, and at his age Vaughan Williams had earned a moment's
respite. It has no movement in sonata form, which itself suggests a
relaxation from the 'progressive' evolution associated with sonata. All the
movements have titles, in Italian, beginning with Fantasia, which hints too
at the English seventeenth-century fantasy in its episodic nature, whereby
one thing leads to another, as in a motet that sets different sections of a
verbal text, though here there is none. Yet the more one looks into the

piece the subtler it seems; and this is inherent in the very concept of the first movement as *variazioni senza thema* – or, as the composer later glossed it, 'variations in search of a theme'. So there would seem to be a search or quest: an element of sonata strife, a hopeful venture at discovery, even if the theme is never found; and the sequence of the variations reveals some affinities with sonata form.

The key is said to be D minor, that of Mozart's more demonic works, not to mention Beethoven's Ninth. Like the Blake songs, however, the music is polymodal rather than diatonic, opening with those pentatonic rising fourths which are almost – so instinctual are they – the breath of life itself. The solo trumpet's fourths are echoed by solo horn and garlanded, in a rocking $\frac{6}{8}$, with false-related triads on the magic instruments, vibraphone, celesta and harp, doubled by pizzicato strings. In the *Sinfonia Antartica* the magic instruments are mostly malign. In the Eighth Symphony they become benign, effecting – after the desolation of the epilogue to the Sixth Symphony and almost the whole of the Seventh – a rebirth *ab ovo*. This may be in part a return to childhood, as in *Hodie* and the more 'innocent' of the Blake songs; but if childhood, like Keats's nightingale, charms magic casements, it also opens on *perilous* seas, in faery lands *forlorn*. We may recall the equivocal nature of Puck, both in folk legend and in Shakespeare's *A Midsummer Night's Dream*.

The trumpet and horn calls, taken up by flute, become a tune in what must count, since there is no theme, as the first variation. The fourths flow into a stepwise undulation between A and C, which in a repeat stretches up to D flat, the diminished fourth. When the rising fourths are transferred to clarinets and bassoon the second of them has become imperfect (tritonal), instead of perfect. Swayings between triads of B flat and D minors launch a subsidiary melody on high violins, at first falling by step in a lilting $\frac{6}{8}$, then in $\frac{3}{4}$. The first variation ends with the rising fourths in crotchets on strings, brass and woodwind, and leads without break into the second variation, which is *presto* and scherzoid. The fourths flicker throughout strings and woodwind; syncopations and cross-accents are rife; tonality is undecided between phrygian C, B flat and F. The impassioned declining scale of the first variation reappears on brass and woodwind, against which rocking fourths, in both quavers and crotchets, are pointed by glockenspiel and other magic instruments.

The third variation, though very different in mood, follows kaleidoscopically, without a break. The magic call of rising fourths is modified, for the second lift is through a fifth, not fourth; movement is in slowish level crotchets, four to a bar. The modality is 'white-note', though it is not clear whether it is aeolian A or dorian D. Serenely introduced on strings, the fourths and fifths grow into lyrical melodies picked out by solo viola, oboe and flute. Cellos and basses too acquire lyrical identity, until the variation climaxes in the scalewise descending motif (C, B, A, A flat, G, F). This triggers a series of variations that have something in common with a sonata development, especially since the lyrical, white-note variation may be thought of as a cantabile second subject. The quasi-developmental variations begin with a fugued scherzo, back in $\frac{6}{8}$, *allegretto*, at first scored for woodwind, with the fourths both perfect and tritonal. Duple are combined with triple metres in an intricate polyphony stabilized on a timpani pedal E. The climax fuses the falling scale thirds in $\frac{3}{4}$ on violins and high woodwind with the fourth-dominated $\frac{6}{8}$ jig on lower strings and bassoons. Since the next variation is slowish, lyrical and in $\frac{4}{4}$, we may broadly think of it as a development from the white-note variation; it is certainly evolutionary, even questing, for the theme searched for begins to define itself as quasi-fugal entries, with perfect fourth, augmented fourth and fifth, spread through the orchestra; the falling scale motif also recurs, quite massively scored.

This may constitute the apex of the quasi-development, and the next variation may initiate a quasi-recapitulation, since it returns to the rising fourths in $\frac{6}{8}$, albeit much faster than at first. The quasi-second subject variation also reappears in what might be B flat, garlanded with the fourths in triplets on strings and woodwind. This leads to the first appearance of a D major key signature and to the movement's coda, which transmutes the sundry variants into a hymnic song, while the fourths continue to babble on cellos, basses and bassoons. Harps are active; but the movement does not end in sonata-like resolution for, with a change back to a key signature of one flat, the original version of the fourths' tune sounds distantly on solo flute, echoed by solo trumpet and horn. The false relations of the magic instruments vanish in a wisp of smoke, leaving a D minor triad distantly on violins:

The kaleidoscopic nature of these variations in search of a theme makes them more unreal than anything in the 'second childhood' of *Hodie*, which has deep roots in English conservatism, if not institutional religion. The brief second movement, scored for wind instruments only, is unreal in a different sense, since it is a march related to social custom and communal life, though the everyday world is viewed retrospectively, even seen through a glass a shade darkly. It is urban music, recalling Vaughan Williams's own works for amateur wind bands, as well as those of Holst and Grainger – and perhaps even the Salvation Army band at the street corner. The main theme is gently comic, in duple rhythm in the phrygian mode on C; after a double bar there is a music-hall section with oompah bass such as Vaughan Williams had raucously or savagely exploited in the Fourth and Sixth Symphonies. Here it is slightly grotesque, as is the tune of the brief trio, which more bucolically lollops in a style appropriate to clowns and fools, wherever they live. The trio, if good-humoured, is a bit mysterious, and in context sad. A da capo of the scherzo has no time to re-establish mirth, in either the modern or the medieval sense. The end is odd, for chromatic semitones inherent in the tune turn into the familiar chromatic wail descending from E to E flat (or from F to E natural), which had proved so disruptive a force in the middle symphonies. Here too the effect is disintegrative, but also momentary. The scherzo is simply wiped off the slate in a *pianissimo* scurry of woodwind.

The third movement substitutes strings for the scherzo's wind, and presents Vaughan Williams's country world in 'second' simplicity, so that it is not so much nostalgic as reborn. After the scherzo's bouncy march rhythms, the lines of this Cavatina are long and flowing, hinting at Elgar's Malvern Hills manner, rarefied. The basic modality is aeolian E, which recurrently oscillates in false relation to C minor. A second theme, hymn-like and symmetrical in $\frac{3}{4}$ as compared with the almost barless main theme, is centred on E flat major, relative of C minor, but veers to E minor, which is translated to major. The impact of this hymn on the first theme is to send it winging through the omnipresent fourth-rising-to-fifth motif, into a pentatonic-tending D major. Solo violin becomes an ascending lark, less ecstatic than the original bird, even a bit wind-buffeted and distraught. Climax comes in alternating thirds and fourths in aeolian F, from which the lark ascends in pure pentatonicism. One can hardly say that his music is a quotation from the original lark since all pentatonic tunes are generically similar; none the less there is authentically lark-like transcendence, so that we hear the da capo of the original theme with new ears. In any case it is transformed, enveloped in swaying triads in false relation: which in turn merge into the hymn, at first in its original E flat, but subtly shifting into E minor, which becomes a paradisal E major. Cello solo *a piacere* momentarily gives the lark a baritone voice (!) in pentatonic E, bringing him down to earth while preserving his spirituality. The cadence is mysterious, not a plagal Amen, but VI I with the C triad flattened, thereby summing up the E minor–C minor dichotomy that has pervaded the movement:

The elliptical, and therefore surprising, structure of this marvellous movement means that it is re-creation, not retrospection, by its octogenarian composer.

The last movement, Toccata, has the key signature of D major, Vaughan Williams's tonality of human fulfilment. But its triple-rhythmed rising third – typical of several other Vaughan Williams D major hymns – first appears softly, is answered in inversion and augmentation by the bass, and is then repeated in augmentation and in the *minor*:

The composer was justified in describing this as 'a rather sinister exordium', and a darker undercurrent is not altogether banished by the riotous hubbub, with magic instruments in full pelt, that dominates most of the piece. Formally, the movement might be described as a sonata-rondo, with the 'Bunyanesque' D major dance-hymn as the rondo theme. The episodes are developmental, but never depart far from the main theme, which appears in many permutations, its thirds stretched to fourths and fifths, sometimes in inversion, augmentation, or diminution. A D minorish episode in the middle, chromatically rotating on itself, hints at sonata, though its fleeting modulations are not dramatic events. As a whole the movement is fiesta rather than symphonic argument, and the unreality of carnival is implicit in the increasing dominance of the magic instruments, which end in a tumult of clanging and tintinnabulating bells (tuned in pentatonic D major). Drama does occur when the thematic fourths are abruptly wrenched into a canonic episode in pentatonic C minor, but D major celebration takes over for the grandly consummatory coda. The final cadence, however, recapitulates the I, VI flat, II, I progression of the first bars' sinister exordium, so *homo ludens* is not, for Vaughan Williams, totally vacuous. The fiesta of this movement is like nothing else in Vaughan Williams's work, and not simply because of the batteries of percussion. It might be called child-like in living in a present moment that is at once folkily English and globally ethnic. Through whatever perturbation, magic renews innocence; and it *is* magic for an old man thus to make a midsummer marriage out of our wintry discontent. The 'flat' cadence genuinely says Amen; texture and scoring are at once savage and sophisticated in a way untypical of British music, at least before Birtwistle. There were both prescience and prophecy in Vaughan Williams's creation of such 'global village' fiesta in the early fifties.

To call the Eighth Symphony slight is clearly inadequate. One would not be tempted so to describe the last, the Ninth Symphony, though it too initially received a lukewarm reception, mostly because by 1956–7 Vaughan Williams was becoming an unfashionable composer whose final works might be written off not as dotages, but as the mixture as before. *That* the Eighth Symphony certainly was not; and if the Ninth (probably with conscious intent) refers back to many aspects of the composer's symphonic pilgrimage, that is hardly surprising from a man of eighty-six. Familiarity with the work persuades one that it is no mere retrospect but a masterpiece: a consummatory work, with the proviso that Vaughan Williams did not believe that his work could or should be neatly tidied up. Though *finis* came with his death the year after the Symphony, his music ends where it had begun, on a question mark.

If the Eighth Symphony is a comedy in the same sense as *A Midsummer Night's Dream* is such, the Ninth is a tragedy whose genesis has a connection with one of the great tragic novels of the late nineteenth century, Hardy's *Tess of the D'Urbervilles*. Vaughan Williams as usual deprecated any ascription of programmatic intention, admitting no more than that there might be some link between his symphony and Salisbury Plain, and that *Tess* had been one of the seminal books of his youth. Certainly there is a parallel between Hardy's haunting evocation of the desolate heath as contrasted with exuberant life and love on the summer farm, and the tense equilibrium, in Vaughan Williams's symphony, between present passion and recollected emotion. Since the symphony deals in tragic experience that harks back to Vaughan Williams's boyhood, and since the central crisis in his creative chronology occurred in his Sixth Symphony, it is hardly surprising that the Ninth should spring from overt references to the Sixth. In that work Vaughan Williams confronted an abyss: into which he nearly tumbled in the *Sinfonia Antartica*. Now, in the mid fifties, after the respite of the Eighth, he had no choice but to consider where, from that abyss, he might – as Eliot put it – 'fare forward, traveller'. The key of the Ninth Symphony, E minor, is the same as that of the Sixth; it is probable that the close thematic relationships between its first movement and the earlier symphony were intentional. He was asking whether, new-born in 'second childhood', he had the strength to discover a tragic rather than nihilistic denouement.

The Symphony opens, *molto moderato*, with soft pedal Es in octave unisons on strings and woodwind, through which trombones, bassoons and bass clarinet murmur a slowly rising scale motif rooted on E, but oppressively flattened: E, F natural, A, B flat, C, D flat. This is a reference back not to the Sixth Symphony, but to the opening of the Seventh, its dourer sequal. There the theme had been associated with the courage and endurance of explorers in a waste land; what more appropriate initiation could there be for a work that asks whether it is possible to begin again, or even to go on? As the theme inches up, the pedal Es on strings are thickened into E minor triads, through which three saxophones wail in parallel $^6_3$ chords; these turn into obsessively alternating thirds (G sharp, G natural, E). Saxophones had been among Vaughan Williams's magic instruments ever since Job's Comforters wheedled in their oily sonority. The saxophones here are more elementally malign, recalling the whining winds of the *Antartica*, as well as the main thematic material of the first movement of the Sixth. Their baleful influence engulfs the whole orchestra which, in a long crescendo, howls in triplets through various permutations of the falling thirds motif, while deep brass and woodwind extend the scale theme, its painful ascent still counteracted by phrygian flattenings. Strings and flutes modify the scale to E, F, A flat, B natural, C, D natural, while the timeless pedal is transferred to timpani. Tritones exacerbate the triplets' descents from their highest point.

The key signature changes from one sharp to two flats, and the song-like theme that steals in on two clarinets and bass clarinet in free canon has some of the features of a sonata second subject. But it is not a new theme, for in this more than any of Vaughan Williams's symphonies every theme is a morphological evolution from what has preceded it. The essence of this melody is still the alternating major and minor thirds, now yearningly longing, rather than explosively fierce. The key is G major-minor; the harp accompaniment shifts between triads of G and E flat, in their minor and major forms alternately. Cantabile strings extend the theme in near-pentatonic E flat lyricism – which fails to survive as the music develops into a tense struggle between the Antarctic rising scale and the descending and alternating thirds. The scoring is dense and modulation is incessant, though E, G and C are polarities as the transmuted themes burgeon. A climax occurs when brass interject the undulating $^6_3$ chords first heard on the saxophones, while strings and woodwind soar in ever longer metamorphoses of the alternating thirds. Figuration is doubled to semiquavers, through which brass barks; the ultimate climax, which takes a long time to come to the boil, is generated from triplets chattering in a medley of thirds and tritones. Even when dynamics subside as horns wail the chromatic organum through still-buzzing triplets, tension increases rather than diminishes. There is a momentary silence, taking a desperately needed breath, before full orchestra yells the alternating thirds theme in massive organum, the tonality being C major-minor. This is the movement's apex; what follows is a coda rather than a recapitulation. After another fraught silence, solo violin sings the lyrical version of the alternating thirds which had sounded as though it might have been a second subject, though it was not thematically new. The key is at first lydian E major, with all the curative and heavenly association of both mode and key. The accompaniment, in diatonic concords on harp and pizzicato strings, veers (as so often) between mediants – E major, C minor, A flat and E flat major and minor. The solo violin melody is clearly an ascending lark and a song–dance of the youthfully beautiful Elihu; and at this point Vaughan Williams introduces another instrument, the flugel-horn, the magical potential of which was revealed when the composer heard one played, to make an echo, whilst he and his wife were on a boat trip on an Austrian lake, in 1956. (The echo played itself back much more magically than the original.) In his introductory notes to the Symphony

Vaughan Williams is meticulous in his instructions: the flugelhorn is 'very important', it must be played with 'a real flugelhorn mouthpiece', and the part must '*never* be played on a cornet'. His insistence on the necessity for the instrument bears on the subtle aural imagination of a composer sometimes accused of accoustical crudity. Could he perhaps have taken a hint from Miles Davis's haunting use of the flugelhorn in his recordings during the fifties? Certainly the jazz trumpeter used the instrument to evoke other-worldly magic comparable with that here created by Vaughan Williams, as the flugelhorn melody mates the ecstasy of the ascending lark to the once-turbulently oscillating thirds. Its magic spell effected, the flugelhorn vanishes; strings softly alight on their original pedal Es, doubled by almost inaudible timpani, while solo cor anglais murmurs the aspiration of the 'Antarctic' rising scale. When the strings stir from their Es to sing the lark's theme, horn and woodwind allow the Antarctic theme, blessed by the return of the flugelhorn, to expand, even to flower:

Yet the end of the movement is again ambiguous. The strings are immobile on an E minor triad, through which the long-silent saxophones bitonally moan their $^6_3$ chords. Are they again Job's Comforters?

There is to be no answer to this question until the finale, which is tragic, but brings the catharsis that tragedy may offer. The slow movement, like the second movement of No. 6, is not tragic, though it is powerfully disturbing and, it would seem, irremediably dichotomous. It opens with the magic flugelhorn, singing a theme that signficantly dates back to the years of *A Sea Symphony*. Appearing in a discarded work called *The Solent*, it clearly signalled a voyage of discovery into an unknown region; and starts with the familiar pentatonic rise, F, G, B flat. The autobiographical significance of such a return to well-springs, in a work dedicated to rebirth, cannot be doubted; nor can we miss the point of Vaughan Williams's modification to the original tune, when the simple modality is sundered by the substitution of a D flat for D:

That D flat is momentous: for the aspiration of youth and flugelhorn is swept away by a sinister, metrically rigid theme in a kind of lydian G minor, the D flat changed to C sharp:

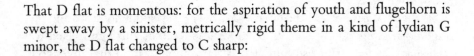

The mood – constricted, constricting, slightly savage – is poles apart from the flugelhorn's tentative song, which bootlessly tries to re-establish itself, encouraged by horns. The jabbing, gawky gait of the march gains in energy, so that even when the flugelhorn chant has the aid of four horns and low woodwind it is impotent. We are told that the grim march was suggested by the legend of a ghostly drummer who roamed Salisbury Plain, but Vaughan Williams's dismissal of this would seem to be justified in that one would not, without the hint, think of a drummer, ghostly or otherwise, in this context. The screwed-up metre and gritty scoring rather suggest some nasty machine, and by inference the kind of world that was obliterating the human qualities in which Vaughan Williams trusted. Youthful aspiration stands little chance against such mechanized remorselessness; indeed when the march stomps in a phrygian G minor, with fifths sometimes flattened and fourths sharpened, the flugelhorn is itself engulfed in the hubbub. Although it re-emerges momentarily, supported by clarinets, it is blurred by wails of alternating thirds on distant strings: a lament that does not rate hope's chances highly. The triumph of evil – as the march thumps in organum fifths on brass, semiquaver figures nag on strings and woodwind, and tenor-drum and triangle bizarrely tickle the beat – is even more scary than the trumpet ostinato in the second movement of Symphony No. 6. That we may still think of as Fate, Destiny, War or any of the dark adversaries that harried the nineteenth-century symphonic hero; in this, however, corruption is within as well as without. The nastiness of the music is grotesque, faintly farcical as well as frightening; and to have admitted this is another instance of Vaughan Williams's 'terrifying honesty'. There are parallels in the symphonic Shostakovich, as well as Mahler.

Strange fruit is born of the horror: for the march suddenly stops and the flugelhorn sings again, softly, at its original pitch, through a haze of *pianissimo* divided strings sustaining a B flat minor triad in first inversion. This might suggest that the 'altered' D flat which had disrupted the original version of the flugelhorn melody has found harmonic resolution. This proves to be merely a dream for, with a tempo change from $\frac{4}{4}$ to $\frac{3}{4}$ and a key shift to E flat major, we enter an oasis of calm at first comparable with the E flat major episode in the cavatina of No. 8. Only whereas that episode was hymn-like, this is deeply romantic; indeed, this is probably the only passage in Vaughan Williams's music that might, in moments of inattention, be mistaken for Bax. The romanticism itself implies insecurity; the melody sways irresolutely through a third; harmonically E flat major fluctuates to the minor; C major and minor triads are substituted for expected tonics. The more freely the lines flow into quaver rather than crotchet movement and the more enharmonically the harmonies shift, the more distraught the dream becomes. Yet this dream, if sad, is potent. It has the last word after a brief resurgence of the drumming march; the coda even reinstates the flugelhorn song in its original form, coloured by clarinet, while strings remotely sustain their first inversion B flat minor triad. This is not peace, let alone resolution. The final C major triad on divided strings with harp harmonics sounds perturbingly other-worldly, for this *is* a dream, and therefore illusory. There is a difference between a dream and a vision.

The scherzo of No. 6 was a tritonal fury; that of No. 9 is sometimes bluff and gruff (*allegro pesante*), but is also very mysterious, with a nightmarish quality to complement the dream the second movement terminates in. The key, unsurprisingly, is F minor, or rather a wriggling between F minor and E major-minor such as pervaded the Sixth Symphony. The rhythm is at first a lurching $\frac{6}{8}$, though note-values are multimetrical; duplet quavers, triplet quavers and semiquavers chatter in sharply etched, prickling, tingling textures. Like the first movement, this scherzo proceeds by continual thematic metamorphosis, so that it is a sophisticated act of discovery, though its goal is uncertain. At first it is clownish, as are parts of the scherzo to the Fourth Symphony and the quick movements in the *Tudor Portraits*. The feeling has soured, though it is, at least initially, comical. Such earthiness is, however, transformed by the same magic as typifies the Eighth Symphony. The magic melody instruments are again active, the saxophones behaving, in the composer's words, 'like demented cats', but also assaying a chorale in parallel triads that sounds solemn rather than libidinous. The phantasmagoric quality increases in the coda, in which strings sing the saxophones' 'chorale' while magic instruments embroider cross-rhythms in triplets and quavers; glimmering with celesta and harp, this nightmare sounds very close to the romantic dream of the coda to the previous movement. But the end of the scherzo is brutal. A tutti on the alternating thirds is hammered in a metrical rigidity even more mechanistic than the second movement's march. With a return to an F minor key signature the movement dissolves in tritonal crazy comedy, with tapping side-drum.

The finale follows without a break and is, despite the retrospections in the composer's last major work, a new start. Early critics found this movement unsatisfactory, which it is not, and puzzling, which it is: but only because Vaughan Williams is tackling so difficult an assignment. The Sixth and Seventh Symphonies had ended in limbo; the newness in the finale to the Ninth lies in its acceptance of 'doubleness' not merely as the genesis of unity, but as itself a formal principle: for as Vaugahn Williams pointed out, the finale is really two movements in one. It is a 'double' movement combining a freely fugal andante tranquillo basically in $\frac{6}{8}$ with an andante sostenuto in $\frac{4}{4}$. It is not a rondo or sonata rondo, for the two movements retain independent courses which overlap but do not, in the manner of a sonata, argue or conflict. How appropriate it is that this renovative conservative should end his life's work with this highly original movement that offers alternative futures – in (almost certainly unconscious) accord with some currently 'advanced' compositional theories.

If the first movement of the Ninth was more morphologically evolutionary than any movement in the composer's previous symphonies, the first part of its finale is evolutionary in the most basic sense, for it is continuous polyphonic growth. The first movement of the Second Symphony of that fine post-Vaughan Williams symphonist Edmund Rubbra was once described as a 'gigantic instrumental motet'. While the description is not entirely accurate, it suggests how Rubbra evolved a dramatic symphonic argument from vocally polyphonic principles. In this finale Vaughan Williams does the same – more exhaustively than he had in the Pastoral Symphony, written thirty-five years earlier. It does not immediately register that the winding $\frac{6}{8}$ theme that initiates the fugue is (almost) identical in pitch with the 'Antarctic' theme that had opened the first movement. But so it is, as it floats upwards in something close to the phrygian mode on E, but with flat fifth, sharp sixth and flat seventh:

The fugal polyphony is free because the imitations are not exact and, when woodwind join the strings, are melismatically transformed. From the intricate polyphony a more lyrical tune in aeolian C minor is formalized, and soon incorporates the familiar major-minor motif of the first movement. What Vaughan Williams calls the 'other' movement begins with a change of key signature to two flats and of time signature to $\frac{4}{4}$. However different the feeling, the level crotchets are a modification of the opening notes of the movement; and the original theme, at the original pitch, soon reappears on oboe, absorbing the rocking thirds also. When solo violin and flute enter the polyphonic web, the music grows incrementally more animated, weaving a filigree of semiquavers. Harp and triangle, if not the full panoply of magic instruments, add a tinsel glitter, leading to a liberating climax when, in almost E major, strings and woodwind transform the main motif (now E, D sharp or natural, B) into untrammelled song.

The 'other' theme returns canonically on brass with pizzicato strings, now patently revealing its affinity with the Antarctic theme of the first movement, with its chromatic oppressions ironed out; we may also hear it as an expansion of the magic flugelhorn melody of the second movement. To say that what happens next is a development section does not mean much since the whole movement is evolutionary; even so, it means a little, since the return of a polyphonic texture is freer, and more developmental, than any previous section. This is probably the most highly wrought polyphony in Vaughan Williams's *oeuvre*, the lines surging in a multiplicity of note-values, transforming the descending triplets of the first movement, combining all the themes in contrapuntal density. Tonality is in flux, yet the tightness of the counterpoint, scored thickly but clearly, makes for a powerful affirmation. It is at this point that a comparison with the first movement of Rubbra's Second Symphony (which predates the Vaughan Williams movement by fifteen or more years) seems valid. An ultimate climax is attained when the 'two movements' become one through their contrapuntal interweaving – which is distinct from the dramatic argument of sonata. The aspiring Antarctic theme, vastly extended, merges into the undulating triplet thirds; the key signature becomes that of E major. Magical harp and celesta double magical flugelhorn and less magical brass, in parallel triads harmonizing the notes B, A sharp, F sharp, G sharp, with tremolando whirrings on strings. Aspiration collapses through the falling third triplets and lands, *Job*-like, on a rocking between E flat and C.

After a brief silence full orchestra chants alternating triads of E major and C major in second inversion, interspersed with the 'other' theme, which we have seen to be a metamorphosis of the first, and of the flugelhorn song. After another brief silence the whole orchestra blazes in E major triads, triple *forte*, dimming to double *piano*: a device three times repeated, the final fade-out being *a niente*. So in this immensely complex movement the interweaving of long, winging polyphonies has germinated new seeds of life; in these resonating E major chords innocence is reborn of long experience. Even so, the two states coexist, like the 'two movements' – which in themselves are neither positive nor negative. Complementarily, both the negative and positive magic instruments share in the triadic tuttis, while the harps ripple in glissandos through their total compass. When the E major tuttis fade, the three saxophones revert to their earlier dubiety, moaning through triads of F and G while the strings sustain paradisal E major. The effect of the harp glissandos is thus paradoxical. They are not religiously consolatory and perhaps, after the Fifth Symphony, Vaughan Williams's music is never that. In the Ninth as in the Eighth Symphony, 'magic' is a blurring of boundaries between the natural and the supernatural; and if in the Eighth dream effaces reality, in the Ninth reality obliterates dream. Of course the music may be asking a further – the ultimate – question: which is which? In this case the harp glissandos may tell us that we are such stuff as dreams are made on, our little lives being rounded with a sleep. The Shakespearian quotation seems more pertinent to the end of the Ninth than to the end of the Sixth, to which Vaughan Williams himself applied it, perhaps as a slightly petulant riposte to lunar and post-atomic theories about the Sixth's epilogue.

Vaughan Williams's last symphony ends, as do so many of his major works, with a diminuendo to silence – *a niente*. It is consistent that for Vaughan Williams sound should exist within the context of silence, just as the known is in the context of the unknowable, the physical in the context of the metaphysical. The last line of the last of the *Four Last Songs*, with words by his wife, tells us that 'music and silence meet, and both are heard'. This we may relate to Prospero's ultimate question about reality and dream, and to the epigraph from Plato's *Phaedo* that Vaughan Williams applied to his *Sancta Civitas*. (It is quoted on p. 135). Another quotation is also pertinent, this time from seventeenth-century England, whence sprang so much of the composer's re-creative doubleness. The writer is Gerard Winstanley, one of those Levellers who, like Bunyan, was a man of God yet not far from a political activist; they come from an address he made 'to his Excellency Oliver Cromwell' in 1651, under the title of 'The Law of Freedom, or True Magistracy Restored':

> And indeed if you would know spiritual things, it is to know how the spirit or power of wisdom and life, causing both motion and growth, dwells within and governs both the several bodies of the earth below, as grass, plants, fishes, beasts, birds and mankind. For to reach God beyond the Creation, or to know what he will be to a man after he is dead, if any otherwise than to scatter him into his essences of fire, water, earth and air of which he is compounded, is knowledge beyond the line or capacity of man to attain to while he lives in his compounded body.

That seems a just assessment of what Vaughan Williams is after in his last symphony, considering it as a summing-up of his long life's work. His testament is that of a man who, though he knows that he does not know, is as sensible of the numinous as he is of mortality: a man who – in the words of Pater, quoted at the beginning of this book – lived in 'an age the intellectual powers of which tend strongly to agnosticism' and to 'the mechanical theory of nature', yet who found 'the supernatural view of things' still credible; or if not credible, at least a necessary ballast to any tenable view of the good life. It is hardly surprising that the last movement of Vaughan Williams's last symphony should be difficult. If it succeeds – as we are slowly but with increasing confidence coming to believe – that makes Vaughan Williams a greater composer, as well as a greater man, than we had imagined. He had seen Traherne's 'strange glory', 'that strangest is of all: yet brought to pass.'

A VALEDICTION:
FORBIDDING MOURNING

A time there was as one may guess
And as, indeed, earth's testimonies tell
Before the birth of consciousness,
    When all went well.

None suffered sickness, love, or loss,
None knew regret, starved hope, or heart-burnings;
None cared whatever crash or cross
    Brought wrack to things.

If something ceased, no tongue bewailed,
If something winced and waned, no heart was wrung;
If brightness dimmed, and dark prevailed,
    No sense was stung.

But the disease of feeling germed.
And primal rightness took the tinct of wrong;
Ere nescience shall be reaffirmed
    How long, how long, how long?

        THOMAS HARDY, 'Before Light and After'

When British music steered out of the doldrums at the turn from the nineteenth into the twentieth century it did so, we observed, through the agency of three composers of genius: Elgar, Delius and Vaughan Williams. Elgar, apparently relishing the pomp and circumstance of Victorian and Edwardian England, celebrated its opulence in a German-based, English-sounding idiom of dazzling technical brilliance, while at the same time revealing that the 'spirit of delight' which gave meaning to its materiality 'cometh but rarely', so that his mature music is simultaneously homage and elegy. Delius, Elgar's polar opposite yet complement, turned his back on everything Edwardian industrialism stood for, seeking renewal in a childhood Eden wherein, through Nature, he might be reborn: a process that occurs by way of the infiltration into his basically Teutonic, Wagnerian technique of the modalism and pentatonicism of folk song. Vaughan Williams, latest born of the triumvirate, alone could start from English roots – from Tudor modality and polyphony as well as or rather than folk song – and could create from those fundamentals a vision of a New Albion that could embrace even the (basically Teutonic) symphony. Elgar was a doubting seeker after a faith; Delius was a fanatical unbeliever trusting nothing except the validity of his senses; Vaughan Williams was a double man and Christian agnostic, dubious of creeds but animated by a Blakean sense of the numinous.

After Vaughan Williams, the English tradition too readily lapsed into passivity. To evade regression called for a synthesis of the re-creative values represented by Elgar and Delius, and for something like Vaughan Williams's difficult fusion of the impulses inherent in New World Whitman, Christian communistical Bunyan, and apocalyptic Blake. Such was hard to come by: so Vaughan Williams's immediate successors, some of whom might be called acolytes, all tended to be regressive, as he himself was not. Their returns may be to the lost agrarian tradition, or to the Anglican Church, or to a mixture of both.

Among the elegists three figures of decisive identity must be mentioned: Gerald Finzi, John Ireland and Patrick Hadley. Finzi's father, like Delius's, had been a successful businessman; one of the consequences was that his son could renounce such a life while pursuing his destiny without pecuniary embarrassment. He became a country gentleman by proxy; studied music with Sir Edward Bairstow, organist of York Minster; and embraced the career of a professional composer – against the advice of the curmudgeonly Stanford. He neither composed prolifically, nor sought with much vigour to promote the music he had created. But what he made was of distinguished quality, and sprang from channels that were deep if narrow. His elegiac agrarianism is rooted in his near-obsession with the poetry of Hardy, settings of whose verse he published in five volumes between 1933 and 1949, though the published songs by no means complete the tally. In their genre, Finzi's Hardy songs are near perfection. No composer, not even Vaughan Williams himself, has created melodic lines that spring so spontaneously from the rhythms of English speech, while attaining musically sustained lyricism; Finzi's piano parts, lying well under the fingers, reanimate the legacy of Stanford with an elegance that Vaughan Williams's piano parts cannot emulate.

Finzi has several manners in his Hardy songs. There are a few bucolically rollicking, 'open-road' numbers, and rather more that explore, with thin textures and crystalline bitonality, stellar landscapes and Hardy's sense of the imperviousness of fate. By far the majority of the songs, however, are valedictory, expressing loss and regret by way of sighing appoggiaturas that have their genesis in 'Malvern Hills' Elgar, and a modal diatonicism that is the legacy of Vaughan Williams. This entails too a partiality for secundal suspensions and for the bitter-sweet pathos of false relation, as is most touchingly evident in the long piano prelude and postlude to 'Proud songsters' – a song dealing with Nature's oblivious but eternal renewal, as contrasted with man's foundering hopes and fears. This music is beautiful and moving, but is not entirely true to Hardy, who has no trace of its enervating nostalgia. The Hardy settings of a later composer Benjamin Britten, in his cycle *Winter Words* (1953), may well by truer to the spirit of Hardy in that they are projected into musical images, even becoming – in for instance the wonderful setting of 'The Choirmaster's Burial' – mini-operas. Britten's version of 'Proud songsters', if less affecting than Finzi's, is closer to Hardy's poem.

The heart-rending false relations in Finzi's 'Proud songsters' have their source in his dichotomy between past and present, country and town. But since the great age of false relation in English music was the seventeenth century – for reasons we have discussed in reference to Vaughan Williams – we are not surprised to discover that Finzi too was devoted to the English nature poetry of seventeenth-century mystics such as Vaughan and Traherne, as well as to that of nineteenth-century romantics like Wordsworth. The best and best known of Finzi's larger works is his setting of prose passages from Traherne's *Centuries of Meditation* and from his poems, to which he gave the apposite title of *Dies Natalis* (1939). Scored for tenor and string orchestra in five quasi-symphonic movements, it parallels Vaughan Williams's works that deal with the Edenic state of childhood and with the potentiality for a new day of birth. Its debt to Vaughan Williams, in verbal sensitivity and in the modal sweep of its paragraphs, is clear, while the pervasive false relations spring both from him and from their source in seventeenth-century string music. The noble appoggiaturas and resonant string texture recall Elgar's great *Introduction and Allegro* and the 'celestial' prologue to Part II of *Gerontius*. Even so, the winging ecstasy the music generates is *sui generis*, and the work is a small masterpiece. If one uses the qualifying adjective 'small', that is because the experience has a certain hermeticism as compared with Vaughan Williams, whose moments of transcendence are never far removed from his life as a man of the twentieth century. On the rare occasions when Finzi attempts a more public manner he is unconvincing. His *Ode to St Cecilia*, written in the convention of Purcell and Handel to specially composed words by Edmund Blunden, may have roots in Anglican tradition but fails to find, in the ceremonial manners of Parry and Stanford, or even Elgar, a substitute for Purcellian baroque glory. Today, or even in 1947 when it was composed, the piece sounds rather pompous. Finzi, introspective in celebrating the past, could find glory only through the sublimatory effect of Nature.

John Ireland is another minor post-Vaughan-Williams composer who has a strong personal identity, most evident in moods of regression and nostalgia. His heart is in his songs, which include settings of Victorian and Edwardian poets, relatable to Vaughan Williams's early Rossetti and Stevenson cycles, although composed a decade or more later. Settings of Mary Coleridge's 'The sacred flame' and 'Remember' are touching examples of the genre, though the dramatic, even melodramatic repetition of clinching lines may tinge them with pretentiousness, closeting them in the Edwardian parlour, from which Vaughan Williams escaped. Closer to Vaughan Williams are the Housman settings, especially the beautiful version of 'The heart's desire', which rivals Vaughan Williams in the folk-like spontaneity of its modal tune, while its subtly wrought, highly chromatic piano part, with scrunchy added notes and cross relations, imparts the bitter-sweet flavour which is Ireland's distinctive characteristic; his idiom, if limited in range, is immediately recognizable. Some of Ireland's best songs are in his Housman cycle, *The Land of Lost Content* (1920–1). The first song, 'The Lent lily', has a vocal line that seems to be a paraphrase of (and conscious tribute to?) the second song of Vaughan Williams's *On Wenlock Edge*, though again the ripe chromaticism of the piano part makes Ireland's view of Housman more introverted, even self-indulgent. His conscious artistry is, in no discreditable sense, still more evident in his settings of old English verse, whether of folk provenance (as in 'The three ravens') or in the form of an Elizabethan lyric (for instance, Daniel's 'Love is a sickness'). Such songs may be correlated not so much with Vaughan Williams as with Peter Warlock's cannily modernized archaism. Ireland's pseudo-Warlock songs are effective examples of a genre in which melodies springing from Elizabethan or folk verse are fused with a harmonic density that owes much to Delius, whose nostalgia stemmed, we noted, from precisely such an equivocation. In Warlock's case the catalyst between flexibility of melody and density of harmony was Bernard van Dieren; and a trace of van Dieren's hyper-subtle harmonic polyphony occasionally finds its way, at second hand, into Ireland's songs. ('Love is a sickness', mentioned above, is a lovely instance.) Vaughan Williams's blunter temperament had no truck with such slightly effete artifice, though he admired Peter Warlock's work in rediscovering and editing early English music.

The basic distinction between Ireland and Vaughan Williams as song writers is that Ireland was essentially a harmonist, as Vaughan Williams was not. It is not therefore surprising that Ireland's solo piano music defines the nature and range of his sensibility even more clearly than do his songs. He wrote for the piano with elegance, grace and, where appropriate, virtuosity, especially in pieces such as 'Amberley Wild

Brooks', 'April' or, in different mood, 'The darkened valley', all of which distil the essence of English rural landscape by way of impressionistic techniques which – whatever they may have picked up from Debussy and Ravel – sound, in relation to Ireland's modal melodies, indisputably English. The watery textures of 'Amberley Wild Brooks', in particular, recreate not only (in Hopkins's words) a 'sweet especial rural scene', but also a simultaneous sense of wonder and regret, mating present with past. Similarly the *London Pieces* catch with precise nostalgia the 'Chelsea' and 'Soho forenoons' of Ireland's youth. More opulently but not less magically the later *Sarnia* cycle evokes the past and present of the Channel Islands, to which the composer became addicted.

All Ireland's best and most typical music, written during the twenties, is in small forms and for modest resources. His large-scale Piano Sonata (1918–20) contains striking music but ultimately succumbs to rodomontade. The Piano Concerto, written in 1930 under the spell of the pianist Helen Perkin, is his most successful attempt at a concert work turned outward to the world, to embrace high romantic afflatus as well as the popular exuberance of his music-hall-style tunes and his flirtings with delicately boogie-rhythmed cocktail-lounge jazz – probably picked up from Ravel and Gershwin. The work was once a Prom favourite and deserved to be. If it is now infrequently heard, it is still alive: which can hardly be said of Ireland's few attempts at the public manner of Parry. Stanford or Elgar, as in the cantata *These things shall be*. The radical sentiments do not accord with the temper of the music, the piece being comparable, in date and character, with Vaughan Williams's *Dona Nobis Pacem* while amounting, in face of that great work, to little more than pious good intention. Ireland, a genuinely distinctive minor composer of piano music and songs, is most persuasive when most private.

The same may be said of our third elegist, Patrick Hadley, though his finest work, *The Trees so High*, scored for baritone solo, chorus and large orchestra, is of symphonic dimensions. Of the pieces mentioned in this postlude *The Trees so High* is probably closest to Vaughan Williams. It is based on a real folk song, which it submits to techniques of variation comparable with those we have observed in Vaughan Williams. It respects the modality of its tunes while colouring its harmonies with a chromaticism redolent of Delius; it retains a strong serenity while eschewing self-indulgence. The later cantata *The Hills* likewise combines pathos and exuberance with a sturdy sobriety: qualities that resemble Vaughan Williams, though Hadley lacks his many-sided energy. In a sense Hadley was a casualty of the First World War, which Vaughan Williams overrode. But for his war wounds, Hadley would surely have created more music and would today seem a more substantial figure.

We can hardly deny the adjective substantial to Arnold Bax, on the evidence of his prolific output, which includes seven symphonies. He cannot, however, be claimed for the 'school of Vaughan Williams', since his extravagantly romantic, pseudo-Celtic chromaticism, though close to Delius, is poles apart from Vaughan Williams: except in an occasional setting of early English verse, such as *This Worldes Joye* or the superb *Ora Mater Filium* for double choir. Nor has Bax anything to do with Anglican Church tradition, Vaughan Williams's central root in England's past, other than folk song. Hadley composed a little music for the Anglican rites as an outcrop of his position as choirmaster at Caius College, Cambridge; but this was not an activity to which he was deeply committed, while Ireland and Finzi were not committed to it at all.

The most distinguished of Vaughan Williams's immediate successors was, however, above all a composer for the Anglican Church, writing music for all its liturgical rites; he was also the maker of one of the major masterpieces of the English choral tradition. Herbert Howells, like Vaughan Williams, was a Gloucestershire man. Born in 1892, twenty years later than Vaughan Williams, he was not actively involved in the rediscovery of English folk song, though it coloured his aural imagination and enabled him, as it had enabled Vaughan Williams, to counter the Brahmsian Teutonicism fostered by Stanford, his teacher at the Royal College. Credit must go to Stanford, who was not notably encouraging to young composers, for recognizing the outstanding talent, perhaps modest genuis, displayed in the chamber works Howells composed in his early and mid twenties. The Fantasy Quartet of 1917 and the Piano Quartet of 1918 are works of true nobility, the later being dedicated to Ivor Gurney and to Choden and Churchdown Hill, Gurney's haunts between Gloucester and Cheltenham. Musically, these works owe more to Vaughan Williams than to Stanford, effecting a compromise between traditional sonata form and modally polyphonic evolution. Howell's songs are fastidiously written, both for voice and piano, and suggest the kind of song Vaughan Williams might have composed, had he had that aptitude. The vocal lines are free and open in their pentatonicized modality; the piano textures luminously flow, preserving linear identity. The harmony always 'sounds' – often chromatic, but also luminous, without Ireland's slightly sticky self-involvement. 'King David', above all, demonstrates how Howells excelled in settings of Walter de la Mare, that exquisite and sometimes profound minor poet whose inspiration so often came from childhood.

Professionally, Howells started out as a cathedral organist at Salisbury. His ecclesiastical appointment was interrupted by serious ill-health, and he spent most of his later working life as a visiting professor at the Royal College and at London University. Even so, his creative affiliations were with the Anglican Church, for the liturgy of which he composed more prolifically than any of his contemporaries. Moreover, his decision to become a composer occurred when in 1910 he heard the first performance of Vaughan Williams's Tallis Fantasia at the Three Choirs Festival, in his beloved Gloucester Cathedral. He must have recognized himself in the music, though he was not a double man as obviously as was Vaughan Williams – he hardly could have been, producing so much music for everyday use in the Church, and manifesting in that music a conservatism based on Merbecke's anglicization of plainsong intonation and on the long tradition of Anglican services and verse anthems stretching from Tallis to Stanford. In his Service for St Paul's or his *Collegium Regale* for King's College, Cambridge, both the stepwise movement of the lines and the rhythmic declamation are founded on the majestic prose of the English Prayer Book; Howells does consistently what Vaughan Williams does intermittently, on his occasional forays into liturgy. But for Vaughan Williams's example, however, it is doubtful if Howells could have effected so moving a metamorphosis of traditional idiom into terms meaningful to us, if not exactly contemporary.

The scoring is usually for four-part chorus with boy trebles and altos, accompanied by church or cathedral organ. The doxologies are often ecstatically pentatonic and rather grand; although specially composed music, they serve a traditional purpose in being used as ritornelles to unify the canticles, which are of course scattered throughout the service. The soaring trebles glorify God with such abandon that tired conventionality is reanimated. That must call for faith, and that it does so is suggested by the liturgical music of Howells that sprang most deeply from a personal source. In 1936, inspired by the death of his nine-year-old son, he composed a Requiem service for unaccompanied voices. This refines the techniques of his everyday liturgical music to a purged austerity that is deeply moving, and is also worthy of the texts the composer selected from the Psalms in the Latin Vulgate and in English, from the Missa pro Defunctis, from the 1662 Book of Common Prayer, and from the Salisbury Diurnal.

Ten to fifteen years later Howells recast and expanded this Requiem into what is incontestably his greatest as well as biggest work. *Hymnus Paradisi* deals, in the composer's words, 'with the transient griefs and indestructible hopes of mankind'; only after many years' gestation could Howells bring into the open the pain latent in the liturgical severity of the Requiem. In a sense, the non-liturgical version dilutes as it enlarges the intensity of the original experience, for one listens to the piece as a concert work, instead of participating in a rite. This does not alter the fact that *Hymnus Paradisi* is one of the high points of English choral tradition. Scored for soli, chorus and full orchestra, it was first heard at the Three Choirs Festival in 1950. Its concatenation of private with public impulses gives the music a potency exceptional in the work of a composer always quietly distinguished, but seldom thus emotionally charged and intellectually vigorous. Derivation from Vaughan Williams is patent in the flexible modal lines, the fluid vocal polyphony, the recurrent false-related triads. The solo writing in the setting of Psalm 23 evokes Vaughan Williams's English Eden – indeed the psalmist's descent into the valley of the shadow of death prompts music closely aligned to that which Vaughan Williams created for his death-confronting Pilgrim; while the victory of *lux perpetua* in the last movement is prefaced by trumpet fanfares over an 'eternal' pedal, as is the music to which Vaughan Williams's pilgrim 'passed over to the other side'. For Howells, one imagines, the *lux perpetua* was not merely a metaphor for a psychological rebirth.

What is unexpected from a composer usually content with small forms is the mastery of large-scale architecture and of harmonic direction which Howells here displays. Intricate textures are deployed with an orchestral expertise that has learned much from Elgar; and as the music approaches climax, Vaughan Williams-like, quasi-Christian transcendence and passionate Elgarian humanity together take off in luxuriantly lucid chromaticism comparable with the most inspired moments in Delius. Since the Sanctus incorporates a setting of Psalm 121 ('I will lift up mine eyes unto the hills'), it is apposite that the choral writing should recall the wordless voices that, in Delius's *A Song of the High Hills*, wing us aloft from the appoggiatura- and care-laden heart. Christian sublimation and Nietzschean inebriation unite in a visionary moment, bringing together the three key figures – Delius, Elgar and Vaughan Williams – who had refired our music at the turn of the century. Howells was not, like those great predecessors, himself a re-creative flame; but he was inspired by their flames as well as by his personal grief to create an incandescent masterpiece, fusing sources on which he no longer needed to be dependent.

In an obvious sense *Hymnus Paradisi* contains more of Howells's essential self than does his liturgical music. Even so, he resembles Vaughan Williams in being an artist for whom self-discovery was also a rediscovery of tradition. Minor works like *Lambert's Clavichord*, or organ pieces such as *Master Tallis's Testament*, the *Sarabande in modo elegiaco* or the *Preludio sine nomine* are keyboard music that looks like deliberate pastiche, yet sounds like Howells. In this they resemble some of the choral music of Edmund

Rubbra, a composer born a decade later than Howells, and substantially reared, by Holst and R.O. Morris, on Tudor polyphony. Although Rubbra was not consistently an ecclesiastical musician as was Howells, his liturgical works both for the Anglican and Roman rites (he was a Catholic convert) make deeply personal music in fulfilling an ecclesiastical function. His *Missa Cantuariensis*, commissioned by Canterbury Cathedral at the end of the Second World War, is a special case in being – except for the unisonal, organ-accompanied Credo – elaborately contrapuntal, conceived on a grand scale for potentially grand events. Yet the idiom is hardly less deeply rooted in Tudor practice than is Vaughan Williams's Mass. The rhythms spring from the words of the 1662 English Prayer book; melodically and harmonically the slightest modal or chromatic alteration may transmute pastiche into reincarnation. This applies still more to the Catholic liturgical pieces such as the *Missa in honorem Sancti Dominici*, composed a few years later: music for unaccompanied liturgical performance that is at the same time of subtly personal expressivity. Consider the marvellous transition from the 'flat' darkness of the Crucifixus to the questioning wonder of the Et Resurrexit, wherein modal alterations create an effect comparable with the serene insecurity typical of Vaughan Williams's more transcendent moments. This seems apposite to a man of hopeful faith in an unstable and materialistic world.

Although this music is in the tradition of Vaughan Williams, it is not influenced by him, except indirectly by way of Tudor polyphony. The same is true of Rubbra's eleven symphonies, on which his reputation most depends: for Rubbra adapted the techniques of modal alteration and polyphonic evolution explored in his vocal music to the wider canvas of the orchestra. Thus he, like Vaughan Williams, was able to create an English symphony that bypassed German hegemony: as has been indicated in our comments on Rubbra's Second Symphony in comparison with Vaughan Williams's Ninth. In later symphonies, notably the Fifth and Sixth, Rubbra refines on the concepts inherent in the Second. These noble works are symphonic arguments which are also religious testaments, their affirmations of faith being manifest in their consistency of figuration, continuity of pulse, and close polyphonic interweaving. They might be called symphonic hymns in the same sense as Bruchner's symphonies, and may for that reason seem a trifle anachronistic in the modern world, as Vaughan Williams's always renovative symphonies do not. None the less Rubbra and Vaughan Williams share common concepts as to what an English symphony is or could be; and parallels may be found not merely in Vaughan Williams's 'religious' Fifth, but in all his later symphonies. Rubbra's Second is Vaughan-Williams-like not only in its contrapuntal density but also, and more obviously, in the fact that its rondo-finale throws up several very good quasi-folk tunes from its polyphonic web.

No English symphonists follow directly in the Vaughan Williams–Rubbra succession. Walton's two symphonies are fine works (especially the earlier of them, first performed in 1930), but they stem from symphonic Elgar rather than Vaughan Williams: while the 'English' false relations omnipresent in the Viola Concerto of 1925 are probably an offshoot of the rediscovery of English seventeenth-century music then being instigated by Walton's friends and colleagues, notably Peter Warlock and Constant Lambert. There is a symphonist of a generation later than Walton who, even more than he, worked and still works within nineteenth-century romantic tradition. He is George Lloyd, a Cornishman born in 1913, who achieved success with his first symphony at the age of nineteen, but suffered a creative hiatus as the result of shell-shock in the Second World War. After some years in retreat as a market gardener, Lloyd returned to composition and has currently reached his crucial Ninth Symphony. His symphonies are increasingly recorded and sometimes performed live, with acclaim: which is understandable, since they have the basic elements of popular appeal, being as direct in melodic impetus as Verdi, and scored with the brilliant lucidity of Berlioz, these two nineteenth-century masters being Lloyd's admitted and admired mentors. Yet Lloyd's symphonies are not mere pastiche, although technically there is nothing in them that might not have been composed in the late nineteenth or early twentieth century; even if they call on folk-like Celtic tunes, this is only in the way of Dvořák or Smetana. Presumably the music owes its vernality to a true naïvety which, as Ronald Stevenson has put it, 'preserved wonder and avoided cynicism'. The Lloyd symphonies are, however, no more than peripheral to the English succession as represented by the symphonies of Vaughan Williams and Rubbra; and the same must be said of the symphonies of a still odder, more phenomenal, composer of Vaughan Williams's own generation – Havergal Brian, a poor boy from the Potteries who, with virtually no cultural background or formal education but by virtue of exceptional intellectual acumen, managed to become a professional composer, producing a vast body of music wherein he defined a unique symphonic world.

In his early days in the late nineteenth century Brian was haunted by German romantic literature, especially Goethe, and his first symphonies are unsurprisingly gargantuan in the tradition of Mahler. His later symphonies became incrementally terser and tougher, more quirky and quixotic, as the years rolled on: as roll they did, for Brian, living a decade longer (even) than Vaughan Williams, wrote thirty-two symphonies, twenty-one of them, incredibly enough, after he had passed the age of eighty. There is something slightly monstrous about so long a career devoted to the production of so much music which the composer – at least for most of this century – did not expect to hear performed. Whether we call the idiom of the symphonies European, or just *sui generis*, it has little to do with Vaughan Williams's concept of an English symphony. Not surprisingly, opinions as to how important, as distinct from extraordinary, Brian's work is vary considerably. The present writer finds the symphonies' idiomatic oddity in itself fascinating, structurally, texturally and orchestrally, though ultimately vitiated by a lack of memorable melodic inventiveness. But it is more to the point that one of Brian's staunchest admirers should be the finest British symphonist of the generation after Rubbra: namely, Robert Simpson who, like Brian and Vaughan Williams, sees symphony (and string quartet) as a spiritual pilgrimage. The logic and power of Simpson's symphonic thought are Vaughan-Williams-like in spiritual ambition as well as integrity, though he is not specifically in the 'English' succession.

With the exception of Simpson – and perhaps in his oddball way Havergal Brian – the composers so far mentioned look, if not backwards, no further forwards than themselves. Increasingly, Vaughan Williams's greatness seems to be synonymous with his uniqueness: he had disciples, but no peer. In discovering himself he discovered too the destiny of English music, looking forward to composers and to realms of experience very different from himself and his own. There is a direct link between Vaughan Williams and Michael Tippett, born more than thirty years later, for the work that in 1939 established Tippett as a major force in our music was a Concerto for Double String Orchestra which, like Vaughan Williams's Tallis Fantasia, owes much to English string music of the seventeenth century, and is intrinsically polyphonic in its doubleness. It shares Vaughan Williams's (and Tallis's) partiality for false relation and for rhythmic contrarieties that have something in common with Afro-American jazz; its slow movement is almost a blues-inflected British folk song. String works of the forties, such as the *Little Suite* and the great *Fantasia Concertante*, similarly remake seventeenth-century conventions; and although Tippett's later music, including the four symphonies, is less directly aligned with Vaughan Williams, we have noted affinities between his *Midsummer Marriage* and magical moments in later Vaughan Williams. If the ecstatic inebriation of Tippett's choral and orchestral *Vision of St Augustine* is wilder than anything in Vaughan Williams, it inhabits a metaphysical world deeply empathetic to the older man.

Britten, born seven years later than Tippett, belongs to the generation usually believed to be in reaction against the 'school of Vaughan Williams'. Certainly in his precocious youth he sought to recontact Europe as an escape from English insularity, as his French and Italian song cycles and his fascination with cosmopolitan Mahler indicate. Yet it is more than an interest in British folk song and a kinship with Suffolk land- and sea-scape that make him seem, at this date, profoundly English; we have commented on the affinity between his obsession with childhood, Eden and rebirth and Vaughan Williams's exploration of such themes in his later years. The music for the Woodcutter's Boy in *The Pilgrim's Progress* is vernally Brittenesque not by conscious imitation, but by consanguinity of mind and feeling. The Christmas cantata *Hodie* occupies a world startlingly similar to Britten's childlike works such as *St Nicholas*, *A Ceremony of Carols*, *Rejoice in the Lamb*, and even the technically sophisticated Christmas cycle *A Boy was Born*, composed when Britten himself was hardly more than a boy. Vaughan Williams had to wait for a second childhood before he could attain to such immediacy; and in music written not merely about childhood but for young people themselves to perform, he cannot reach the miraculous identity with the embryonic minds of children of all ages that Britten achieves in *Noyes Fludde*.

None the less Vaughan Williams shares with Britten a knack of creating works for young people which are socially regenerative – something people *do* together – rather than artefacts for concert performance. Vaughan Williams's use of congregational hymns can be as thrilling as that of Britten in *Noyes Fludde* and for the same reason: for the time being we as audience or congregation are involved in an act of praise or a cry for mercy, being banded together, in child-like wonder and/or apprehension, to confront the wondrous and possibly *in*apprehensible. One suspects that Britten's use of Anglican Church traditions was similar to Vaughan Williams's; he loved the sense of belonging that the Church offered, its continuity between past and present, without needing to accept Church doctrine. There is, however, a significant difference between Britten's use of a congregational hymn and that of Vaughan Williams. Britten in no discreditable sense exploited hymns that had become household words. Vaughan Williams did that too – in for instance the remarkable *Fantasia on the Old 104th*. But he also composed hymns of his own which have become part of popular tradition. Tunes such as *Sine Nomine*, *Down Ampney* and the Bunyan hymn 'He who would valiant be' survive because they are musically strong as well as readily memorable. It is partly, one suspects, a chronological matter: by Britten's day it was more difficult to identify oneself with such hymns than it had been in Vaughan Williams's.

Although direct links between Vaughan Williams and composers of a post-Britten generation may seem improbable, it looks at this date as though there may at least be parallels between them. Peter Maxwell Davies had his initiation in Viennese serialism; yet even in his young days he wrote music for children which has English and medieval affiliations, as in the magical *Magnum Mysterium*, wherein the vocal writing is characterized by a serene insecurity like that of Vaughan Williams. More recently, since he went to live in the Orkneys, his music has betrayed overt elements of folk culture. Many of his Orkney works are ritualistically theatrical and explore melismatic linearity; his more orthodox symphonies and concertos may now be said to be within, if without manifesting the conscious influence of, the Vaughan Williams succession. (The Violin Concerto, though not one of Davies's best works, is especially interesting in this context.) Moreover, the central work in Davies's career is his opera *Taverner*, which is about a double man contemporary with Thomas Tallis.

The most advanced among British composers of Davies's generation, Harrison Birtwistle, also has points of contact with Vaughan Williams in his concern with English primitive rituals, mumming plays, Punch and Judy shows and folk mythology. His major work, the opera-rite *The Masks of Orpheus*, is violent to a degree that far outstrips even Vaughan Williams's Fourth Symphony – as is hardly surprising, given the world we have made. Even so, its 'body music', its compulsive rhythms of earth and moon and sea, live in realms not remote from those of Vaughan Williams. Already, Birtwistle sounds as rudimentarily English as the grand old man, and the consanguinity is likely to be more apprehensible as time goes by. Another English composer, slightly younger than Davies and Birtwistle, has likewise been preoccupied with English folk-rites and children's games, combining body music with a sense of the numinous. John Tavener – a remote descendant of the Tudor composer with nearly the same name – is a specifically religious composer whose concerns and techniques overlap with those of Vaughan Williams, especially in the mysteriously moving *Celtic Requiem*.

That there should be links between Vaughan Williams's music and that of America is natural enough. Inspired in youth by Walt Whitman and faithful to him throughout his life, Vaughan Williams was a pioneer as well as a pilgrim. American composers of the forties found aspects of his symphonic style congenial to their pioneering instincts, though most of these New World symphonists now sound cinematic, even when they are as technically resourceful as Peter Mennin, or as genuinely noble in sensibility as Howard Hanson. By far the most impressive of these symphonists is Roy Harris, a major composer with or without the impact of Vaughan Williams. His Third Symphony of 1939 remains a key work in the story of American music. Indeed it amounts to an audible rendering of the making of America; and although Harris never produced another work with so decisive a punch, his later pioneering works preserve an indigenous identity.

The American connection is no longer confined to the pioneering aspects of Vaughan Williams. His presence may also be sensed behind the medieval monody and Renaissance polyphony of several West Coast composers, notably Lou Harrison, whose American orientalism (by way of Java and Bali) echoes elements latent in Vaughan Williams's music from *Flos Campi* onwards. This is not merely a matter of fashion; it reflects Western man's growing disquiet about his foundering values and self-instigated destruction both of his civilization and of the natural universe in which it subsists. Vaughan Williams's perennial youth and his purity of heart find responses, conscious and unconscious, in the vernal music of Lou Harrison which, without pretension or presumption, renews the human spirit. There are further links between this West Coast music and the more benign types of minimalism (such as Daniel Lenz and Harold Budd); while between that and the more gentle kinds of youth-orientated pop there are no longer barriers – as the racks of record and tape shops literally prove. Vaughan Williams would not have despised this vulnerably hopeful music, though he might have considered it half-baked.

It would seem from the above that comments on the limitations of Vaughan Williams's insularity are no longer valid, if they ever were. Physically an imposing figure, he now casts a more formidable shadow than he did at the time of his death, for the sound reason that he embraced our past, present and future. Everyone admits that he was a great man and an English institution. We should not underestimate this aspect of his life's work: one of the last examples of which was a cantata for the massed voices of schoolchildren and adolescents, while one of his earliest creative activities had been his compilation of a new English hymnal. Although the young Vaughan Williams had been an organist and choirmaster, at St Barnabas, South Lambeth, from 1895 to 1899, he accepted the invitation (in 1902) to remake the hymnbook only with reluctance, since he was not formally a Christian. If on reflection he agreed to undertake the task, that was for the sound reason that the Church gave people each week 'the only music in their lives, and it was all too often unworthy both of their faith and of music itself'. Cecil Sharp had put his name forward because he thought that Vaughan Williams's familiarity with English folk song meant that he was rooted in a 'people's music' antecedent to hymns ancient as well as modern: a music of which the manliness and humanity might safeguard hymnody from then current bathos and sentimentality. He was right. Vaughan Williams warmed to the task; spent a number of years over it, instead of the two months the publisher had said it would take him; and not only cleaned up, both musically and poetically, the orthodox hymn repertory, but also composed about a dozen new tunes himself, at first published anonymously, but acknowledged in the second revised version of the hymnal issued in 1933. All these tunes are fine and at least two of them ('Sine nomine' and 'Down Ampney') are so magnificent and so memorable that they have become part of popular consciousness. Some other tunes, if less memorable, are hardly less fine – such as the modally severe 'Whitegates' ('Fierce raged the tempest'), the mysteriously folk-like 'Mantegna' (Into the woods'), and 'Cumnor' ('Servants of God'), which is both modal and asymmetrical and therefore, perhaps, tricky for congregational use. All these noble tunes effect a communal affirmation if not, strictly speaking, an act of faith. This may be why they are so impressive as people's music: in a faithless age we find strength, which may be not so far from faith, in their integrity.

We have suggested that such an achievement parallels, and does not pale beside, the composer's art music. His symphonies and cantatas were often of some technical sophistication. Even so, they always functioned within the context of human life as it was and might be; and became an inner drama of Everyman, heard by large numbers of people in concert hall, on radio, disc and tape. If performances of the music fell off during Vaughan Williams's unfashionable period after his death, they never ceased, and are again becoming more frequent. In art music as in hymnody his Christian agnosticism and temporizing temperament may be his greatest strength, forging links with common men and women. Delius, advocating 'courage and self-reliance', said that 'humanity is incredible. It will believe anything to escape reality'. Such stern rejection of compromise earns our admiration; but in the long run it is possible that Vaughan Williams was the braver, for in respecting the Church and possibly the State without believing in them he was paying tribute to man's hopeful good intentions, however horrendous his actions – especially in the name of God – may often be. Delius showed us how courageously we might die; Vaughan Williams showed us how courage-ously we may go on living, within the premises of what we have and the potentiality of what we might have. For most people life seems preferable to death: which is why it increasingly seems that Vaughan Williams matters, at the end of our baleful century, not principally because he was a good man and an English institution, but because he was a great composer. The words Meredith wrote of the skylark who was so seminal in Vaughan Williams's evolution may be applied, appropriately enough, to the composer himself:

> Yet men have we, whom we revere,
> New names, and men still housing here,
> Whose lives, by many a dint
> Defaced, and grinding wheels on flint,
> Yield substance. ...
>
> And they are warriors in accord
> With life to serve, and pass reward,
> So touching purest and so heard
> In the brain's reflex of yon bird:
> Wherefore their soul in me or mine,
> Through self-forgetfulness divine
> In them, that song aloft maintains
> To fill the sky and thrill the plains
> With showerings drawn from human stores,
> As he to silence nearer soars.
>
> George Meredith, 'The Lark Ascending'

VAUGHAN WILLIAMS AND MUSICAL SYMBOLISM

All composers have 'fingerprints' whereby one may recognize that the music is theirs rather than someone else's. Such fingerprints are less conspicuous in composers who live in relatively stable societies wherein the public values are accepted by almost everyone; but even then a real composer will manifest his identity in discreet departures from the norm. Vaughan Williams lived in an unstable society, however deeply he may have respected tradition: so his music became a personal pilgrimage, wherein his 'language' changed in a changing world. There is an equilibrium between the private and the public life, though the stress falls differently at different times and in different places.

Musical meaning derives in the first place from the acoustical behaviour of sounds. As Derrick Cooke has demonstrated in his great book *The Language of Music*, intervals, rhythmic patterns and harmonic progressions have physiological and psychological effects which seem to have remained constant through most musics in most cultures. But specific cultures have refined on those meanings, giving them connotations peculiarly relevant to themselves. Pentatonic formulae are basic to most oriental musics, though the precise tunings given to intervals in Indian, Balinese, Chinese and other cultures vary – usually in accord with some concept of musical cosmology. In our own equally tempered, harmonic musical world, a IV, V, I progression in Handel is a formula, even a cliché, of his time, to which he may give unusual and personal applications. Bach is a more specialized case, for the elaborately codified language he evolved was partly a deduction from past traditions and present commonplaces, and partly his own invention.

Many of Vaughan Williams's fingerprints, as commented on in this book, spring spontaneously from the way sounds function: his fourth-rising-to fifth-rising-to-octave motif is an acoustic phenomenon basic to all European music (and to most other music) since time was, though Vaughan Williams gives it, as the totality of his work evolves, a significance peculiar to himself. The same is true of less basic formulae, such as his partiality for parallel fourths and fifths on the analogy of medieval organum and for the phrase that lifts through a minor third and then declines; and his near-obsession, from the Tallis Fantasia onwards, with linearly alternating major and minor thirds and with harmonic cross-relations. Such fingerprints are simultaneously manifestations of acoustical behaviour and parts of European tradition; on both counts Vaughan Williams unconsciously refashions them to make them part of *his* language, which in turn itself becomes part of tradition. The process of conversion is in his case more than usually clear because his evolving pilgrimage is so consistent and so well defined. If the obsessional recurrence of his fingerprints may sometimes seem like a limitation, that is because a composer living in a society that does not offer clearly audible accoustical norms will be pressurized to discover, even to invent, his own. For a composer such as Vaughan Williams, who had no doubt that music is a language with communicable meanings and social relevance, the making of a language is the technical complement to the search for a faith.

Particularly interesting, in the context of Vaughan Williams's language, is the matter of mode and key. Medieval and Renaissance modes acquired in their own day specific emotional connotations, which had acoustical bases in the intervallic structure of each mode which, in the disposition of its tones and semitones, was different from the others. Why one mode should have been associated with a particular kind of experience – the lydian with healing, and so on – is another question. In that case one might suggest that the prominence of the devilish tritone (F to B natural) meant that tonal disturbance was inescapable – until it was resolved upwards into the godly perfection of the fifth (F to C). Similarly the flat second in the phrygian mode may have imparted to it a certain oppressiveness, and by inference an awareness of suffering, whereas the open major third and sharp seventh of the ionian mode gave it buoyancy and vigour. But it is impossible to codify the effect of modes systematically; however the process happened, certain physiological and psychological effects did, though the course of time, accrue to certain modes, and coloured the ways in which composers, both consciously and unconsciously, used them, as they lived in a given society, working for a given court or church. Intuitively, the 'folk' also no doubt made tunes in one mode rather than another because it was apposite to the feelings – of joy, pain, love, hate, fear or hilarity – of which they were singing. Vaughan Williams's modal melodies function in much the same way, though no more than the folk did he think about the mode before the melody happened; his polymodality is, of course, more complex than the modality of Tudor polyphony, let alone that of a rural folk tune. Despite this basic empiricism, some of Vaughan Williams's modal practices are conventional and traditional; the flattening of the modality for the Crucifixus and Sepultus of his Mass accords with sixteenth-century precedent.

The modes were derived from Nature in so far as they were

precipitated from acoustical facts. When modern man, dressed in a little brief authority, took over as potential arbiter of his destiny, the modes fell into abeyance. In his post-Renaissance society European man relished his self-reliance in man-made contrivances, based on Nature's cycle of fifths, but now codified into a harmonic and tonal system which was an aural equivalent to the order he hoped to impose on every aspect of civillized life. The absolute monarch was playing God; similarly, the 'laws' of equal-tempered diatonic tonality, operating within the cycle of fifths, were a pseudo-science which was believed to be definitive. The French composer Rameau, himself a friend of the Encyclopaedists, was at once a vigorous creator or maker and a theorist who explained the behaviour of sounds in ways acceptable to himself and to his contemporaries.

In equal-tempered tonality, which is essential if harmonic progression within the cycle of fifths is to be possible, all scales must be identical since each semitone is equal: the emotional effect of D major cannot be distinct from that of C major, whereas the dorian mode is distinct from the ionian because the intervals that comprise it are differently disposed. None the less the classical baroque era, in its rage for order, built up an elaborate system whereby the different major and minor keys were invested with psychological properties. There was an acoustical reason for associating D major with power and glory because it was the key of natural trumpets, and a good key for instruments of the violin family to play brilliantly in, owing to the ready availability of open strings. But there was no acoustical reason why D major's relative, B minor, should have become associated with tragic experience, pain and pathos, except that it was the relative of D major and by inference could be construed as its polar opposite and complement. All that matters is that the symbolism of key, in classical baroque music, worked: as the hierarchy of keys on which Bach's Mass in B minor is constructed wondrously testifies. The Mass is not really in B minor but in B minor and D major, with the latter slightly more prevalent. D major and B minor are the positive and negative poles; the subdominant (G major) is the flatter key of blessing and benediction, with *its* relative (E minor) as the key of crucifixion. A major and F sharp minor are intensifications of D major and B minor, enhancing joy or pain; E major, being the sharpest major key in common use, is paradisal – and comparatively rarely attained,. Flatwards progressions work in similar ways. F major and B flat major were associated with pastoralism and the earth; C minor with human strife tending to darkness; F minor – the flattest minor key in common use – was the key of funereal experience and of the infernal regions. And so on.

Although such rigid classification weakened with the decline of the classical baroque and of the absolute autocracies who created it, these symbolic attributes of key were too deeply entrenched to be lightly surrendered. Mozart has his benign G major, tragic G minor, radiant A major, demonic D minor, strifeful C minor, nobly enlightened C major, and so on, used in comparable contexts in instrumental works and in operas wherein words and action offer clues as to their meanings. Beethoven still writes 'dynamic' works in C minor (Pathétique Sonata and Fifth Symphony), benign ones in G major (Violin Sonata opus 96, Fourth Piano Concerto), 'infernal' ones in F minor (Apassionata Sonata. Quartet opus 95), and uses D major and B flat major in association with power and glory, both natural and supernatural (Ninth Symphony, *Missa Solemnis*, Hammerklavier Sonata). Schubert composes his final triptych of piano sonatas in keys (C minor, A major, B flat major) perserving their traditional connotations, and continues to write heavenly, or at least Edenic, music in E major – as the words of his songs testify; while his Young Nun is storm-buffeted in F minor. Unsurprisingly, the archaistic Bruckner never abandoned classical key symbolism, though his heavenly regions seem to have risen up the cycle of fifths from E to B and even F sharp major. Tchaikovsky's E minor and F minor Symphonies relish their precedents in the desperations of the past. Debussy and early Messiaen find their heavens way up in F sharp and C sharp major, bristling with celestial sharps.

Clearly the choice of one key rather than another must have been, as the centuries rolled on, an instinctive reflex. Composers did what had always been done; and in the course of time an audience's response to a work in a given key would be coloured by its foreknowledge of other, especially very famous, pieces in the same key. This is a bonus the composer did not count on, though he may have been glad of it. He chose one key rather than another because instinct and precedent told him to. He did not need to think about it, though some composers must have done so more than others. It is improbable that Vaughan Williams consciously reflected on the symbolism of key (and mode) which is so elaborately evident in his music, but the consistency of his approach fascinates. Consider the sequence of his symphonies. The first, *A Sea Symphony*, is, though tonally free, the most conventional. It begins in or just off D major as the key of power and glory, for the first movement concerns man the explorer and pioneer. The slow movement, veering between E minor-major and C minor, does so with traditional implications, for C minor is strife in relation to crucifying E minor – which E major may resolve into a bliss that may be either dream or vision. In the scherzo modalized G minor and unmodalized B flat major function in traditional ways. The finale tempestuously seeks the benediction of G major, but ends in mediant relation to it – very quietly in E flat major which, if 'down' from G major, is 'up' in relation to the D major the work had started in: which suggests that the voyage is far from over.

Most of the works of the early years use classical-romantic tonality in similar ways. *Toward the Unknown Region* moves from an aeolian D to an unambiguous F major, reinforcing our sense that the quest ends in a region earthily known rather than unknown. This may be fair enough for a young artist at the start of his pilgrimage. In the stormy first movement of *On Wenlock Edge* dorian G minor has traditional associations both with the transposed mode and the later history of diatonic G minor. In the second song E major is traditionally heavenly, though precariously so. In the last song A major implies, as is its wont, youth and hope, albeit fraily. The *Fantasia on a Theme of Thomas Tallis* is a special case because it was a conscious modification of Tudor modal practice. Such too is the basis of the unaccompanied Mass, which we saw to be not 'in' G minor; and in most of the works after the Tallis Fantasia the orientation is as much modal as tonal. Such equivocation between relatively just modality and unjustly tempered tonality is the heart of Vaughan Williams's 'doubleness': as becomes evident in that small, semial work *The Lark Ascending*, which for much of the time has a key signature of one sharp, though it is not in G major or E minor but is poised between modalities of E, G and C, while the lark himself is usually pentatonic. One of the consequences of the polymodality of the war-time and post-war works was that during the twenties Vaughan Williams produced his most harmonically adventurous music, since works such as *Sancta Civitas*, the *Magnificat* and the Piano Concerto have surrendered a serenely accepted (folk-like) modalism without acquiring the will-full certitude of tempered tonality. Quasi-oriental arabesques flourish in this music, as well as whole-tone sequences that are themselves tonally rootless. Even so, *Sancta Civitas* seems to be seeking, if not finding, a resolution of its phrygian E minor into a traditionally celestial E major, while G major retains its benedictory consolation. By the end of the twenties we find this polymodality developed on a grander scale. The God-Satan dichotomy in *Job* generates modal-tonal tugs-of-war, often gyrating around tragic G minor and hopeful A major or heavenly E major. The Sons of the Morning dance in a blessed G major, which becomes a triumphant D, though the end is neutrally in a cross between G dorian and B flat major.

Such modal-tonal dichotomies date back at least as far as the London Symphony, though then their structural significance was less defined. Vaughan Williams's maturation is technically evident in his mastery of polymodality in his middle symphonies, the Fourth being a bombshell tonally as well as in other ways. Of course its key is infernal F minor: and of course it adheres, as it hangs on for grim life, more closely to classical principles of tonality than do most of the works contemporary with it. Its order is very man-made, in the face of desperate odds; the rigidity of the Epilogo Fugato, which is more chromatic than either modal or tonal, just saves the day. In their more exuberant way – gravitating around hopeful A major rather than grisly F minor – the *Tudor Portraits* belong tonally to this phase: as the central Fifth Symphony does not. As we noted in our analysis, this is called Symphony in D major, but is not in that key (with sharp seventh) until its epilogic end. Its basic modalities are as much G and C as D, which is why its final resolution into the traditionally glorious key is so potent in effect. The triumph is one of faith rather than, in Beethovenian terms, of the human will, but it is none the less a triumph. D major, throughout Vaughan Williams's later work, is a key of human fulfilment, which may or may not contain hints of transcendence.

But the Fifth Symphony, if a victory for faith, was not an end but rather a half-way house in its composer's creative life. The Sixth Symphony was another bombshell, more ambiguous than the Fourth. It is said to be in E minor, the painful connotations of which – both in its form as the flat-seconded phrygian mode and as the crucifying tonality of the baroque – are potently manifest. The first movement, we noted, cannot decide whether it is in E minor or F minor, generating chains of major-minor thirds from the dubiety. It seeks and briefly attains the bliss of E major, with pentatonic and lydian tendencies; but bliss is obliterated in the scary second movement and the tritone-infested scherzo, while the epilogue floats in a no-man's-land between phrygian E minor and F minor, fading into a $^6_4$ triad of E minor. Traditional key associations may persist, though they are radically metamorphosed. This is true also of the Seventh Symphony, which takes off from the Epilogue to No. 6 and remains the most tonally obscure of Vaughan Williams's symphonies, as befits its 'lost' state. Though it ends on a pedal G, the tone is barely audible, and the wordless voices' $^6_4$ triads waver as will-less as the winds and waves. When, in the penultimate intermezzo, recollections of happiness past momentarily surface they do so in a modal D major – a quasi-folk-song from the loved earth, on which feet will not founder.

D is the key of the Eighth Symphony, the product of Vaughan Williams's last decade. The first movement is aeolian D minor, with 'magic' ambiguities, but there is little doubt that the work will progress towards D major apotheosis in its finale. This is not an answer to the perturbations of the Sixth and the near-nihilism of the Seventh, for the

Symphony is deliberately lightweight, marking time before the final leap. This occurs in the last, Ninth Symphony which is again, significantly, in E minor, beginning as a modified phrygian mode. The purgatorial implications of E minor are incarnate in this *opus ultimum*, which is the most complexly organized of Vaughan Williams's symphonies, and needed to be. Within its amalgam of modality and tonality the traditional polarities appear and reappear, striving towards the goal of E major, which is achieved in the finale, though in a manner mysteriously open-ended. So Vaughan Williams dies as he had lived, sturdily human, passionate and compassionate, but with the ultimate mysteries still unknown and, except in fleeting moments of transcendence, unknowable. Vaughan Williams's handling of modality and tonality in his last symphony is his ultimate realization of an awe-inspiring question-mark. Our analysis discovered comparable subtlety in the one- or two-voiced writing of the Blake songs, a complementary *opus ultimum*, rarefied into something rich and strange.

The works of Vaughan Williams's 'second childhood', notably *Hodie*, are less tonally-modally ambivalent; the odd (invented) mode on G in which it opens is clearly destined to reach apotheosis in the diatonic G major of the last movement. One suspects that Vaughan Williams accepted, even fell into his key relationships because there were precedents in the past. Sometimes this is overt, even naïvely so, as when he conventionally writes his *Benedicite* in resonant D major, his *Te Deum* in G. These, being ceremonial as well as liturgical pieces, must accede to custom; far more commonly, however, Vaughan Williams transmutes modal and tonal precedents because his personal idiom changed with the growth of his mind and sensibility. Traditional modality and tonality were reborn in the light of his pilgrimage: as were the 'fingerprints' of his idiom and as was he himself. This is what Beethoven, within more clearly defined tonal assumptions, did also; and while this does not mean that Vaughan Williams is a composer of Beethoven's stature, it does mean that he has Beethovenian qualities. Given his different, in some ways more difficult, environment, that is something, and may be more than enough.

INDEX

Anglican church, 45
apocalypse, theme of, 131–5
Arne, Thomas, 6–7
Arnold, Matthew, 206–7
Arundell, Dennis, 124
Attey, John, 215
Auden, W.H., 33, 96

Bach, Johann Sebastian, 128,
  158, 159, 161, 188, 209,
  260, 262
Bairstow, Sir Edward, 245
Barnes, William, 16, 25
Bartók, Bela, 42, 100
Bax, Arnold, 29, 238, 249
Beethoven, Ludwig van,
  19–20, 136, 145, 157, 161,
  168, 169, 171, 179, 207,
  263, 266
Benedicite, 184, 204, 266
Birtwistle, Harrison, 233,
  256
Blake, William, 6, 7, 16, 17,
  56, 58, 61, 135, 139, 141,
  142, 143–57, 185, 220
  mythology of, 145–6, 157,
  169
  see also Job; Ten Blake Songs
Borrow, George, 27, 207
Boult, Sir Adrian, 8, 218
Brahms, Johannes, 14, 15
Brian, Havergal, 253–4
Bright, John, 175
Britten, Benjamin, 96, 108,
  160, 246, 255
Bruckner, Anton, 6, 263
Budd, Harold, 257
Bull, John, 31
Bunyan, John, 55, 58, 118,
  121–3, 133, 142–3, 171,
  181
  *see also Pilgrim's Progress,
  The*
'Bushes and briars', 31
Busoni, Ferruccio, 6, 158,
  159–60, 161, 208, 209
Butterworth, George, 42,
  77, 86, 207
Byrd, William, 31

Calvin, John, 122
'Captain's apprentice, The',
  31
chaconne, 183
Charles I, 120
Chaucer, Geoffrey, 95
Cheesman, Alfred, 43
Church of England, 45–6
Civil War, 48, 60, 119–20,
  143
Clare, John, 61
Clough, Arthur Hugh, 207
Coleridge, Mary, 206, 219,
  247
Coleridge, Samuel Taylor,
  17
Collingwood, R.G., 144
Concerto Accademico, 158–9
Concerto for Oboe and
  Strings, 187–8, 225
Cooke, Deryck, 260
Coverdale, Miles, 212
Crashaw, Richard, 106, 107,
  120
Cromwell, Oliver, 120–1,
  133
'Cuckoo, The', 31

Darwin, Charles, 1
Davies, Peter Maxwell, 256
Davies, Sir John, 46
Davis, Miles, 236
De La Mare, Walter, 43,
  249
Debussy, Claude, 196, 248,
  263
Defoe, Daniel, 133
Delius, Frederick, 10–13, 23,
  29, 60, 116, 117, 174, 186,
  244, 245, 247, 248, 249,
  258
  A Mass of Life, 10–11
  Requiem, 11–12, 114
  Sea-Drift, 12–13, 19, 49
  A Song of the High Hills,
  10, 19, 251
Dieren, Bernard van, 43,
  247
'Dives and Lazarus', 28

Dona Nobis Pacem, 143, 163,
  171–6, 248
Donne, John, 121
double choir, in Tudor
  church music, 50
Down Ampney, 50, 255, 258
Dryden, John, 133

Elgar, Sir Edward, 7–8, 12,
  29, 39, 80, 84, 85, 96, 188,
  231, 244, 245
  The Dream of Gerontius,
  8–10, 18, 19, 20, 23, 24,
  116, 186, 246
  *Introduction and Allegro for
  Strings*, 9, 246
  Pomp and Circumstance
  marches, 7
Eliot, George, 134
Eliot, T.S., 7, 14, 28, 66, 75,
  80, 90, 91, 187, 221, 234
Emerson, Ralph Waldo, 17
English Hymnal, 50
English Prayer Book, 45
Epithalamium, 107, 114–15
equal temperament, 262

false relation, 47–8
*Fantasia on English Christmas
  Carols*, 28
Fantasia on the Old 104th, 207
*Fantasia on a Theme of Thomas
  Tallis*, 47–53, 49, 68, 69,
  78, 80, 87, 126, 147, 178,
  181, 209, 254, 264
Farnaby, Giles, 31
Finzi, Gerald, 67, 245–6, 249
Fisher, H. A. L., 2
Five Mystical Songs, 106
Five Tudor Portraits, 96–105,
  127, 239, 265
*Five Variants on Dives and
  Lazarus*, 190
Flemish Farm, The 188
Fletcher, John, 43, 105
Flos Campi, 107–10, 130, 140,
  147, 151, 154, 184, 204,
  207, 215, 216, 225

267

INDEX